University of Glasgow Publications
in French Language and Literature

1

WORDS OF POWER

University of Glasgow Publications in French Language and
Literature

Series Editor: James A. Coleman

Consultant Editors: Colin Smethurst, Kenneth Varty

Department of French, University of Glasgow,
Glasgow G12 8QL, Scotland

First published 1987.

Printed by Glasgow University Printing Department.

ISBN 0 85261 209 5

WORDS OF POWER

Essays in Honour of
Alison Fairlie

**edited by
Dorothy Gabe Coleman
and
Gillian Jondorf**

Glasgow 1987

Table of Contents

Editors' Note.   vii

Alison Fairlie: a personal appreciation   1
    Odette de Mourgues

'Death is a fearful thing...': Lucretius, Montaigne   5
and the sonorities of death
    Gillian Jondorf

Giraudoux's use of detail and *Amphitryon 38*   27
    Alison Finch

Polyphonic poets: Rabelais and Queneau   43
    Dorothy Gabe Coleman

Some reflections on problems of language in Corneille   69
    Gwyneth Castor

Verga's *Il Marito di Elena* and the art of the inexplicit   89
    Judith Davies

'Zut, zut, zut, zut...': novels where consciousness   115
of language is a fictional theme (Proust, Constant,
Flaubert, Stendhal, Gide)
    Christine M. Crow

Théophile Gautier's *Voyage en Italie*: the
description of experience, or the experience
of description
Joan Driscoll

139

Vallejo, Heidegger and Language
Lorna Close

163

Definition of the enemy as self-definition:
a commentary on the role of language
in Unamuno's *Niebla*
Alison Sinclair

187

Towards a poetry of silence: Stéphane
Mallarmé and Juan Ramón Jiménez
Mervyn Coke-Enguídanos

227

Sticks and stones: the weaponry of words
in *Vous les entendez?*
Valerie Minogue

243

Austerity (poem by M.C.-E.)

267

Editors' Note

This volume of essays, although it reflects the contributors' affection for and gratitude to Alison Fairlie (now retired from her personal professorship in the University of Cambridge), is not a conventional *Festschrift*. All the contributors are old Girtonians and they have composed the book in collaboration, each knowing what the others were doing. It is Alison Fairlie's activity as Director of Studies in Modern Languages at Girton for twenty years which has inspired the writers, all of whom were her pupils. We have built a book arising from the experience of being taught by her as undergraduates and expressing some of the central things we learned, from her, to look for and appreciate in literature.

The book centres on two main themes: the first is allusiveness, what a literary work gains in strength and richness by 'echoes' from other writers or other European literatures. The second is the paradox that part of the value of literature lies in its attempt to communicate, in language, what language itself cannot say. The essays by Jondorf, Finch and Coleman represent the first theme, with that by Coleman forming a bridge to the second theme, continued by the essays from Close, Castor, Driscoll, Davies, Sinclair, Coke-Enguídanos, Crow and Minogue. The book is completed by a personal appreciation by Alison Fairlie's friend and colleague of long standing, Professor Odette de Mourgues, and, as an afterword, a poem by Mervyn Coke-Enguídanos.

The editors wish to thank James Coleman for his invaluable help and advice, and the Council of Girton College, who generously supported this tribute to one of the College's most distinguished Fellows.

Dorothy Gabe Coleman
New Hall, Cambridge

Gillian Jondorf
Girton College, Cambridge

Alison Fairlie

A personal appreciation

Alison Fairlie's reputation as a scholar and as an outstanding literary critic is well established. Anyone interested in Constant, Baudelaire, Nerval or Flaubert has found an unfailing source of intellectual pleasure and enriching stimulus in the writings she has devoted to these major authors. Her most recent book, *Imagination and Language*, a felicitous synthesis of essays, has made even more obvious the qualities of her approach to literature: more particularly the impeccable precision of her informative comments, her insight into the complexity of the text, linked with an exceptional sensitivity to the slightest vibrations of language and also - perhaps her most precious gift to her readers - the imaginative revelation of the fascinating patterns which constitute the vital structure of a poem or novel.

From the evidence of her written criticism it is easy, up to a point, to guess how lucky the Girton Modern Linguists were to have her as director of studies and supervisor. I say 'up to a point', for the full realisation of her achievement in the career she chose to adopt deserves further comment. One may be an eminent scholar, a brilliant critic and yet be an indifferent teacher. To begin with, the temptation is great for some academics to sacrifice teaching, which takes so many hours and so much mental energy, to the more enticing pursuit of one's own personal research. This was never the case with Alison Fairlie even when combining the two activities entailed a more strenuous life.

The importance she attached to her role as a teacher was, moreover, fully justified by some innate traits in her which, I think, account in great part for her remarkable success with students. Perhaps most striking is a very rare asset which I would call intellectual generosity, served by a sympathetic and irrepressible interest in the idiosyncracies of the human mind. With a great deal of technical skill she turned the traditional Cambridge system of college teaching to its best advantage. The supervisor's task, as she conceived it, was not primarily to impart knowledge, nor was it to impart a ready-made *grille* as a short cut to literary criticism, but to give a student the opportunity of making the best of her own ideas. The careful reading of the submitted essay, often with marginal annotations, the thoughtful listening to the supervisee's views on a book or a literary problem were the preliminary to her quiet rejoinder 'Yes, but...', which tactfully warned against facile over-simplification, treacherous irrelevancies or shaky use of words, and compelled her interlocutor to reassess the scope of the question, to give it a clearer focus while discovering its many-sidedness. I have myself, on occasion, suffered and greatly benefited from the famous 'Yes, but...' after what I had rashly thought to be an altogether convincing argument. Few people, I am sure, have ever mastered as she has the subtle art of being exacting without being dismissive.

The respect for the personality of each student and warm concern for any latent individual talent, as well as the soundness of her critical judgment, may partly explain her extraordinary flair in selecting candidates to be admitted to read Modern Languages at Girton. As a result, for many years not only she herself but all the specialists of different languages in the college had the immense satisfaction - and

2

also the responsibility - of supervising a great variety of stimulating undergraduates, among them some of the best brains in our field of studies.

Her sagacity in the choice of her students and the impulse she gave to the creative originality she had so keenly detected at its early stage are reflected in the essays which compose the present volume. The fact that, although grouped into a harmonious whole, they are not limited to a given period of literature nor solely to France, nicely lights up the fan-like pattern of her wide-ranging influence. The impressive quality of this contribution to literary studies, with each essay so markedly individual, will delight Alison Fairlie and will also touch her deeply, coming from those who, no longer her pupils but now teachers and writers themselves, have remained lifelong friends.

O. de MOURGUES.

'Death is a Fearful Thing...': Lucretius, Montaigne and the Sonorities of Death

Gillian Jondorf

Montaigne tells us more than once how much he enjoys Lucretius, and it is clear when we read his comments (especially in III, 5; 5, p.127) that it is as a poet that he appreciates him, tasting and trying the words on his tongue, relishing them, urging us to share his pleasure, to say the words with him.[1] But while intensely alert to the richness, energy and majesty of Lucretius's poem, while reacting to it and acted upon by it, Montaigne also acts upon it himself, so that lines from Lucretius become 'convertis en sang et nourriture', undergoing small and sometimes subtle changes.

One *essai* where this is prominent is I, 20, *Que philosopher, c'est apprendre à mourir*, because quotations from Lucretius are very abundant here, and also because there is obviously an overlap between the theme of the *essai* as announced in the quotation from Cicero which forms its title, and Lucretius's purpose in *De Rerum Natura*. Lucretius wanted to free men's minds from fear, including the fear of death, so that they could lead better lives. Montaigne in I, 20 is urging, and practising, the contemplation of death as a means of overcoming the fear of death, and he finds useful material in Lucretius, particularly in Book III of *De Rerum Natura*. In the first part of my essay I shall look at how Montaigne acts upon Lucretius to present, in I, 20, a certain view of death. I shall then compare this to familiar writings on death, which may lead us back to a different aspect of Montaigne.

As soon as we look at Montaigne's use of Lucretius in this *essai* we begin to see how he adapts and changes Lucretius's words so that the 'allegations' are not just ornaments to his prose, but parts of a new whole. One of the things which give Montaigne's prose its characteristic texture is his use of quotations, exact or adapted, to utter his own thoughts while at the same time sharing with us his delight in the qualities of Latin.

The first quotation from Lucretius in I, 20 illustrates one of Montaigne's idiosyncratic ways of using 'allegations'. Although in this *essai* Montaigne quotes mostly from Book III of *De Rerum Natura*, this first quotation is from Book IV:

> Qui capite ipsc suo instituit vestigia retro.
>
> (I,20; p.113, adapted from *DRN* IV.472)[2]

There is a double form of adaptation here, of thought and image. Montaigne is talking about the man who solves the problem of death by never thinking about it and thus has to 'brider l'asne par la queue' and go through life backwards, unable to look where he is going. This back-to-front man was in Lucretius a topsy-turvy man ('retro' has been substituted by Montaigne for 'sese'), image of the sceptic who with upside-down logic claims to *know* that he knows nothing.[3] Further, Montaigne has not only altered the text of Lucretius, but altered it in order to use a comic transformation of Lucretius's comic image in support of something that Lucretius himself would not say. Lucretius certainly does not think that a man's mind should be fixed on death, but that death is nothing to us:

LUCRETIUS AND MONTAIGNE

Nil igitur mors est ad nos neque pertinet hilum

(*DRN* III.830)

a position which Montaigne is closer to later in his life, as can be seen in an addition further on in the same *essai*:

|||Elle [la mort] ne vous concerne ny mort ny vif: vif, parce que vous estes; mort, parce que vous n'estes plus.

(I,20; p.129)[4]

Montaigne's adaptation of Lucretius can be seen again in the most famous passage of *Que philosopher, c'est apprendre à mourir,* the prosopopeia of Nature. Simone Fraisse says of this passage: 'Quatre grandes pages de Montaigne reprennent pas à pas les arguments développés par Lucrèce dans la prosopopée de la Nature.'[5] But this is rather misleading. When we look at the quotations from Lucretius used by Montaigne in the prosopopeia, several things are immediately noticeable. The first is that the series of Lucretian quotations begins and ends with quotations which are not only not from the Lucretian prosopopeia, but are not even from the same book. They are from Book II, which is scientific rather than philosophical and deals principally with the movements, shapes and characteristics of atoms. The first Lucretian lines worked into Nature's speech contain the lovely image of the runners in the race of life passing on the torch to those who take their places:

inter se mortales mutua vivunt
et quasi cursores vitaï lampada tradunt.

(I,20; p.126, adapted from *DRN* II.76, 79)

Here too, Montaigne has taken liberties with text and meaning. In Lucretius, the argument at this point concerns the proposition that the sum of things, *rerum summa*, never diminishes. The lines which conclude the section run thus:

sic rerum summa novatur

semper, et inter se mortales mutua vivunt:
augescunt aliae gentes, aliae minuuntur,
inque brevi spatio mutantur saecla animantum
et quasi cursores vitai lampada tradunt.

(DRN II.75-9)

(Thus the sum of things is constantly renewed and mortals live by exchange one with another. Some species increase, others diminish, and in a brief space of time the generations of living things succeed one another and like runners hand on the torch of life.)

By picking out lines 76 and 79 Montaigne drops the reference to other species, he removes the connexion between human mortality and the constant *rerum summa*, and brings together the words *mortales, vivunt* and *vitai*. The quotation, like all but two of those used in the prosopopeia, was added in the 1588 edition, and there is great aptness and elegance in its placing. It forms a bridge between Nature saying 'Vostre mort est une des pieces de l'ordre de l'univers; c'est une piece de la vie du monde' and a passage in which the words 'mort', 'mourir' and 'vie', 'vivre' are closely juxtaposed, just as 'mortales', 'vivunt' and 'vitai' are in the doctored Latin. The 'ordre de l'univers' is an idea closely related to the lines not quoted by Montaigne, those referring to the *rerum summa* and to the balance between species; the interplay between life and death, displayed verbally by both writers, illustrates what Nature calls (in the sentence following the quotation) 'cette belle contexture des choses', by its 'weaving together' of the ideas of life and death which we commonly, erroneously, suppose to be mutually antagonistic. At the same time the 'belle contexture' of Montaigne's text is made still denser and richer by the quotations not only from Lucretius but from Seneca and Manilius, with other possible allusions woven in as well.[6]

If we look now at the other quotation from Book II, the one which closes the series of quotations in Nature's speech, we could make almost the same comments on it. It consists of three lines:

> Nam nox nulla diem, neque noctem aurora sequuta est,
> quae non audierit mistos vagitibus aegris
> ploratus, mortis comites et funeris atri.
>
> (I,20; pp.129-30, adapted from *DRN* II.578-80)

(For no night follows day, nor does any dawn follow night, without hearing, mixed with the sickly wailings [sc. of the newborn] the lamentations that accompany death and gloomy funeral rites.) By changing Lucretius's words 'nec nox ulla' to 'nam nox nulla' Montaigne makes more emphatic the alliteration in 'n' and also makes the quotation syntactically more independent ('for no night' instead of 'nor any night'), thereby making it seem to refer only to death and mourning, which is the context in which he has placed it:

> |Tout ne branle-il pas vostre branle? Y a-il chose qui ne vieillisse quant et vous? Mille hommes, mille animaux et mille autres creatures meurent en ce mesme instant que vous mourez:
>
> ||Nam nox ulla diem...

In the passage as quoted by Montaigne it is not clear what it is that is mingled with the laments of mourners; Lucretius in the prceding lines had already expressed it as

> vagor
> quem pueri tollunt visentes luminis oras
>
> (*DRN* II.575-6)

— the cry of the newborn. A reader of Montaigne familiar with the Lucretian context will therefore understand what 'vagitibus aegris' refers to, and appreciate this as another allusion to the 'belle contexture des choses' which weaves life and death so closely together, an example indeed of the 'vitai lampada' being handed on to the next generation. On the other hand a reader relying only on Montaigne will presumably take the 'vagitibus aegris' to be the utterance of the 'mille hommes, mille animaux et mille autres creatures' who die at the same instant as any one of us. As in the earlier part of Book II from which Montaigne borrowed the image of the Athenian torch-race, Lucretius is discussing, in the lines leading up to *DRN* II.575-80, order in the universe and in particular, here, the Epicurean doctrine of ἰσονομία or equilibrium, and the perpetual battle between creation and destruction. Montaigne could once again be alluding (by means of the context of his quotation) to the 'ordre de l'univers' with which Nature opened her speech. But since this hint of optimism would occur only to a reader familiar with the context of the quotation, the use of Lucretius's line 580 with its reference to lamentations, death and funerals ended Nature's speech on a sombre and disturbing note in the 1588 edition. By a long insertion in the Bordeaux copy Montaigne later allowed Nature to finish her speech in more coaxing, less intimidating tones.

Let us look now at the quotations from Book III which punctuate the speech of Nature. In the following list of lines from Book III of *De Rerum Natura* quoted or adapted by Montaigne in Nature's speech, double bar-lines indicate lines added in 1588, an asterisk indicates that the quotation is inexact (i.e. adapted, but sometimes very slightly) and quotations whose line-numbers are underlined are from the first of the two speeches made by Lucretius's Nature, the rest being in the poet's own voice:

||<u>938</u> ||<u>941-2</u> ||1080   <u>944-5</u>   1090-1* ||885-7*

||919, 922 ||926* ||972-3* ||968

This list tells us quite a lot about Montaigne's use of Lucretius in his prosopopeia. First of all, most of the quotations are not from Lucretius's prosopopeia (and none from Nature's second speech, *DRN* III.954-62). Secondly, the order in which the quotations are used is not the order in which they occur in Lucretius. We can see this more clearly if we number from one to twelve, in their order of use by Montaigne, the Lucretian passages cited. In this series, numbers 1 and 12 are from Book II and the remaining ten occur in the following order in Lucretius (underlining again indicates quotations from the first speech of Lucretius's Nature):

7, 8, 9, 2, 3, 5, 11, 10, 4, 6.

Thirdly, the asterisks indicate that, as with the quotations from *DRN* II already discussed, Montaigne alters what he quotes. Clearly, Montaigne's Nature is not merely playing echo to Lucretius's. Montaigne does not quote exactly, does not follow Lucretius's order, and uses very little of the material of the Lucretian prosopopeia (and the second speech not at all). Not that this setting out of line-numbers gives a complete tally of Montaigne's imitation of Lucretius in the speech of Nature, for sometimes he seems to have Lucretius's turns of phrase in his mind even when he does not quote him directly. For example in 'vous vous fuyez vous mesmes' (I,20; p.126), near the beginning of the speech, meaning that in wishing to escape death we are trying to evade part of our own nature, there seems to be an echo of Lucretius's

hoc se quisque modo fugit   (*DRN*   III.1068)

(so each man runs away from himself). Here Lucretius is referring to the restless, weary self-hatred of men who lack philosophy and who therefore, like the men addressed by Montaigne's Nature, do not understand their own mortality. Once again the text is enriched by allusion, even when there is no direct quotation.

However, if there are hidden similarities which are not made apparent by a tally of quotations, there are also large differences, notably in tone, in spite of the use of Lucretius's own words. Or because of this use, in that the lines quoted by

LUCRETIUS AND MONTAIGNE

Montaigne's Nature from Lucretius are mostly not from the Lucretian prosopopeia. The tone of Lucretius's Nature is harsh and fierce. She begins to speak abruptly ('repente') and three times the verb 'increpare' (to scold) is used for her speech, along with 'incilare' (to blame), 'inclamare' (to rebuke) and the phrases 'litem intendere' (to bring a charge) and 'voce acri' (with stern tones or in harsh words). Montaigne uses the neutral 'dit-elle' of Nature's discourse, and at the end of the speech comments 'Voilà les bons advertissemens de nostre mere nature' (I,20; p.131). Lucretius's Nature is not only harsh but abusive. When addressing 'one of us' ('alicui nostrum') she calls him 'stulte' in the second of a pair of lines of which Montaigne quotes only the first:

cur non ut plenus vitae conviva recedis
aequo animoque capis securam, stulte, quietem?

(*DRN* III.938-9)

(Why do you not withdraw, like a guest who has had his fill of life, and attain untroubled rest with a calm mind, you stupid man?) In her second speech, addressed to an older man ('grandior... seniorque'), she calls her hearer 'baratre' (gallows-bird, reprobate) with a play on words when she adds that this 'baratrus' will not be thrust into the 'barathrum' or pit of Hell, because it does not exist and because his constituent atoms will be needed for new generations.[7]

M.F. Smith suggests, plausibly, that the rhetorical device of personifying Nature and making her deliver these sharp rebukes allows Lucretius to speak his mind without offending Memmius (his *dédicataire*) and other readers.[8] He wishes to say these things to them, but not in his own voice. When he speaks in his own person, as he does in most of the passages quoted by Montaigne, his tone is milder. Montaigne's rhetorical purpose is presumably somewhat similar, although the tone is so much gentler. In much of the rest of the *essai* he meditates, argues and exclaims in the first person plural, allying himself with his reader, facing the common problem of

humanity:

> |||Quelle sottise de nous peiner sur le point du passage à l'exemption de toute peine!
> Comme nostre naissance nous apporta la naissance de toutes choses, aussi fera la mort de toutes choses, nostre mort. Parquoy c'est pareille folie de pleurer de ce que d'icy à cent ans nous ne vivrons pas, que de pleurer de ce que nous ne vivions pas il y a cent ans. (I,20; p.125)

The prosopopeia, on the other hand, allows Montaigne to address the reader with imperatives, although the brusque opening of '|Sortez, dit-elle, de ce monde' gives way to more coaxing ways of saying the same thing:

> ||Si vous avez faict vostre proufit de la vie, vous en estes repeu, allez vous en satisfaict... (I,20; p.126)

> |Faites place aux autres, comme d'autres vous l'ont faite. (I,20; p.128)

Montaigne however maintains the 'personality' of Nature more fully and thoroughly than Lucretius does. In the twenty-five lines spoken by Lucretius's Nature there is only one sentence containing the first person singular, and this provides the only instance of Nature saying something which Lucretius could not say in his own voice:

> nam tibi praeterea quod machiner inveniamque,
> quod placeat, nil est: eadem sunt omnia semper.
> (*DRN* III.944-5)

(As for my devising or inventing anything new to please you, there is nothing; all things are always the same.) Montaigne does not fail to quote these great lines, in which Nature shifts from the tone of an exasperated parent to the solemn contemplation of the *rerum summa*. But in addition he

introduces them by a paraphrase which by its use of the word
'passe-temps' emphasises the irritated parent ('nostre mere
nature') and makes us feel that the right translation of
'placeat' would be 'amuse' rather than 'please': '|Je ne suis pas
deliberée de vous forger autres nouveaux passe-temps' (I,20;
p.128). In Montaigne, this is not the only place where we are
reminded, by the use of the first person, that this is the
speech of Nature. Near the beginning of her speech she asks
'|Changeray-je pas pour vous cette belle contexture des
choses?' (I,20; p.126), with a suggestion of legitimate pride in
the 'belle contexture' which is her own work. Then, in the
passage leading up to the quotation of lines 944-5, she talks
with the same kind of pride about 'mes quatre saisons' as
being 'les actes de ma comedie'. Then with the same kind of
ingenious sleight of hand that we have seen Montaigne
practising on other quotations, she uses a quotation from
Lucretius which is conveniently in the first person plural, so
that for a moment she seems to present herself and us as
equally bound by the necessity of time (Lucretius in this line,
DRN III.1080, refers in his own voice to himself and all men
bound to die), and equally ingeniously follows it with a line
from Virgil (*Georgics* II.402) to make a new poetic fragment,
perfectly appropriate to the context of 'mes quatre saisons':

|Ce sera tousjours cela mesme,
||versamur ibidem, atque insumus usque.
Atque in se sua per vestigia volvitur annus.

(I,20; p.127)

(We turn round in the same place and stay in it all the time;
and the year turns round upon itself and retraces its own
journey.) This identification of Nature with her children is
carried even further in her eighth quotation, which consists of
two lines which are not consecutive in Lucretius:

||nec sibi enim quisquam tum se vitamque requirit,
nec desiderium nostri nos afficit ullum.

14

LUCRETIUS AND MONTAIGNE

(I,20; p.128. *DRN* III.919, 922)

(No-one misses himself or his life, and we feel no longing for ourselves.) By leaving out the intervening lines Montaigne makes the quotation appropriate for Nature, who is talking about the absence of regret after death, whereas Lucretius is talking about sleep (as lines 920 and 921 make clear) and arguing, by analogy with sleep, the absence of regret after death. The quotation did not need as much doctoring, however, as the one before it, which had to be changed from:

nec videt in vera nullum fore morte alium se
qui possit vivus sibi se lugere peremptum
stansque jacentem   (*DRN* III.885-7)

(and he does not see that in real death there will be no other self alive to mourn his own death, standing by his own body) to:

||in vera nescis nullum fore morte alium te
qui possit vivus tibi te lugere peremptum
stansque jacentem   (I,20; p.128)

(Do you not know that in real death there will be no other you alive to mourn your own death, standing by your own body?) The change from third person to second person makes the words harmonise with Nature's direct address to mankind, and the change in the opening words of line 885 reinforces this by providing a finite verb in the second person. Montaigne could not make the obvious, and smaller, change from 'videt' to 'vides' without destroying the scansion. As it is, he has changed the first foot from a dactyl to the more weighty spondee and at the same time, by suppressing 'nec', made the syntactic connexion smoother, as in his alteration of *DRN* II.578, whereas the 'nec' in lines 919 and 922 (quoted above) fit well into Montaigne's sentence, which begins with 'Ny'.

Nature brings herself into her discourse three more times, all three instances being found in the long insertion which Montaigne added to the end of the speech in the Bordeaux copy. In the first she aligns herself not with man but with 'la destinée', defending it and herself against man's complaint, and asserting their authority (again the tone suggests an exasperated parent): '||||Pourquoy te pleins-tu de moy et de la destinée? te faisons-nous tort? Est-ce à toy de nous gouverner, ou à nous toy?' (I,20; p.130). The second instance occurs almost immediately, when Nature justifies, patiently and from a standpoint of superior wisdom, her provision of death:

||||Imaginez de vray combien seroit une vie perdurable, moins supportable à l'homme et plus pénible, que n'est la vie que je luy ay donnée. Si vous n'aviez la mort, vous me maudiriez sans cesse de vous en avoir privé. J'y ay à escient meslé quelque peu d'amertume pour vous empescher, voyant la commodité de son usage, de l'embrasser trop avidement et indiscretement. Pour vous loger en cette moderation, ny de fuir la vie, ny de refuir à la mort, que je demande de vous, j'ay temperé l'une et l'autre entre la douceur et l'aigreur. (I,20; p.130)

The image of Nature adding 'quelque peu d'amertume' to death may seem slightly illogical, since her speech is devoted to the task of reconciling us to death and persuading us that it is not bitter, but it forms a witty converse to Lucretius's famous image of the honey round the rim of the cup of bitter medicine (*DRN* I.936-42). Lucretius has sweetened the draught of science and philosophy with 'musæo lepore', the charm of the Muses, in order to encourage us to drink it: Montaigne's Nature has on the contrary added 'amarum absinthi laticem', a drop of bitterness, to the sweet draught of death lest her children drink it too readily.

Lastly, in case mankind has not believed her authoritative voice, Nature (in an anecdote borrowed by Montaigne from Diogenes Laertius) refers to a mere man to support her case;

or rather, shows him off with a touch of complacency as a well-taught pupil: '|||J'apprins à Thales, le premier de voz sages, que le vivre et le mourir estoit indifferent; par où, à celuy qui luy demanda pourquoy donc il ne mouroit, il respondit trèssagement: "Par ce qu'il est indifferent " '. (I,20; pp.130-31) If Montaigne's Nature, 'nostre mere nature', is a more convincing presence than Lucretius's, it is because by deictic means (such as the frequent use of the first person and the oscillation between 'vous' and 'tu' for the address to man, as Nature shifts from admonition to tender coaxing) Montaigne creates a distinctive voice for her. Exhorting, teasing, reassuring, chiding without anger, she seeks to reconcile her wayward child to her benevolent laws. Montaigne's prosopopeia does not follow Lucretius 'pas à pas'; it uses Lucretius's text, reworks it by selective and adapted quotation, alludes to it, brings in lines from other parts of Lucretius and from other authors to create something new. The whole passage provides a fine illustration of how cleverly and richly imitation and allusion can work.

Considered as pleasing prose, this essay is immensely successful. The way in which Montaigne weaves Lucretius into his discourse in ingenious, inventive and delightful. A positive attitude to death is firmly expressed in epigrammatic images:

|Il faut estre tousjours boté et prest à partir.　　　　(p.119)

||| ... le sault n'est pas si lourd du mal estre au non estre, comme il est d'un estre doux et fleurissant à un estre penible et douloureux.　　　　(p.123)

|Ils vont, ils viennent, ils trottent, ils dansent, de mort nulles nouvelles　　　　(p.116)

By a 'belle contexture' of words, life and death are wound and bound together:

|||Le continuel ouvrage de vostre vie, c'est bastir la mort.

Vous estes en la mort pendant que vous estes en vie. Car vous estes après la mort quand vous n'estes plus en vie. Ou si vous aymez mieux ainsi, vous estes mort après la vie; mais pendant la vie vous estes mourant, et la mort touche bien plus rudement le mourant que le mort, et plus vivement et essentiellement. (p.126)

The whole is enlivened by wit. In the passage just quoted, for example, there is the ironic 'Si vous aymez mieux ainsi'; do we like it better? Certainly not! — but it comes to the same thing anyway. And the use of 'vivement' is ironically apt: of course it touches us more 'vivement' when we are still 'vif'.

This is excitingly clever writing and it does offer one way of confronting the intractable problem of death; Montaigne's way, here, is to thread the idea of death so tightly and so insistently into the idea of life that while we read the passage we must cease to think of them as opposites, and must accept death as an absolutely inescapable condition of life (which of course it is) and indeed as the necessary condition which makes our life what it is. Montaigne does not offer us easy consolation (such as 'There is no death'), but the picture of a life shaped and conditioned by the fact of death; and by the wit and vigour of his writing he not only carries conviction but delights us so that we receive the message with a sort of joy. There is a difference between the pleasure Montaigne gives, and what Lucretius says he means to do with his honeyed words. Montaigne is more like the later *moralistes*, like La Fontaine or La Rochefoucauld or La Bruyère, who can shock and delight us at the same time. When La Bruyère writes 'L'on craint la vieillesse, que l'on n'est pas sûr de pouvoir atteindre' we are simultaneously stung by the clear perception of a disagreeable, even painful truth, and delighted by the wit, concision and balance.[9] The cleverness and elegance do not distract us from the pitiless unveiling of human frailty, far from it, but in a sense they compensate us for that frailty. It is depressing to think about old age, frightening to think about the possibility of dying before reaching it, but La Bruyère by expressing these frightful things in such perfect form has triumphed over the very frailty he reveals, and in some measure triumphed over death.

There are other powerful ways of writing about death, with very different intentions from any we may impute to Montaigne or Lucretius. I am thinking of language which is used deliberately to evoke the fear of death. This can be done for more than one purpose. The language of the service for the Burial of the Dead in the Anglican Book of Common Prayer constantly juxtaposes life and death, as in Lucretius's and Montaigne's word-patterns and in Nature's 'belle contexture'. But it goes much farther and juxtaposes the horror of physical decay — 'and though after my death worms destroy this body' — with the promise of resurrection — 'yet in my flesh shall I see God'. Beside the grave, there is mention both of the flower-like brevity of the life of man 'who fleeth as it were a shadow, and never abideth in one stay', and of 'the bitter pains of eternal death'. But at the committal, the words that express most painfully and with seeming finality the mortality of man, 'earth to earth, ashes to ashes, dust to dust', are followed immediately by 'in sure and certain hope of the resurrection to eternal life'. Because the belief in resurrection and immortality is so strong in Christianity (but not in Judaism), Christian liturgy (but not Jewish) can afford to give full and terrible expression to death and mortality, and presumably does so for edifying purposes. It is perhaps because Montaigne has no consoling belief in immortality to offer (although he acknowledges the existence of such a belief) that in *Que philosopher...* he gives only subdued expression to either the fear of death or the natural, if silly, human protest at death. When fear is glimpsed, it is controlled and limited by an accompanying phrase (my italics for the limiting phrases):

|*si elle nous faict peur*, c'est un subject continuel de tourment, et qui ne se peut aucunement soulager   (p.112)

|*si elle nous effraye*, comme est il possible d'aller un pas

avant, sans fiebvre?   (p.112)

Autrement de ma part je fusse en continuelle frayeur et
frenesie (but for the fact that he has tamed his fear of
dying by constant thoughts of death).   (p.118)

The almost zestful stress on mortality in the Burial Service
is an example of language being employed ritually, with
sacred texts (the Psalms, St Paul) used to build a drama of
death, burial and resurrection. The fear of death can also be
evoked in imaginative writing, and seldom, perhaps, has this
been done for English readers with more chilling effect than in
the terrifying speech in *Measure for Measure* which follows
shortly upon the line used for the title of this essay. In Act III,
Isabella tells Claudio that he may live only at the expense of
her honour, a bargain which she expects him to repudiate. At
first he does so, but soon fear takes over:

Isab.   What says my brother?
Claud.   Death is a fearful thing.
Isab.   And shamed life a hateful.
Claud. Ay, but to die, and go we know not where;
        To lie in cold obstruction, and to rot;   120
        This sensible warm motion to become
        A kneaded clod; and the delighted spirit
        To bathe in fiery floods or to reside
        In thrilling region of thick-ribbed ice;
        To be imprison'd in the viewless winds,   125
        And blown with restless violence round about
        The pendent world; or to be worse than worst
        Of those that lawless and incertain thought
        Imagine howling — 'tis too horrible.
        The weariest and most loathed worldly life   130
        That age, ache, penury and imprisonment
        Can lay on nature is a paradise
        To what we fear of death.
                    (*Measure for Measure*, III.i, 117-33)

Claudio's fears are of the unknown; to die is 'to go we know not where', and he suggests a series of possibilities ('or to reside... or to be worse'). All refer to physically painful or at least unpleasant sensation; even the loss of feeling is described in terms of becoming the passive object of manipulation ('a kneaded clod') and the fate of the spirit is imagined in physical terms ('to bathe in fiery floods', 'to be imprison'd in the viewless winds', 'blown with restless violence').

Intellectually we can see that Claudio's speech is illogical, his fear is of a kind mocked by Lucretius, who argues that once we understand and believe that death is the end of individual consciousness, and that we shall not be there to watch our own decay (see for example *DRN* III.885-7, quoted above), we shall not fear it. This is logically forceful but psychologically inept.

Claudio simultaneously dreads the loss of individual consciousness ('this sensible warm motion to become / A kneaded clod') and imagines it surviving (he fears that he will be aware of being a 'clod'). This contradictory thought is surely very common in spite of Lucretius's efforts to eradicate it (by assuring us that once we have died we shall be dead), and the recognition of a common error contributes to the emotional power of Claudio's speech. This speech is powerful as a statement about death not because it offers consolation or a remedy for fear, but precisely because it conveys fear, and muddle-headed fear at that. Terrifying, hellish images in the speech are reinforced by the uneasy rhythms of the run-on lines, and abundant alliteration and assonance intensify the effects of the most blood-chilling parts of the passage (e.g. lines 123-24, 125-26, 127). Brief hints of the pleasures we must forgo at death ('warm motion'; 'delighted spirit') emphasise the bleakness to come. Literary echoes play their part: in the 'fiery floods', 'thick-ribbed ice' and 'viewless winds' we feel close to the underworld visions of Virgil and Dante, and the last four lines of Claudio's speech recall the lines attributed to Maecenas, quoted disapprovingly by Seneca and quoted from Seneca, in abbreviated form, by Montaigne:

|||Debilem facito manu,
debilem pede, coxa,
lubricos quate dentes:
vita dum superest bene est.

> (II,37; 4, p.228: adapted from Seneca, *Epist.* CI.11)

(Maim my hand, cripple my foot, lame my hip, loosen my teeth; as long as life remains, I am content.) As Montaigne says just before quoting this, '|Tant les hommes sont acoquinez à leur estre miserable, qu'il n'est si rude condition qu'ils n'acceptent pour s'y conserver!'

When Montaigne wrote the *essai* just quoted (II,37; *De la ressemblance des enfans aux peres*) he had already, as he says, 'pratiqué la colique par la liberalité des ans' and in quite a short space of time has suffered 'cinq ou six longs accez et penibles' (and even in the unusually unexcitable language of medical textbooks, the pain of urinary calculi is described as 'excruciating' and 'extreme agony'). He has learned something from his illness: '|J'ay aumoins ce profit de la cholique, que ce que je n'avoy encore peu sur moy, pour me concilier du tout et m'accointer à la mort, elle le parfera; car d'autant plus elle me pressera et importunera, d'autant moins me sera la mort à craindre' (II,37; 4, p.230). Thanks to his illness he now has no need of the arguments and exhortations of 'philosophy'. But even as he says this he admits, by implication, that they were no good anyway ('ce que je n'avoy encore peu'). Perhaps he would not despise Claudio. Indeed we do, in the later Montaigne, catch glimpses of a man on whom death after all can make covert and insidious attacks ('|||Je voyais nonchalamment la mort, quand je la voyois universellement, comme fin de la vie; je la gourmande en bloc; par le menu, elle me pille' (III,4; 5, pp.76-7)). We see him, also, faced with the realities of old age: '||cette chetive condition où mon aage me pousse' (III,5, *Sur des vers de Virgile*; 5, p.83); '‖Tout asseché que je suis et appesanty' (*ibid.*, 5, p.92); '[L'amour] ‖me divertiroit de mille pensés ennuyeuses, ‖‖de mille chagrins melancholiques, ‖que l'oisiveté nous charge en tel aage ‖‖et le mauvais estat de nostre santé' (*ibid.*, 5, p.157). In this last extract the additions in the Bordeaux copy give the prose a 'contexture' which is deeply moving, almost shocking. 'Mille pensées ennuyeuses' have worsened into 'mille chagrins melancholiques'. Old age, originally accompanied by the harmless 'oisiveté' now has piled on to it the 'mauvais estat de nostre santé'. Illness and pain (precursors of death but also forces which reconcile us to dying) are the problems now, not death itself, and illness and pain are not abstract notions with which to create enchanting word-patterns, they have precise physical effects ('asseché', 'appesanty'). Yet they too have been conquered.

What we have in the opening pages of *Sur des vers de Virgile* is not a meditation on old age but a recognition of its impositions and drawbacks, and a description of the strategies Montaigne adopts for dealing with it, giving his mind holidays among thoughts which are 'folastres et jeunes', enjoying the pleasures of memory and the memories of pleasure, moving towards the end 'à reculons' (like the back-to-front man whom he mocked in *Que philosopher...*). His attitude is patient, humorous, resourceful — and utterly different from Seneca coping with a bad attack of asthma by cheerful and brave thoughts ('cogitationibus laetis et fortibus') which turn out to be thoughts of death (*Epist.* LIV.3,4). Here then in Montaigne is something which (like the Burial Service) shows the enemy and the victory, except that here the victory lies partly in admitting that you are bound to lose in the end. Montaigne is not, like Claudio, in a state of unresolved muddle and fear, he is lucid and resolved to remain, as he says 'maistre de moy, à tout sens' (5, p.81).

But there are other moments when the sound of Montaigne's language strikes oddly at our feelings. In the Burial Service and in Claudio's speech, the English reader hears a certain knell-like quality in the language: 'earth to earth, ashes to ashes, dust to dust'; 'round about / The pendent world: or to be worse than worst'. Repetition and assonance of this kind clearly have no necessary or exclusive association with the theme of death, and in Ronsard, for example, are often associated with amorous obsession or with beautiful movements of curling hair, swirling drapery, twining ivy, rippling or turbulent water. But when we hear a similar beat and surge in Montaigne it often occurs in passages where fear seems to be hovering:

|Et nous, et nostre jugement, et toutes choses mortelles, vont coulant et roulant sans cesse. (II,12; 3, p.399)

|tant plus il serrera et pressera ce qui de sa nature coule par tout, tant plus il perdra... (*ibid.*; 3, p.399)

|Car c'est chose mobile que le temps, et qui apparoit comme en ombre, avec la matiere coulante et fluante tousjours, sans jamais demeurer stable ny permanente;
(*ibid.*; 3, p.402)

||Le monde n'est qu'une branloire perenne. Toutes choses y branlent sans cesse: la terre, les rochers du Caucase, les pyramides d'Ægypte, et du branle public et du leur.
(III,2; 5, p.28)

Certainly one could cite passages where Montaigne uses this sort of pattern differently, as in De l'experience when he recommends enjoyment of the pleasure of the moment: '||Quand je dance, je dance; quand je dors, je dors' (III,13; 6, p.243); or when in De la diversion he comments '||Peu de chose nous divertit et destourne, car peu de chose nous tient' (III,4; 5, p.74). Yet in the passages quoted above from the *Apologie de Raimond Sebond* (II,12) and from *Du repentir* (III,2) the assonances and repetitions certainly add a rather menacing quality to Montaigne's perception of change and instability, and give us a forlorn sense of man's awful helplessness in a world of time and flux. We cannot say, on the basis of a fortuitous resemblance of sound patterns, that Montaigne is as frightened of Heraclitean flux as Claudio of death. What we may suggest is that to an English reader whose ear is tuned to the harmonies of the Book of Common Prayer or to the King James Bible, or who has ever been struck by Claudio's speech (and other Shakespearean examples come readily to mind), some of Montaigne's sonorities will have a special ring, so that the evocation of time and change will borrow something of Claudio's anguish, and the Prayer Book's power to terrify.

Literature is created by readers as well as writers, and while sixteenth-century French literature is in any case richly allusive, every reader will also bring his own allusions and associations to what he reads, as Montaigne no doubt was doing when he read Lucretius. Reading literature of the past is a form of time-travel: we need not, indeed we cannot, travel without baggage.

NOTES

1. The quotations from Montaigne will be taken from Jean Plattard's edition in the series 'Les Textes Français', 6 vols. (Roche, 1931-33; reprinted with the same pagination by the 'Société Les Belles Lettres', Paris, 1946-8). This edition uses single, double or triple vertical bars to mark material from the 1580 edition, the 1588 edition and the Bordeaux copy respectively. I have marked all quotations in this way, so the presence of the symbol does not necessarily mark the beginning of a passage from the stratum indicated. I have given page references to this edition, with the volume number in Arabic numerals, save that for quotations from *Que philosopher...*, which is in the first volume, I give only the page number. The question of Montaigne's interest in Lucretius has been discussed by many critics, notably P. Villey, W.G. Moore, S. Fraisse, M. Metschies, M.B. McKinley.

2. Quotations from Lucretius, for which I have used the abbreviation *D R N* followed by book number and line number, are from the 'Oxford Classical Texts' edition of *De Rerum Natura* by Cyril Bailey (2nd edition, Oxford 1959). I have also consulted Bailey's three-volume edition with commentaries (Oxford, 1947) and the commentary in E.J. Kenney's edition of *DRN* Book III (Cambridge,

1971). The translations from Lucretius are my own.

3. *D R N* IV, 469-70, the lines in which Lucretius points out the illogicality of scepticism, are quoted by Montaigne with slight alteration in the *Apologie de Raimond Sebond* (II,12; 3, p.248).

4. Although the question of Montaigne's knowledge of Greek is moot, and scholars debate how to interpret his own claim that it amounted only to 'une puerile et apprantisse intelligence' (II,10; 3, p.113); 'une moyenne intelligence' in editions up to 1588), it is tempting to hear in this sentence an echo of Epictetus (see Diogenes Laertius, X, 125).

5. S. Fraisse, *Une Conquête du rationalisme: l'influence de Lucrèce en France au seizième siècle* (Paris, 1962), p.174; on the following page this critic rightly points out the difference in tone between Lucretius's Nature and Montaigne's. J. Plattard also speaks (in a note in his edition, 1, p.221) of Montaigne offering 'une paraphrase du discours de la Nature aux hommes sur lequel se termine le IIIe livre de Lucrèce'; this is inaccurate as regards both Montaigne and Lucretius. Plattard, like some other modern editors, follows P. Villey's slip in assigning *D R N* III, 941-2 to *D R N* II (see *Essais, ed. cit.*, 1, p.127n.).

6. Among the most obvious are allusions to Seneca; for example compare Montaigne's '||| Le continuel ouvrage de vostre vie, c'est bastir la mort. Vous estes en la mort pendant que vous estes en vie' (I,20; p.126) and Seneca's 'Ante ad mortem quam ad vitam praeparandi sumus' (*Epist.*, LXI.4) or 'Cotidie enim demitur aliqua pars vitae, et tunc quoque, cum crescimus, vita decrescit' (*Epist.*, XXIV.20).

7. *D R N* III, 955, 966. In line 955 Bailey gives 'baratre' in one edition, 'balatro' in the other. The textual crux need not concern us, except that 'baratre' is better for the joke.

8. Lucretius, *De Rerum Natura*, ed. M.S. Smith, Loeb Classical Library (London and Cambridge, Mass., 1975), p.261n.

9. *Les Caractères*, ed. R. Garapon (Paris, 1962; repr. 1976), XI (De l'Homme), 40, p.313.

Giraudoux's 'Cocasserie' and *Amphitryon 38*

Alison Finch

There is little general agreement among Giraudoux's critics about his style. Most of them hold it to be important, as witness the number of works whose titles refer to it,[1] but in some his language arouses unease, in others enthusiasm, in still others a mixture of the two. And sometimes real contradictions are to be found: Celler, for instance, stresses the surprisingness of Giraudoux's style, and suggests that his taste for detail is the mark of a caricaturist who enjoys 'idées étrangères au sujet immédiat'; whilst Albérès gives us a systematic Giraudoux whose precision implies a world 'soumis au déterminisme', and whose 'rapprochements audacieux' suggest a hidden harmony in the cosmos.[2] These opposite approaches both yield valid insights, but remain rather foreshortened.

Other judgments of Giraudoux's style are open to argument or to redefinition. The frequent superlatives picked out by many critics are not so specifically Giraudoux's province as they imply, but rather a traditional 'italicising' narrative device used as much by Mme de La Fayette and Stendhal as by Giraudoux.[3] Similarly, Giraudoux is sometimes said to be 'modernist' when he is only slightly refurbishing well-established raconteur's or playwright's devices.[4] Perhaps, however, the two most significant judgments of his style are that it is 'essentialist' or that it is 'précieux' — significant because, in the first case, made with unique force by Sartre,[5] and, in the second, because made so frequently.[6]

Sartre argues that Giraudoux is 'essentialist' because he presents personality, physical attributes, and settings as striving towards perfect harmonisation with an ideal version of themselves. He quotes, in support, such phrases as this one from *Choix des Elues*: 'Les canines d'Edmée, si nettement canines'; or: 'Aucun péril ne flottait autour de ces têtes, elles étaient éclatantes, elles faisaient signe au bonheur comme des phares, chacune avec son système lumineux; Pierre le mari avec ses deux sourires, un grand, un petit, qui se suivaient à une seconde toutes les minutes; Jacques, le fils, avec son visage même, qu'il levait et abaissait; Claudie, la fille, phare plus sensible, avec ses battements de paupières'. One may, however, introduce a few caveats. First, Sartre is basing his attack on a novel, not a play. In Giraudoux's novels, which can be diffuse and fanciful, such statements stand out as ostentatiously absolute, whereas in the more rigorously-structured plays, they depend on, or create, more immediate dramatic tensions. Second, in many respects Giraudoux's presentation of character and perception is not dissimilar to that of the Sartre who cleverly condescends to him, in as much as even Giraudoux's strikingly 'essentialist' phrases can imply a view of personality which Sartre would not disclaim. If Alcmène is 'la belle Alcmène, toujours égale à soi' (II vii; vol. I, p.191), it is because she is abjuring the self-indulgence Sartre suggests should be abjured — because she has no wish to step into an extravagant role, and has decided that the pleasures of the heroic adventure are ones which do not measure up to her own appreciation of the 'thingness' of things ('je me solidarise avec mon astre ... Ne me parle pas de ne pas mourir tant qu'il n'y aura pas un légume immortel': II ii; vol. I, p.162).

Giraudoux does, of course, play on both sides of personality in *Amphitryon 38*, with its skilful eat-your-cake-and-have-it end: part of Alcmène's 'humanity' is her attraction to Jupiter and some dreaming of the infinite. But what predominates is the dependence of humanity's joys on its limits, and this leads, in *Amphitryon 38* and elsewhere, to an implicit mistrust of deities and of abstractions; both Sartre and Giraudoux prefer to see immediate sensory responses as a truer gauge of reality, and both share an interest in contradiction and in the uniqueness of individual moments. Both have learned from one particular, and relatively modern, emphasis in French literature: that which opposes the ambiguities of physical perception to constructions erected by the intelligence.

Sartre's charge of 'essentialism' may be queried on other grounds. He overlooks, for instance, the fact that 'les canines d'Edmée, si nettement canines', is humorous: first because of the fang-like quality conveyed (reinforced by 'nettement', which helps to conjure up the sharp outline of the tooth itself); but, equally, because Giraudoux is provoking his readers to wonder whether there is such a thing as a canine which is more canine than others. If Giraudoux writes such 'essentialist' phrases, is he not setting up a comic pretence (here based on etymological play)? And does not this comedy assume an 'existentialist' norm? Giraudoux and his public are perfectly aware that they live in a world in which things never correspond to models of themselves, and that is one of the attractions of his style (whether humorous or not): rather than inviting us into a never-never world, it is creating an enjoyable tension between what Giraudoux has imagined, and what he and his audience sense to be the 'truth of the matter'.

To describe Giraudoux's style, or certain aspects of it, as 'précieux' may also raise more problems than it solves; the first being how to define 'précieux'. It is of little help to go back for such a definition to the seventeenth century, where the context of 'preciosity' — either in poetry, or in the salons — was very different from that of drama in the twentieth century. (Indeed, rather than to seventeenth-century 'précieux' writing, Giraudoux's style often corresponds more closely to the description of 'baroque' poetry given by Odette de Mourgues in her reappraisal of the terms 'metaphysical', 'baroque' and 'précieux'.[7]) For most people, 'précieux' implies 'over-deliberate play', 'hyper-sophisticated wit'; but clearly another difficulty arises here. What is deliberate for one may be over-deliberate for another, what is hyper-sophisticated for A may be merely sophisticated for B! Claude-Edmonde Magny herself remarks that 'preciosity' is relative to the comprehension of the reader and the sum of sympathy he has to offer.[8] A final problem — arising directly from this — is that for some, 'précieux' will be a pejorative term, but for others a neutral, even appreciative, statement of fact; both Prévost and Magny use it in the latter way.[9]

Suppose we forgot, for a moment, that Giraudoux had ever been called 'essentialist' or 'précieux', and suggested instead that what, more simply, characterises his style is an unusually, and sometimes irritatingly, intense interest in physical detail; what might we find? Such a description, although broad, could cut across anxieties as to whether Giraudoux is being 'précieux' here but not there, flippant in one scene of *La Guerre de Troie* but not in another; a unity could be traced between minor and major twists of the plot, characterisation, humour, and even the most solemn statements.

The immediate dramatic impact of the details in Giraudoux's plays is perhaps what has most confused readers trying to assess his worth as a writer. These details often seem to be hovering on a borderline between apt illustration and 'cocasserie': are they purely 'cocasses', for instance, in Amphitryon's proclamations about the protection of the citizens from unfortunate events — events like insects, storms and hiccups (I ii; vol. I, p.131)? When Egisthe, praising the palace acoustics, says they are part of its design, the architect having wished to overhear the discussion of his fee (I iii; vol. III, p.20), is this an 'arbitrarily' joking addendum? To whatever degree they may be judged 'cocasses', details like these have two functions: first, they provide the unpredictability which is the source of much good drama, in the form of entertaining asides or tiny vignettes which pop up and down again with a Jack-in-the-box effect. Second, such surprises are also, of course, the mainspring of much comedy. Giraudoux's details often puncture what preceded them, suddenly focussing attention on an 'insignificant' physical attribute or action — sneezing, hiccuping, wearing down shoe-heels. To follow the lofty generalisation with the bathetic detail is a device that humorists have always used, but Giraudoux exploits it with an especially wide variety of comic tones. Sometimes, with a switch of style, he shifts from a large picture of abstractly presented events to a smaller occurrence, as when Alcmène says she is prepared to accept all the variations of human life, 'de la naissance à la mort, j'y comprends même les repas de famille' (II ii; vol. I, pp.162-3). And there is a similar humorous coupling of grand with particular in Alcmène's remark to Jupiter:

> Sur beaucoup de points, à commencer par votre création d'ailleurs, et à continuer par votre habillement, je n'ai pas du tout vos idées. (III v; vol. I, p.218)

Even where the drop in tone is not so sharp, it is still often an 'informative' detail that will come to interrupt an atmosphere growing too intense: Mercure, describing Alcmène's and Amphitryon's love-making, says: 'Il la flatte de la main, ainsi qu'on flatte un jeune cheval ... C'est un cavalier célèbre d'ailleurs' (I i; vol. I, p.128).

If this is 'cocasserie', it is of a kind essential to witty drama.[10] But it is frequently the case that Giraudoux's details are not as 'cocasses' as they might at first seem. When Ulysse says that condemned nations are recognisable by the particular way they sneeze or wear down their heels (II xiii; vol. II, p.324), the sneezing suggests momentary physical weakness, the worn-down heels shabbiness and an uneven gait: not so quirky an illustration, then, of the lack of military bearing or prowess in question at this point. When Alcmène says, 'L'air de la nuit ne vaut d'ailleurs rien à mon teint de blonde ... Ce que je serais crevassée, au fond de l'éternité!' (II ii; vol.I, p.162), she is not making an *ad hoc* extension to Jupiter's image of her transformation into a star, but is using the bathetic reference to chapping to suggest how chilling, and wintry, endless space and time can seem. Or again, Sosie, describing the desirability of peace, stresses how good it is to sleep amongst

> rats qui ne connaissent pas le goût de la chair humaine ...
> Quelle plus belle panoplie que vos corps sans armes et tout
> nus, étendus sur le dos, bras écartés, chargés uniquement
> de leur nombril...

(I ii; vol. I, p.132)

This final comical detail carries an immediate, uncomplicated effect precisely because the belly-button is not an entirely arbitrary part of the body to select in this context. (Indeed, it is central...) Formerly functional, the belly-button is now purely ornamental. So the citizens' navels evoked here, in a series, are an appropriate symbol for armour, weapons, etc., that were once used but are now decorative — as in a panoply displayed on a wall, say. Even if one gives 'panoplie' its other meaning ('full suit of armour'), the belly-button could still suggest the middle point of a buckler. Giraudoux's 'détails cocasses' usually have, therefore, a comic representativeness.

Giraudoux's careful exploitation of detail also has important effects on his characterisation. When major, and many minor, figures in his plays use bathetic detail, it is often they who are being amusing, rather than comic in themselves; the audience will laugh with, not at, them. When they build from one detail to another, creating tableaux, they appear to be skilled manipulators of language in their own right. Through this control of detail, then, and by becoming 'poets' or humorists, Giraudoux's characters can achieve a witty intelligent dignity that has few counterparts in twentieth-century French theatre.

Plot too is affected by Giraudoux's love of detail. The fact that many dramatic reversals are built round it (Andromaque's eyelid-movement tips the 'weighing' between Ulysse and Hector: II xiii; vol. II, p.327) curiously both reinforces and weakens the audience's impression of inevitability. And to present 'Fate' as an indistinct image built up from small points, rather than as a conviction of doom, defuses a sense of disaster *and* intensifies it, showing that history can work through unexpected means:

> *Hector:* ... On croit lutter contre des géants, on va les vaincre, et il se trouve qu'on lutte contre quelque chose d'inflexible *qui est un reflet sur la rétine d'une femme.*
>
> (I ix; vol. II, p.281) (my italics)

This concentration (and occasional over-concentration) on detail owes much to certain of Flaubert's and Proust's emphases. Like them, Giraudoux frequently suggests that the physical response to individual moments is to be treasured, whether it brings welcome or unwelcome truths; he suggests this in a perhaps more direct, less flippant way than some critics have realised. The guarantee of Hélène's second sight is not so much her vision in colour as the fact that this colour enables her to 'see' future details; and it is through details that Hector tries to persuade her to see this future differently, and that she expresses her straining to do so: 'Je ne vois scintiller ni la ferrure du mât de misaine, ni l'anneau du nez du capitaine, ni le blanc de l'œil du mousse' (I ix; vol. II, p.280). In *Electre* too, where there are more overt attempts to define and state than elsewhere in Giraudoux's drama, characters will, nevertheless, unexpectedly turn to detail to give their statements the hallmark of truth.

> *Le président:* Tout a plutôt tendance à s'arranger dans la vie. La peine morale s'y cicatrise autrement vite que *l'ulcère*, et le deuil que *l'orgelet.*
>
> (I ii; vol. III, p.15)

GIRAUDOUX'S *AMPHITRYON 38*

Egisthe: On peut même s'étonner ... que [les coups des dieux] ne soient pas plus divagants... Que ce soit la femme du juste *qu'assomme un volet par grand vent*, et non celle du parjure ..., en général, c'est toujours l'humanité qui prend... (I iii; vol. III, p.22) (my italics)

When Electre maintains that she tried to stop Oreste falling, she conveys the urgency of her attempt by means of the details that one by one slipped through her grasp — blue tunic, arm, finger-tips — and Clytemnestre, contradicting her, contradicts the detail: 'La tunique, entre nous, était mauve' (I iv; vol. III, p.34). Almost any page of Giraudoux's drama or fiction will show, at varying levels of humour, gravity, or would-be poignancy, a similar high valuing of detail.

It is, however, in *Amphitryon 38*, the wittiest and most tightly structured of Giraudoux's plays, that this affectionate attention to the particular most aptly reinforces characterisation and plot, and even finds a place in an argument about the interplay between religious and non-religious feeling. The descriptions 'précieux' and 'essentialist' surely become still more redundant here than elsewhere. In this play, at least, we must discuss Giraudoux's 'cocasserie' in the context of his constant suggestion that the human beings who both appreciate, and consist of, transient, evanescent, sometimes contradictory, *features* are superior to the gods who plan and talk in *abstractions*. 'La terre s'aime en détail, le ciel en bloc' (II v; vol. I, p.74).

Two qualities of divinity, as Giraudoux portrays it in *Amphitryon 38*, are its capacity to think in generalisations but its lack of intuition as regards examples; these deities are unintimate. Alcmène brings out this gap between theory and illustration when she says that the gods 'ont pitié des malades, ils détestent les méchants. Ils oublient seulement de guérir, de punir' (III v; vol. I, p.212). But there are clearer indications elsewhere of the gods' penchant for the general: first, in Jupiter's own choice of vocabulary at key moments. His description of his creation is — Homais-like — abstract and

34

pompously technical:

> recourant aux vibrations diverses de l'éther, il a fait que
> par les chocs des doubles chocs moléculaires, ainsi que par
> les contre-réfractions des réfractions originelles...
>
> (II ii; vol. I, p.160)

etc. Second, in Léda's comments about both Jupiter and his effect on the women he has loved: he has 'Beaucoup de suite dans les idées et peu de connaissance des femmes', and his tendency to abstraction is contagious: the 'old-girls' reunions' of his past mistresses hold not 'orgies divines', but, with Platonic implications, 'orgies d'idées générales' (II vi; vol. I, pp.184, 186). And Mercure himself suggests that the gods try to fit an unpredictable humanity into a mould for which it is really too varied: 'Devant nous l'aventure humaine se cabre et se stylise' (I i; vol. I, p.129).

What is this 'aventure humaine'? There are numerous remarks about it in *Amphitryon 38*, usually so caught up with the comedy of the moment that the audience is scarcely given time to pause over them; but what they stress is its changeability and paradoxical nature. Mercure humorously suggests, for instance, that it is of the essence of being human to follow transient fashions, thereby imposing absurdities on one's body:

> *Mercure*: Avez-vous le désir de séparer vos cheveux par
> une raie et de les maintenir par un fixatif?
> *Jupiter*: En effet, je l'ai.   (I v; vol. I, p.148)

To be human is to have the capacity, good or bad, to be swayed: 'Si l'homme savait pousser l'obstination à son point extrême, lui aussi serait déjà dieu' (III i; vol. I, p.198). It is to be casual, even careless: Mercure came to earth 'comme un vrai humain, par laisser-aller' (I i; vol. I, p.126); and it is to feel *conflicting* wishes:

> *Mercure*: Mais enfin, que désirez-vous?
> *Jupiter*: Ce que désire un homme, hélas! Mille désirs
> contraires. (II iii; vol. I, p.169)

And humanity is also physically changeable:

> *Mercure*: Ce que je constate devant un corps vivant
> d'homme, c'est qu'il change à chaque seconde,
> qu'incessamment il vieillit.
>
> (I v; vol. I, p.147)

Many similar statements in *Amphitryon 38*, skilfully shifting between the serious and the playful, or fusing the two, suggest what kinds of dignity it is right to attribute to a humanity necessarily more bound up with 'le passage' than 'l'être'. The largest paradox about the characters of the play — as seen by the gods — is that their enclosure within themselves does not exclude a great confidence about life and the universe. This confidence can be comical because overweening (neatly pinpointed by the Jupiter who has at last assumed plausibly human form: 'pour la première fois, je me crois, je me vois, je me sens vraiment maître des dieux': I viii; vol. I, p.148); but Giraudoux also proposes its importance in other tones.

When Jupiter says that there is in Alcmène 'quelque chose d'inattaquable et de borné qui doit être l'infini humain' (II iii; vol. I, p.166), he must be singling out, as this impregnable, short-sighted quality, a biological sense of 'I am, and that's all that matters'. In *Amphitryon 38*, this sense is more than enough to stand up to the idea that the 'I' must die — that is why Jupiter suggests it is an infinite (thereby provoking us to consider other paradoxes of the 'infinite'). It is a blind but wonderful absorption with the self and its sensations — a treasuring of, precisely, the fleetingness that Alcmène believes escapes Jupiter's control. He did not even create it, as she suggests half-gravely, half-humorously:

Il a créé la terre. Mais la beauté de la terre se crée elle-même, à chaque minute. Ce qu'il y a de prodigieux en elle, c'est qu'elle est éphémère: Jupiter est trop sérieux pour avoir voulu créer de l'éphémère. (II ii; vol. I, p.159)

It is, on the other hand, obvious to what degree Alcmène herself values 'l'éphémère', the sensory detail. She expresses her love for Amphitryon through it: 'Tu as modifié pour moi le goût d'une cerise, le calibre d'un rayon: c'est toi mon créateur' (II ii; vol. I, p.161); and she conveys their harmony by describing herself as 'moi qui mange avec moins de plaisir si tu te sers d'une cuiller quand j'ai une fourchette' (III iii; vol. I, p.204).

This opposition between human care for passing details and divine indifference to them so thoroughly permeates the play that it may affect our reading of speeches whose immediate impact is 'simply' one of ingenious anachronism. If Mercure praises the lawns of the planet Earth, not — say — its forests; if the soldier summoned to war in the middle of the night has a farewell snack of pâté with white wine; and if the changes wrought by Amphitryon in Alcmène's perception are the result of human ingenuity imposed on nature (his invention of fruit-tree grafts and window-pulleys), — these anachronistic features, set in the context of the plot, also suggest that any of Earth's physical details is enjoyable in its own right, whether culled from 'brute' nature or from pleasant living and later civilisations (I i, I ii, II ii; vol. I, pp.126, 135, 161).

In many authors, a valuing of the transient is inseparable from a fascination with quirky details; La Bruyère is one evident example. But in *Amphitryon 38*, this fascination is also used to suggest not just the contrasts I have outlined so far, but wide-ranging reservations about religious belief. Giraudoux's comedy at the expense of the gods goes further than may at first be realised, and further than that of his nineteenth-century predecessors who also parodied images of the Greek and Roman gods. It has of course been seen that in

Giraudoux 'le dieu est finalement berné: la sympathie de l'auteur va aux hommes',[11] and it is obvious that, whatever Alcmène's finally mixed feelings, Giraudoux is weighting the scales against his gods in many ways. He not only portrays them as schoolboyish, occasionally stupid, and too splendid when they *are* splendid,[12] but also, more subtly, as lacking the finesse and sophisticated insights shared between author and a theatre-going public well-schooled in the 'mechanisms' of love by Racine, Marivaux and others.[13] Indeed, the gods find it more difficult to be gods than humans do to be humans:

Mercure: Il nous faut au moins amonceler par milliers les miracles et les prodiges, pour obtenir d'Alcmène la minute que le plus maladroit des amants mortels obtient par des grimaces. (I i; vol. I, p.129)

These aspects remain at a safely comic level, reinforcing a certain condescension we may feel towards the gods of antiquity, dead as dodos for us. However, it is clear at other points that Giraudoux is being humorous at the expense not just of the pagan gods, but of any deity, including 'our' god, that of the Bible. The audience cannot help being reminded of the grandeurs of Genesis, as much as of Greek myth, when Alcmène doubts whether Jupiter fully created his own creation; was he responsible for 'Les pins parasols, les pins cèdres, les pins cyprès, toutes ces masses vertes ou bleues sans lesquelles un paysage n'existe pas'? Did he create colour? the rainbow perhaps, but Alcmène's favourite colours? (II ii; vol. I, p.160). Darwin, expressing a similar doubt, is supposed to have remarked that God must have been extremely fond of beetles to have created hundreds of thousands of species of them.

Alcmène raises another general question not confined to the Greek gods: that of the apparent arbitrariness and parsimony of divine intervention in the affairs of the earth (III v; vol. I, p.212). The trumpeter too voices a fundamental problem: the relation of a hypothetically perfect creator to the evils of the existing world, particularly those inflicted by nature. Jupiter must not be shown the lame or handicapped: 'C'est un sacrilège que de prouver à notre créateur qu'il a raté le monde... D'autant plus qu'il prétend nous avoir créés à son image' (III ii; vol. I, p.199). This speech as a whole is deftly comic, but is nevertheless couched in strong language: '*prouver* à notre créateur qu'il a *raté* le monde'. And the 'créateur' is again not just the Greek god; those are Biblical words: 'Il prétend nous avoir créés à son image'.

The very choice of myth — that of a god who decides to give the world a son by fertilising a woman — may remind the audience, however dimly, of certain aspects of the New Testament; they may, too, contrast Mary's response to the annunciation with Alcmène's belief that purely human ties are more precious than love between godhead and mortal.[14] And the extended and brilliant word-play on 'divin', 'terrestre', 'conjugal', is comic not just because of the constant shifts between the literal and sentimentally superlative meanings of 'divin', but also because divinity *per se* is being made to seem preposterous, and easily outwitted — by no major onslaught, but unintentionally:

Jupiter: Quelle nuit divine!
Alcmène: Tu es faible, ce matin, dans tes épithètes, chéri.

(II ii; vol. I, p.156)

A certain 'morality' of perception is, then, wittily put forward in *Amphitryon 38*; this 'morality' proposes connections between religious feeling and a penchant for abstractions, and contrasts such feelings with a liking for detail. These connections and contrasts shape the repartee and situations of *Amphitryon 38* more firmly than elsewhere in Giraudoux. But the qualities, and the faults, of his other works doubtless spring from a similar implicit longing to look constantly aside at tangible detail 'just here', rather than the unknowable 'out there'. To see this longing as 'précieux' or 'essentialist' leaves too many gaps in our understanding of

Giraudoux.[15]

NOTES

1. E.g. G. du Genêt, *Jean Giraudoux, ou Un Essai sur les rapports entre l'écrivain et son langage* (Vigneau, 1945); H. Sørenson, *Le Théâtre de Jean Giraudoux: Technique et Style* (Acta Jutlandica, 1950); R.M. Albérès, *Esthétique et Morale chez Jean Giraudoux* (Nizet, 1957). Full bibliographical details of works cited will be given only in the first reference to them. References to Giraudoux's plays will be taken from the 4-volume edition by Grasset (1958-59) and will give act and scene number followed by volume and page number (thus: I iv; vol. II, p.257).

2. See M.M. Celler, *Giraudoux et la métaphore: Une étude des images dans ses romans* (Mouton, 1974), pp.24-5; R.M. Albérès, e.g. pp.86-7, 96, 97, 106.

3. See, for example, Celler, pp.31, 32.

4. Thus his use of colour in a certain scene of *La Guerre de Troie n'aura pas lieu* is said to derive from the nuancing of modern painting (Sørensen, p.217), whereas the intention is surely to make the scene a *crudely* brilliant one (this is the moment at which Hector is asking Hélène to imagine the setting against which she will be returned to the Greeks). (And, more widely, R. Cohen thinks Giraudoux's most important achievement was 'a reversal of the moralistic naturalistic tradition which had stifled dramatic development for at least 300 years', whereas Giraudoux shows, for example, a debt to the dramatic use of disguise in Marivaux and Beaumarchais and to certain uses of quiproquo farce in nineteenth-century comedy. See R. Cohen, *Giraudoux: Three Faces of Destiny* (University of Chicago Press, 1968), p.136.)

5. In 'Jean Giraudoux et la philosophie d'Aristote: A propos de "Choix des Elues"', *Nouvelle Revue Française*, 1940, pp.339-54.

6. See especially C.-E. Magny, *Précieux Giraudoux* (Seuil, 1945); and also, for instance, P.A. Mankin, *Precious Irony: The Theatre of Jean Giraudoux* (Mouton, 1971); J. Prévost, 'Jean Giraudoux et la préciosité', *Confluences*, 1944, pp.85-8; Celler, p.71; Sørensen, p.183.

7. The baroque poets Théophile de Viau, Saint-Amant and Tristan, she says, 'consider nature as a succession of landscapes to be enjoyed for their own sake and depicted with some precision; and precision for them consists in putting the stress on concrete details in a landscape ... one may wonder if the note of deliberate irresponsibility, of delightful gratuitousness, in some of

Théophile's and Saint-Amant's poetry was not a great asset... Their way of coming almost irrelevantly upon a delicate flower or a moonbeam gives a magic touch to the isolated object...' (O. de Mourgues, *Metaphysical, Baroque and Précieux Poetry* (Clarendon Press, 1953), pp.93, 99.)

8. *Précieux Giraudoux*, p.54.

9. In the works mentioned above, n.6.

10. Giraudoux as lecturer (making remarks germane to this essay) will for similar purposes swoop into immediacy: 'Je crois bien que je vais être obligé, malgré tous les efforts que je fais contre ce fléau depuis ma naissance, et *surtout depuis une demi-heure*, d'aborder les idées générales' (my italics). (In a lecture of 1930; quoted by Albérès, p.7.)

11. Albérès, p.357.

12. They have a taste for practical jokes (I i; vol. I, p.128); Mercure's actions summon Amphitryon back when it is vital for Jupiter's purposes that he be kept away (II iii; vol. I, p.167); Jupiter's disguise is too shiny, and his wrongness about the eyes aptly (and touchingly) exemplifies all that is non-human about him (I v; vol. I, pp.145-6).

13. *Jupiter*: Tu la suis d'abord, la mortelle, d'un pas étoffé et égal aux siens, de façon à ce que tes jambes se déplacent du même écart, d'où naissent dans la base du corps le même appel et le même rythme? ... Puis, bondissant, de la main gauche tu presses sa gorge... (I i; vol. I, p.126).

14. It is the prime motor of the play that Jupiter himself has realised this, and has refused any quasi-magical possession of Alcmène because this would mean he had to 'toucher son corps de mains invisibles pour elle, et l'enlacer d'une étreinte qu'elle ne sentirait pas' (I i; vol. I, p.125).

15. The final, and major, acknowledgement of this essay is to Alison Fairlie, who first aroused my interest in Giraudoux, as in so much else.

Polyphonic Poets: Rabelais and Queneau

Dorothy Gabe Coleman

Queneau spoke of Rabelais' works in this way,

> d'après leur auteur, [elles] sont comparables à un os à moelle, et, à mon sens, toute oeuvre digne de ce nom ... car toute oeuvre demande à être brisée pour être sentie et comprise, toute oeuvre présente une résistance au lecteur, toute oeuvre est une chose difficile; non que la difficulté soit une signe de supériorité, ni une nécessité: mais il doit y avoir effort du moins vers le plus.

('Drôles de goûts', in *Volontés*, No.11, novembre 1938, pp.2-3)

Here he touched a nerve of literature: all great works demand an act of reader-conspiracy. Reading literature entails the continuous development of the power of intelligent discrimination. The meaning is the work itself, to be re-experienced every time the reader wishes to renew that experience. The difficulty is perhaps more acute in French literature for 'great French writers have of course based their art on a catching up of the great works of the past, where an essential part of the aesthetic pleasure lies in the reader's ability to recognise creative variations on a familiar theme, to follow on the score the echoes, the harmonics and the departures from known tradition'. (Alison Fairlie, *Imagination and Language*, Cambridge 1981, p.297) I wish in this essay to suggest various aspects which are present in both Rabelais and Queneau: the allusiveness, the difficulty, the creation of poetry through prose, the treatment of words as living things, the playing with words, and the undermining of the narrative convention.

Let us start with the best example from Rabelais on words/ non-words, communication and persuasion/non-persuasion. In the fifty-fifth and fifty-sixth chapters of the *Quart Livre* Rabelais tells us how Pantagruel and his companions, in their voyage near the Arctic Circle, encounter and hear sounds but cannot see anyone or anything around: the episode of the *parolles gelées*.[1] The tone is one of joy and delight: they are out of sight of land and *en plaine mer* feasting and *gringnotans* — biting into their food. (Rabelais elsewhere has *Grand grignoteur, beau mangeur de soupes*, so the associations around this *grignotans* are the hearty giants, soup-consuming, wine-bibbing and tongue-smoking in Chapter 1 of *Pantagruel*.) The narrative is in the first person plural — we are 'in on' the story. Pantagruel is the first to hear and not to see and he invites us to listen,

> nous feusmes attentifz, et à pleines aureilles humions l'air, comme belles huytres en escalle ...

This is a beautifully absurd simile: *humer* can be drink (Rabelais has a *page à la humerie* elsewhere); it can be *avaler en aspirant*, sucking in the air. But the image falls apart. The two sensations, that of hearing and that of tasting are hilariously put together and we are expected to laugh. Furthermore it is impossible to know whether Rabelais is grammatically saying 'nous ... humions l'air, comme nous humerions de belles huytres' or 'nous ... humions l'air, comme de belles huytres le humeraient'.[2] The reader is perhaps allowed to have associations around oysters: their colour — the juicy grass-green of Marennes oysters; their smell,

> D'un tas d'huîtres vidé d'un panier couvert d'algues
> Monte l'odeur du large et la fraîcheur des vagues
>
> (Samain)

their taste — briny, piquant, giving the eater a shock of freshness, a seawater flavour. Added to these sensations is the knowledge that by night oysters open to drink in dew. Set back in its context, there are marine associations — the company is in full sail and feasting; the suggestion of Pantagruel and company gustily eating; the enormous sound of sucking, of greedily swallowing with a noise of the lips and throat, of slurping and gulping and we can almost imagine the juices mopped up by good bread and a fine bottle of white wine. The comparison adds to the air of enjoyment.

Then 'we' hear even words — *Ce que nous effraya grandement* — and Panurge is given the task of showing panic. The rest of Chapter 55 does not concern us and so we move on to the central episode, the fun and games of all the company with these melting words,

> ...Tenez, tenez, dist Pantagruel, voyez en cy qui encores ne sont degelées.

> Lors nous jecta sus le tillac plenes mains de parolles gelées, et sembloient dragée perlée de diverses couleurs. Nous y veismes des mots de gueule, des motz de sinople, des motz de azur, des motz de sable, des motz dorez.
> Les quelz, estre quelque peu eschauffez entre nos mains, fondoient comme neiges, et les oyons realement, mais ne les entendions, car c'estoit langage barbare. Exceptez un assez grosset, lequel ayant frere Jan eschauffé entre ses mains, feist un son tel que font les chastaignes jectées en la braze sans estre entonmées, lors que s'esclattent, et nous

feist tous de paour tressaillir. 'C'estoit, dist frere Jan, un coup de faulcon en son temps'.

Panurge requist Pantagruel luy en donner encores. Pantagruel luy respondit que donner parolles estoit acte des amoureux. 'Vendez m'en doncques, disoit Panurge. — C'est acte de advocatz, respondit Pantagruel, vendre parolles. Je vous vendroys plus tost silence et plus cherement, ainsi que quelques foys la vendit Demosthenes, moyennant son argentangine.'

Ce nonobstant il en jecta sus le tillac trois ou quatre poignées. Et y veids des parolles bien picquantes, des parolles sanglantes, les quelles le pillot nous disoit quelques foys retourner on lieu du quel estoient proferées, mais c'estoit la guorge couppée; des parolles horrificques, et aultres assez mal plaisantes à veoir. Lesquelles ensemblement fondues, ouysmes hin, hin, hin, hin, hin, ticque, torche, lorgne, brededin, brededac, frr, frrr, frrrr, bou, bou, bou, bou, bou, bou, bou, bou, tracc, tracc, trr, trr, trr, trrr, trrrr, on, on, on, on, on, ououououc, goth, magoth et ne sçay quelz aultres motz barbares; et disoyt que c'estoient vocables du hourt et hannissement des chevaulx à l'heure qu'on chocque. Puys en ouysmes d'aultres grosses, et rendoient son en degelant, les unes comme de tabours et fifres, les aultres comme de clerons et trompettes. Croyez que nous y eusmes du passetemps beaucoup.

The episode is not original (hardly any of the scenes and episodes in Rabelais are original). Plutarch had told the story as had Castiglione and Calcagnini, the former in 1528 in a famous chapter of *Il Cortegiano* and the latter in 1541 in a collection of moral fables of which two are concerned with 'frozen words'. But Rabelais' telling of the story is magnificent, elaborated with great imaginative detail and enlivened by his inventive genius.

Pantagruel, like the soft, cuddly bear he is in this episode, is quite excited: *Tenez, tenez* holds a hint of eagerness as he throws a handful of unthawed words on deck. The concept of words being touched, thrown from one to the other, being seen as things in reality — hail, frozen raindrops, *grésil*, pellets of ice crystals, is pleasingly played with. Rabelais describes the physical characteristics of words; we are given an opportunity of handling these curious objects, of holding them up to the light and inspecting them, and by warming them in our hands, of transmuting them once more into their appropriate sounds. The words are unintelligible to Pantagruel and his companions. But there is a joy in poetic creation here: the relationship between words and objects; the real life that words seem to have, an animated movement which is on the confines of articulation. The *langage/matière* is above all the concern of Queneau but we can see it too in this episode. Rabelais elaborates on one of the mysteries of language — how words have colours, shapes and sounds which are 'tangible'. They seem to be *dragée perlée*: Cotgrave gives for *dragée* 'any ionkets, comfets, or sweet meats, served in the last course' and for *perlée* 'rough, rugged, or not smooth'. Thus, Urquhart's translation is accurate — 'rough Sugar-Plumbs'. The white *dragées* of twentieth-century France whisper birth in the family or a wedding; the fragrance, the feel of them and the look of them are essentially French. Added is the colour of the words, like the colour of Rimbaud's vowels, like the 'parfums, les couleurs et les sons se répondent' or Gautier's 'j'entendais le bruit des couleurs'.

Rabelais extends the conception of word-colours in the next sentence: 'we' 'see' *des motz de gueule* — this, the first of a series of heraldic terms, means red; then there are green or vert words, words of blue or azure, of black or sable, of golden and 'or'. Woven into them are hints of another association: *des motz de gueule* given by Cotgrave as 'a wanton or waggish iest, an obscene or lascivious conceit'; *des motz dorez* — 'This means also fair words' (Urquhart). 'We' then warm them and the ice crystals melt *fondoient comme neiges* — an agreeable simile as it conjures up for the reader the tactile sensation of snow melting in our hands and the joy of children playing with snow. When they melt 'we' can actually hear them but 'could not understand them, for it was a Barbarous Gibberish' (Urquhart). Then, with a nicety and an appropriate singling out of frère Jean — who is always boisterous, brave, loving to eat and drink burlesquely, bold and courageous in the three books in which he appears — we see that he has a pretty big word whose sound is the same as *chastaignes jectées en la braze sans estre entonmées* — without having been pricked, they explode with much noise like a cannon-shot.

The next paragraph is a dialogue between Panurge and Pantagruel around the word *parolles* — giving or selling words like a lover or lawyer and the giant saying he would prefer silence but... *Ce nonobstant* opens the following paragraph where the verbal thickness and the manipulation of words are remarkable. We talk of *parolles* being bloody — the bleedingness of words, the plasticity of *picquantes* — the very sharpness of language, and we are thinking about them as objects. We feel the strange, almost magic power that words have of striking fear, of charming and stimulating people and evoking visually and resonantly a battle of long ago; it is a power which perpetuates past events so that even if unintelligible to clear reason they have this element of survival, of bursting forth in the imagination of men. The extreme jubilance of the whole company is expressed when they are playing with these pretty coloured words, the jumbled jigsaw of thawing words, caught at the level of mere sounds. We have the rather thin laughter of *hin, hin, hin, hin, hin*, the copious blubbering of *bou, bou, bou, bou, bou, bou, bou, bou*, the sharp *ticque, torche, lorgne* which Cotgrave gives as 'voices or words, whereby, as by our thwicke thwacke, &c, a beating, or cuffing with the fist, &c, is expressed', the crashing and roaring of *frr, frrr, frrrr* — louder and louder as the consonant *r* grows in number and the spluttering and mumbling of *brededin, brededac*. This theme of the potency of words, their layers of meaning, the way they are charged with more than their normal semantic load or the associations of their immediate context is to recur many times in French literature. Non-words have their own potency: Baudelaire's *l'irrésistible Ouf!* or Proust's *Zut, zut, zut.* Although *Ouf!* or *Zut!* are non-words, they can simultaneously act as words and express the difficulty of finding words in which to render experience. Clearly, the tone of Rabelais' 'Frozen words' is brawling and primitive; there are hints of something the company cannot understand; there is also a comic astonishment which makes me think of the frogs' chorus in Aristophanes — Brekekeke, coax, coax.[3] Queneau wrote in 1955 a statement that could have been the climax to this episode in Rabelais,

> Le langage oral comprend, outre les mots plus ou moins organisés en phrase, un nombre incroyable de grognements, raclements de gorge, grommellements, interjections, qui participent à la communication et qui ont une valeur sémantique; et, naturellement, il faut tenir compte aussi de la part de la mimique.

Rabelais and Queneau are interested in oral French, that is to say, language considered in its entirety, including also the full complement of gestures, grunts, coughs and so on.

Rabelais is a universal man: Franciscan, Benedictine, lawyer, medical doctor, *évangéliste*, comic writer and humane humanist. Queneau is also a universal man: poet, mathematician, philosopher, historian, philologist, painter, translator and writer. He has been influenced by Rabelais, even likes Trouillogan as the best character in fiction and the two have in common 'poetic prose'. What do I mean by poetic prose? Following Longinus and Montaigne — both exciting literary critics — I mean imagination, judgment, sensitivity, word-consciousness and the interlocking of rhythm and imagery so that we can say 'J'ayme l'alleure poëtique, à sauts et à gambades. C'est une art, comme dict Platon, legere, volage, demoniacle'. (*Essais*, I, 28) A dense, ambivalent texture which can only be grasped if we read it as poetry with the willingness for a phrase to be obscure in itself but expecting that the context around it will eventually make clear the meaning. In fact, Rabelais starts the tradition of prose/poetry writing that includes *Don Quixote, Moby Dick*, Flaubert's *Bouvard et Pécuchet* (a favourite book of Queneau), Joyce and Queneau. This tradition has as its main intention the disruption of conventions, shocking the reader out of his normal safe universe and forcing him to accept the position of participation. When Smollett wrote:

> Although nothing could be more ludicrous and unnatural than the figures they [the romances of the Middle Ages] drew ... Cervantes, by an inimitable piece of ridicule, reformed the taste of mankind, representing chivalry in the right point of view...
> (cited by Miriam Allott, *Novelists on the novel*, p.43)

the Cervantes who appears here is the colossus who broke down the knight-errantry that the whole of Europe had admired for the previous three centuries. The hero of such adventures made unnatural difficulties for himself in order to give the reader the pleasure of seeing him overcome them and win the heroine. In the *Prologue* to *Pantagruel* in 1532 Rabelais also writes a list of *chansons de geste* mingled with books of pure fantasy:

> Fessepinte, Orlando furioso, Robert le Diable, Fierabras, Guillaume sans paour, Huon de Bourdeaulx, Montevieille et Matabrune.

but above all the *Chronicques Gargantuines*. Both sixteenth-century authors are self-consciously writing a comic and parodic work. The first half of the sixteenth century saw the last heyday of chivalric romances and *chansons de geste*: the popularity of the *Amadis* in the reign of François Ier, the addition of more magic, more *merveilleux* and more *aventures galantes* to stories that were known; 79 adaptations of *chansons de geste* between 1478 and 1549 — all this made good reading for lords and ladies.

In the first chapter of *Pantagruel* there is then the parody framework of a *chronique*. There is a meticulous accuracy in the account of wildly grotesque and impossible events followed by the first-person narrator:

> affin que je n'erre, car de cela me veulx je curieusement guarder...

where the accuracy and the first-person tone are totally out of keeping with what is being narrated. In the history of the *enfleure tres horrible* Rabelais alternates between presenting information and commenting on it in a burlesque fashion. The first-person narrator addresses the reader directly: for instance, the swelling of the shoulders, the *couilles*, the legs, the nose, the ears and the *membre viril* are dealt with and immediately after the *membre viril* comes the remark 'vous sçavez le reste de la chanson' implying women's insatiability and demandingness in sexual matters.

To view the highly comic, the disorientation and the parodic form in Queneau's whole work we can take the first page of *Les Fleurs bleues* and judge that he demands participation of the reader in the same way Rabelais does. The novel was published in 1965 and it starts with a virtuoso display of verbal fireworks.

> Le vingt-cinq septembre douze cent soixante-quatre, au petit jour, le duc d'Auge se pointa sur le sommet du donjon de son château pour y considérer, un tantinet soit peu, la situation historique. Elle était plutôt floue. Des restes du passé traînaient encore çà et là, en vrac. Sur les bords du ru voisin campaient deux Huns; non loin d'eux un Gaulois, Eduen peut-être, trempait audacieusement ses pieds dans l'eau courante et fraîche. Sur l'horizon se dessinaient les

silhouettes molles de Romains fatigués, de Sarrasins de Corinthe, de Francs anciens, d'Alains seuls. Quelques Normands buvaient du calva.

Le duc d'Auge soupira mais n'en continua moins d'examiner attentivement ces phénomènes usés.

Les Huns préparaient des stèques tartares, le Gaulois fumait une gitane, les Romains dessinaient des grecques, les Sarrasins fauchaient de l'avoine, les Francs cherchaient des sols et les Alains regardaient cinq Ossètes. Les Normands buvaient du calva.

Tant d'histoire, dit le duc d'Auge au duc d'Auge, tant d'histoire pour quelques calembours, pour quelques anachronismes. Je trouve cela misérable. On n'en sortira donc jamais?

Fasciné, il ne cessa pendant quelques heures de surveiller ces déchets se refusant à l'émiettage; puis sans cause extérieure décelable, il quitta son poste de guet pour les étages inférieurs du château en se livrant au passage à son humeur qui était de battre.

Il ne battit point sa femme parce que défunte, mais il battit ses filles au nombre de trois; il battit des serviteurs, des servantes, des tapis, quelques fers encore chauds; la campagne, monnaie et en fin de compte, ses flancs. Tout de suite après, il décida de faire un court voyage et de se rendre dans la ville capitale en petit arroi, accompagné seulement de son page Mouscaillot.

Parmi ses palefrois, il choisit son percheron favori nommé Démosthène parce qu'il parlait, même avec le mors entre les dents.[4]

Queneau is all out to disorientate us. The universe is an

unfamiliar one. The words of the sub-title in Greek by Plato mean 'dream instead of dream'. The duc d'Auge is on his own looking *un tantinet soit peu* at the historical situation which is fuzzy, in a jumble, higgledy-piggledy. We realise it is a jumble of styles from the highly literary — *ru voisin* — to the very colloquial *calva* for *calvados*. The number of puns is collossal: for example, *deux Huns* is a pun on *deux uns*; *les Eduens* are the Haeduans, a race that invaded Gaul and a pun on *et du un*; *Francs anciens* are both the barbaric Franks and the old franc as opposed to the new one; *Alains seuls* are the Alani, another lot of Barbarians, but we hear a pun on *linceul*, a shroud; *Le Gaulois fumait une gitane* — literally the Gauls and the gypsy race, but they are also French cigarettes; *cinq Ossètes* are a people of the Caucasus but there is also a pun on *cinq ou sept*; then the battery of meanings using *battre*: *battre le fer pendant qu'il est chaud* — the proverbial meaning 'strike while the iron is hot' is rendered hilariously funny when Queneau pluralises *fer*; *battre la campagne* means 'to scour the country' but also 'to be delirious' and also became the title of a book of Queneau's poetry published in 1968 — three years after the publication of *Les Fleurs bleues*; *battre de la monnaie* is 'to mint money' whereas *battre monnaie* is 'to raise the wind' and finally *se battre les flancs* is 'to cudgel one's brains'.

Queneau said in *Bâtons, chiffres et lettres* that he did not see any real difference between novels and poems (Gallimard, 1950, p.43). Any writer can 'faire rimer des situations ou des personnages comme on fait rimer les mots; on peut même se contenter d'allitérations' (p.42). We see many examples of this in the first page we are analysing. For example, *se dessinaient les silhouettes molles de Romains fatigués* is echoed by *les Romains dessinaient des grecques*. Or we see the almost refrain of *Quelques Normands buvaient du calva* and *Les Normands buvaient du calva*. Or *dit le duc d'Auge au duc d'Auge*. The very names of the characters — Mouscaillot, Cidrolin, Onésiphore, Biroton, Démo/Sthène, Stéphane — have the same comic fantasy as names in Rabelais — Riflandouille, Humevesne, Baisecul, Bridoye, Nazdecabre — or those of

Molière — Flipote, Sganarelle, Madame Pernelle, Galopin, Gorgibus.

The questioning, undermining and reviving of the act of narration are profoundly manipulated by both Rabelais and Queneau. From the beginning of the prologue to *Pantagruel* we are drawn into the mesmerising, word-spinning account presented by the created author and we never leave it. This disruptive technique relies on a *je*, a *nous*, an *on* and the pseudonymous Alcofribas Nasier narrator who in the *Quart Livre* speaks as a member of the company, observing the behaviour and joining in the fun. In *Les Fleurs bleues* two men dream each other up. The two main characters — Le duc d'Auge and Cidrolin — (note that the calling them so is a hint of Normandy — any dish called after the *pays d'Auge* (chicken, veal, pork, fish or vegetables) comes to the table afloat with cream; it is appropriate that Maupassant should be writing *Boule de Suif* in Normandy and the *pays d'Auge* is an area of the finest Calvados; Cidrolin — from *cidre*, the other local drink in Normandy) — are two halves of a dream: we never know where we are: there are no transit signs, no moment of transition between the two. There arc clues almost hidden by Queneau that the scene is shifting — there is always a phrase suggesting sleep, or at least lying or sitting down to take a nap: for example the first change-over, *le duc d'Auge finit par s'endormir*. (cf.p.6. Cidrolin lies on his couch, his eyes covered by a handkerchief; this is followed by *Le duc d'Auge s'éveillait*; or p.7. when the duke *mangea copieusement, puis alla se coucher et dormit de fort bon appétit*; we suddenly see Cidrolin being awakened by two nomads.) In the blurb Queneau says 'est-ce le duc d'Auge qui rêve qu'il est Cidrolin ou Cidrolin qui rêve qu'il est duc d'Auge?'. On the third page of the novel we read 'le duc d'Auge finit par s'endormir' followed immediately by 'Il habitait une péniche amarrée à demeure près d'une grande ville et il s'appelait Cidrolin'. In this way we never stop at a single focus point: we are carefully never given one (cf.p.6, p.7, p.11, p.14, p.17, p.20, p.22, p.27, p.32, p.37, p.42, p.49, p.55, p.62, etc.). So we follow their careers and do not know which is the more important: we read of the adventures with le duc d'Auge from 1264 when he meets Saint Louis, through 1439 when he buys cannonballs, through 1614 when he discovers an alchemist, through 1789 to 1964 when he meets Cidrolin who has nothing to do in life except dream and repaint the garden fence.

The leitmotifs in *Les Fleurs bleues* are numerous: for example the *considérer, un tantinet soit peu, la situation historique* which we met on the first page is repeated on p.43. 'il se lève et se pointe sur la plateforme du donjon de son château pour y considérer un tantinet soit peu la situation historique'. (cf.p.123 when the 'duc examina la situation'; or p.1189 when Lalix 'alla prendre un second café pour considérer un tantinet soit peu sa situation présente'.) Phrases such as *encore un de foutu* or *essence de fenouil* are uttered by both characters; the duc d'Auge dreams that he is leading the life of Cidrolin (e.g. p.24, p.27) whilst Cidrolin tells of dreams that put him in the time of Saint Louis, Louis XI, Louis XIII (p.139). There are characters that appear in both halves of the dream like Onésiphore; Cidrolin suddenly speaks in the context of a dialogue between the duc and Adolphe, vicomte de Péchenay. The whole novel is circular in pattern with the last thing being little blue flowers — *s'épanouissent déjà de petites fleurs bleues*, thereby echoing the *fleurs bleues* which come in the duc d'Auge's first conversation with the horse.

My third point is the problem of allusiveness in both Rabelais and Queneau. Literary tradition in sixteenth-century France was too new to be anything but artificial, that is in the sense of artifex, produced by art as opposed to spontaneous nature. It is well-known that Rabelais — perhaps more than the other sixteenth-century giant of French prose, Montaigne — used Greek and Roman writers, medieval writers, sermon-writers like Menot and Maillard, macaronic writers like Folengo, writers of the Old and New Testaments, with the appearance of carelessness in his crowded universe. His indebtedness to the past is colossal. Flaubert — who admired him tremendously ('Rabelais, d'où découlent les lettres françaises') — linked him together with Ronsard and Montaigne and thought they were creating a literature which was going to be highly allusive for the next four hundred years. The effectiveness of an allusion depends on the assumption that readers are as civilised as authors. Creative activity is involved in reading the best of French literature. Even the seventeenth century — whose utterances on Ronsard and Du Bellay are well known from Boileau's words,

> Ronsard
> Réglant tout, brouillant tout, fit un art à sa mode ...
> Ce poëte orgueilleux, trébuché de si haut,
> Rendit plus retenus Desportes et Bertaut.
> Enfin Malherbe vint et le premier en France,
> Fit sentir dans les vers une juste cadence...

— looked back on the sixteenth century, whilst Diderot a century later writes,

> Les Grecs ont été les précepteurs des Romains, les Grecs et les Romains ont été les nôtres; je l'ai dit, et je le répète: on ne peut guère prétendre au titre de littérature sans la connaissance de leurs langues.

We have only to read the first poems of a writer such as Baudelaire to see how firmly grounded he was in Latin poetry: for instance in 1837 he won at school a second prize for his Latin verses; no.8 in his *Premiers poèmes* is from Ovid's *Turpe senex miles*; in the 1855 edition of *Les Fleurs du Mal* we find lines from D'Aubigné starting the work; we can study *Le Cygne* for his large-scale borrowing of Virgil or *L'Amour du Mensonge* for his borrowing from Racine's *Athalie*. A year before his death in 1945 Valéry showed how close Latin poetry was to him,

> Quoique latiniste des moins sûrs de soi, cette mince et

médiocre connaissance qui m'est restée du langage de
Rome m'est infiniment précieuse.

And, of course, he had been translating Virgil's *Eclogues*
between 1942 and 1944. He sees himself in a tradition which
stems from the Greeks and from poets like Virgil, Catullus,
Horace, Propertius and Ovid. Far from being an abnormal
literary phenomenon he is a typical product of a
Roman-Graeco-French culture. And it is in sixteenth-century
France that the literary habit of allusiveness becomes firmly
established.

Queneau's allusiveness is oblique. He creates two horses —
Démosthène and Stéphane: they are both gifted with human
speech and a fondness for punning; called Sthène and Stèphe
they are hilarious puppets. When the duc *et compagnie* arrive
in Paris in 1264 Stèphe feels impelled to use these terms
about the capital city,

Alme et inclyte cité.

To which Sthène answers,

Silence! ... Si l'on nous entendait parler, notre bon maître
serait accusé de sorcellerie.

We cannot help remembering chapter six of *Pantagruel*, the
episode of the Limousin student and Pantagruel. The chapter
starts,

Quelque jour, je ne sçai quand, Pantagruel se pourmenoit
après souper avecques ses compagnons, par la porte dont
l'on va à Paris. Là rencontra un escholier tout jolliet qui
venoit par icelluy chemin, et, après qu'ilz se furent saluez,
luy demanda:
'Mon amy, d'ont viens tu à ceste heure?'

A familiar question which receives in reply,

'De l'alme, inclyte, et celebre academie que l'on vocite Lutece.'

The student goes on with this latinisation of French,

'Nous transfretons la Sequane au dilucule et crepuscule; nous deambulons par les compites et quadrivies de l'urbe; nous despumons la verbocination latiale, et, comme verisimiles amorabonds, captons la benevolence de l'omnijuge, omniforme, et omnigene sexe feminin.'[5]

This was very funny and satiric for contemporary readers and it goes on for a whole chapter; the Latinisms may prevent twentieth-century readers from hearing the sexuality and the gastronomy in the text. Pantagruel eventually loses his temper and reduces the poor student to a typical Limousin dialect,

'Vée dicou! gentilastre. Ho, sainct Marsault, adjouda my! Hau, hau, laissas à quau, au nom de Dious, et ne me touquas grou.'[6]

Queneau is able to recreate the episode, putting it in the mouths of horses and following it with a *Brr* from the duc,

Et son page itou (very slangy)
— Brr, fit Mouscaillot.

A little further on in *Les Fleurs bleues* the duc d'Auge protests that he does not intend to go on a crusade,

Et ... vous croyez que c'est en allant en Tunisie qu'on l'arrachera des infidèles, le sépulchre! La Tunisie! Pourquoi pas le pays des Amaurotes ou des Hamaxobiens? Tant qu'il y est, notre saint roi, pourquoi n'irait-il pas jusque chez les Indiens ou les Sères? Pourquoi ne s'embarque-t-il pas sur la mer Océane jusqu'au-delà de l'île de Thulé peut-être bien qu'il trouverait par là une terre inconnue avec des

infidèles supplémentaires à ratatiner?
— Modérez-vous, messire, murmura l'abbé Biroton.

We notice first of all a borrowing from *Pantagruel*, chapter 23: the name of a tribe *Les Amaurotes* — a name that Rabelais had himself found in Thomas More's *Utopia*. This clue leads us on to the allusions to *Gargantua* chapter 33, the episode of Picrochole and his advisers. This magnificent chapter is a masterpiece of imaginative writing: Picrochole's dream-conquest of all the territories of Europe and Asia Minor. Another clue to the parodying allusiveness in the Queneau passage is in the mention of Tunisia — which is the first land to be conquered by Picrochole. He is an automaton, a toy manipulated by Toucquedillon, and his advisers the *comte Spadassin* and *capitaine Merdaille* (note the comic effect of their names) — with his mind fixed on things which are impossible of reaching. Rabelais plays with tenses: *'Je ... le prendray à mercy'*, says Picrochole of conquering Barberousse, and at Rome where *'Le pauvre Monsieur du Pape meurt des jà de peur'* we are still in the future,

Par ma foy ... je ne lui baiseray jà sa pantoufle.

Then we are in the conditional, back to the future — greater dreams of all the ancient lands in Asia Minor : *'Voirons nous ... Babylone et le Mont Sinay?'*, then suddenly the present — *'nous sommes affolez'*, another future, then a past historic, then the present tense looking to the half-army which is fighting with *ce villain humeux Grandgousier*, another present and so on. Picrochole's imagination flies high above the world of sense. This automaton is dominated by anger — as indeed his name suggests — and he is quickly disposed of by Rabelais — *Depuis ne sçait on qu'il est devenu. Toutefoys l'on dict qu'il est de present pauvre gaignedenier à Lyon, cholere comme davant...* This episode is tucked into the Fable of *La laitière et le pot au lait* by La Fontaine,

RABELAIS AND QUENEAU

Qui ne fait châteaux en Espagne?
Picrochole, Pyrrhus, la laitière, enfin tous,
Autant les sages que les fous?

And it is equally well hidden in Queneau.

Another allusion is doubly comic in that the story is about wooden horses in *Gargantua* and about the talking horse Sthène in Queneau. The episode is in *Gargantua*, chapter 12: the boy giant has wooden horses at the top of the house; he plays with them, makes them leap and skip forward all the time; then le seigneur Painensac and company visit Grandgousier one day and finding the accommodation skimpy ask Gargantua where are the stables. At which, the boy leads them up and up, via stairs and turrets to a large room,

> Voicy ... les estables que demandez; voylà mon genet, voylà mon guildin, mon lavedan, mon traquenard.

The joke is against the silly seigneur de Painensac. The duc d'Auge tells of the difficulties in the capital,

> C'est en visitant votre grande tour que tout faillit mal tourner, continua le duc. Sthène voulait monter jusqu'au troisième étage, il a dû se contenter du premier.

Cidrolin wants to know how the other horse fared,

> Stèphe? Il n'a pas voulu monter. Il avait le vertige.

There are a number of subtle suggestions which hark back to Rabelais. There are numerous *revenons à nos moutons* (admittedly it had occurred firstly in *Pathelin*, but surely it became current jargon only after Rabelais?) and once *revenons à nos moutons qui sont d'ailleurs des chats*. Once or twice we hear what can be linked to Rabelais: for example, the duc saying, nous méritons un bon repas. A boire et de l'andouille.

Or, near the end of the book, they all feast,

> Et nous commencerons par de l'andouille, maître d'hôtel, nous continuerons par de l'andouillette, maître d'hôtel, et nous terminerons par de douillettes friandises, maître d'hôtel. Voilà ce qu'on appelle un repas bien enchaîné. Et foin du caviar et autres moscoviteries! Et champagne!

An author who is as cultivated and humorous as Queneau cannot but parody and make allusions to previous literature. The allusiveness is everywhere: for example, there are references to *Salammbô* (1862), the novel of ancient Carthage by Flaubert, introduced gaily after real people like Saint Augustine ... Jugurtha ... Scipion ... Hannibal. There is a whisper of Hugo in the phrase *c'était l'heure où les houatures vont boire*: it calls up for us *Booz endormi* with the line,

> C'était l'heure tranquille où les lions vont boire.

There is a fleeting reference to that beautiful poem by Malherbe, *Consolation à Monsieur du Périer, Gentilhomme d'Aix-en-Provence, sur la mort de sa fille*, when Queneau has the duc d'Auge say,

> Comment? le roi n'est pas en son palais du Louvre aux barrières duquel veille la garde?

The poem is a consolation on death the great leveller, striking even kings: the soldiers guarding them in the Louvre cannot protect them against death,

> Le pauvre en sa cabane, où le chaume le couvre,
>   Est sujet à ses lois:
> Et la garde qui veille aux barrières du Louvre
>   N'en défend point nos rois.

Ronsard had the reputation of reading the whole of Homer in three days. Queneau makes Sthène have that good name. There is an allusion to a line from Apollinaire's *Signe*,

Mon automne éternel, ô ma saison mentale

and as a last example this sentence,

Pour tout vous avouer, dit Sthène, je m'ennuie un peu loin du château et souvent je me demande quand je reverrai mon écurie natale qui m'est une province et beaucoup davantage.

This alludes to the famous sonnet by Du Bellay, *Heureux qui comme Ulysse a fait un beau voyage*, one of *Les Regrets* (1558) which was written while in Rome with his cousin the Cardinal Jean Du Bellay (Rabelais' patron). Du Bellay's lines are,

Quand revoiray-je, helas, de mon petit village
Fumer la cheminée, et en quelle saison
Revoiray-je le clos de ma pauvre maison,
Qui m'est une province, et beaucoup davantage?

Du Bellay had written the manifesto of the Pléiade. Thus, in just a few words, Queneau conjures up much that is important in French literary history.

My fourth point is the difficulty of language in both writers. Queneau said of *Les Fleurs bleues*,

J'ai écrit d'autres romans avec cette idée de rythme, cette intention de faire du roman une sorte de poème.

In both writers there is an opulence of vocabulary due to the multiple origins — learned, technical, archaic, slangy, erotic, Latin, latinisation of French words — and they both create new words. The coinages work since we follow the basic structure — the morphology and syntax of French — and add non-existent vocabulary on to it. Under the veil of reforming the French language where the spoken is so far apart from the written, Queneau devised a spelling to render the spoken word: *houatures* equals *voitures*; *ekcetera* equals *etcœtera*, *sandouiche* equals *sandwich* and so on but the attempt at radicalisation of literary French was not a success and we can compare the parsimony of *néo-français* in *Les Fleurs bleues* to the greater use of it in *Zazie dans le métro* which came out six years before. But his neologisms are more creative: for example, *calembourderai* comes from *calembour*; or *migrer* — the French had always had *immigrer* and *émigrer* but not *migrer*; or *faitdiverse* — a noun made into an adjective; or the beautifully appropriate *voletaille* which are the low ranks of the restaurant hierarchy, who are running hither and thither to please their superiors — the associations being with *voleter*, fluttering and flying, and, of course, *canaille*. Rabelais creates a word which is half way between the recognisably intelligible and the purely fantastic,

> pissoient aux pissoirs, crachoient aux crachoirs, toussoient aux toussoirs, resvoient aux resvoirs ...

We do not stop to think what a *toussoir* is because it is already defined by analogy with *pissoirs*. In Rabelais the images are mainly auditory like *mors comme porcs* or Panurge *à cause de ses lunettes, oyoit des aureilles beaucoup plus clair que de coustume* — there is no logic at all in such phrases. By turning upside down the normal meaning of words, Rabelais transforms them into metaphors. The world shows a tendency to abuse metaphors. Often it is poetry that reverses this degradation of language. Rabelais plays with clichés, proverbs and commonplace expressions: for instance frère Jean is *clerc jusque ès dents* — the stock phrase is usually used with *armé* — *armé jusque ès dents*. The contrast between *armé* and the meek *clerc* is richly comic and poetic because the effect depends on the combination of disparate conventional elements ending in incongruity. Rabelais is always on the edge of the fantastic as in the famous list of Sorbonne men,

> Sorbillans, Sorbonagres, Sorbonigenes, Sorbonicoles, Sorboniformes, Sorbonisequens, Norborisans, Borsonisans, Saniborsans.

By playing with the order of letters in a word, by adding a Latin suffix like *sequens* or the French suffixes derived from the Latin, he can take the reader far away from the topical, satirical digs at the Theological Faculty of the Sorbonne into a world of fantasy where the reader's whole delight is in looking at the way he is creative in language.

Similarly with Queneau. At the very beginning of *Les Fleurs bleues* we hear Sthène saying 'let's go and see if Notre Dame is finished' (it is 1264 at this point of the story),

> Si on traîne tellement, on finira par bâtir une mahomerie. Pourquoi pas un bouddhoir? un Confuciussonnal? un sanct-lao-tsuaire?

Mahomerie — slang or invention of a place where Mahomet is worshipped; *bouddhoir* — means both a Buddha and a *boudoir*; *Confuciussonnal* — suggest both Confucius and a confessional and *sanct-lao-tsuaire* — meaning both Lao-Tsu and a sanctuary plus the punning on *suaire*, plus a hint at *sainct suaire de Chambery* (*Gargantua*, chapter 27).

Valéry said of Rabelais that he was among writers 'qui savent vivre où mènent les mots'. His style reflects his *joie de vivre* through enumeration and alliterative and explosive sounds as in this famous sentence,

> L'odeur du vin, ô combien plus est friant, riant, priant, plus celeste et delicieux que d'huile.

The combination of apparent spontaneity and symmetry makes for aesthetic satisfaction. The ebullience, the vitality, the opulence and the seemingly effortless and unlimited flow of language are crucial, so that even when we ought to be scandalised when Gargantua's mother produced a child and milk that were declared an impossible proposition by the Sorbonne the comic coinage makes us laugh at the association of the serious with the *invraisemblable,*

mammalement scandaleuse, des pitoyables oreilles offensive et sentant de loin heresie.

The affinities between Rabelais and Queneau are great. But do they count as influences? I am daring here a hypothesis: Queneau has been influenced by Rabelais but in a strange and unusual fashion. Rabelais' importance in the English critical tradition is great: Bacon was fair to the jester, so were Sir Thomas Browne and the Scottish translator Urquhart; Kingsley wrote *The Water-Babies* with *Pantagruel* and *Gargantua* largely in mind. But it was in an offshoot of the critical tradition that Rabelais shone: the Irish/Celtic writers of the eighteenth century Swift (1667-1745) and Sterne (1713-68) whose *Tristram Shandy* was a continuation of the Menippean Satire model that Rabelais had proposed. In the twentieth century another Irishman responds to Rabelais — James Joyce and we may look at the first few lines of his *Finnegans Wake* to see him at work,

riverrun, past Eve and Adam's, from swerve of shore to bend of bay, brings us by a commodius vicus of recirculation back to Howth Castle and Environs.
     Sir Tristram, violer d'amores, fr'over the short sea, has passencore rearrived from North Armorica on this side the scraggy isthmus of Europe Minor to wielderfight his penisolate war: nor had topsawyer's rocks by the stream Oconee exaggerated themselse to Laurens County gorgios while they went doublin their mumper all the time: nor

avoice from afire bellowsed mishe mishe to tauftauf thuartpeatrick: not yet, though venissoon after ...

The reader is immediately disorientated; very little punctuation; an unreal orthography; tricks played by language; a traffic in staple words and out-riggers of association on each syllable. The humorous play with language, from the French *pas encore* to the *bellowsed* and the *venissoon after* makes us realise that the piece must be read aloud before we can understand it. The poetic sound of 'from swerve of shore to bend of bay', followed by the prosaic comically long Latinism 'commodius vicus of recirculation', which is a very peculiar rhythm — the Latin phrase bang in the middle, disrupting the English sentence —, the apparent nonsense of many a sentence — all this makes us lose our bearing and yet, curious to go on reading. Joyce works through a macaronic language: to the English language he adds provincialisms, pronunciation faults, neologisms, jargon and blocks or combination of several words to form one new word. In addition he pours in French, German, Italian, Greek, Sanscrit, old Irish and Russian. He can form a word from a French prefix and a Greek root or he can gloriously parody in

Wallalhoo, Wallalhoo, mourn is plein

which is the first line of the second section of Hugo's *L'Expiation,*

Waterloo! Waterloo! Waterloo! morne plaine.

Joyce's style is such that it refuses to place the reader in a familiar universe. Joyce too is universal: educated by Jesuits, student of medicine, multilinguist, a cosmopolitan Irishman living in Europe and a man who had a more-than-Rabelaisian humour.

In *Entretiens avec Georges Charbonnier* (Paris, 1962, p.12), Queneau replies to the question of influence, par Joyce d'abord, et puis par *Lord Jim* ... je n'ai pas trouvé d'exemple et d'inspiration dans la littérature française.

Joyce, Queneau and Rabelais are masters of encyclopædic tradition and all three play with styles, with tones, with ironic levels and with the sound of spoken word. Words are musicalised in that the meaning, the shape, the sound and the alliteration become the primary incentive for using them. They mesmerise the reader with language. Later on in the same interview Queneau develops his idea of all novels being either an *Iliad* or an *Odyssey*. Those having the shape of an *Odyssey* include *Don Quixote* and 'Rabelais aussi, bien sûr, Rabelais, c'est une Odyssée'. And so, we have come the full circle round. Queneau has a Rabelaisian method of seeing, hearing, repeating, coining which in the end looks but is not obscene,

Ils se tordent les bras
Ils se mordent les yeux
Ils se déchaussent les dents
Ils se frottent les oreilles
Ils s'écrasent les doigts du pied
Ils se saignent le nez
Ils se heurtent les tibias
Ils se noircissent les paupières
Ils se tapent sur le ventre ...
Ils se dépiautent.
Ils se mutilent.
Ils s'émiettent ...

(*Chiendent*, Gallimard, pp.141-2)

In Colletet's *Life of Rabelais* there is a tribute which could equally serve as an epilogue to Queneau's life,

car il est certain qu'il fut très-sçavant humaniste, et très-profond philosophe, théologien, mathématicien, médecin, jurisconsulte, musicien, arithméticien, astronome, voire mesme peintre et poëte tout ensemble.

NOTES

1. The edition used throughout is by Jourda (Garnier, Paris, 1962, 2 vols.).

2. See La Fontaine's variation on the oyster in *Le Rat et l'Huître*, VIII.9.

   Par un doux zéphyr réjouie,
   Humait l'air, respirait, était épanouie,
   Blanche, grasse, et d'un goût, à la voir, non pareil.

   See also Maupassant, *Bel-Ami*, Paris 1926, I.V.p.99

   Les huîtres d'Ostende furent apportées, mignonnes et grasses, *semblables à de petites oreilles* enfermées en des coquilles ... (my italics)

   Urquhart's translation,

   According to his command we listen'd, and with full Ears suck'd. in the Air, as some of you suck Oysters...

   is his personal interpretation and not a good version; nonetheless it is worth noting.

3. Rabelais owned a text of Aristophanes.

4. *Les Fleurs bleues*, London, 1971, pp.3-4.

5. Molière could use perfectly the Latinised jargon of medicine: Diafoirus finds Argan's pulse *'duriuscule pour ne pas dire dur'* or Sganarelle in *Le Médecin malgré lui* feels buoyant when he realises that no-one knows Latin,

   en faisant diverses plaisantes postures. Cabricias arci thuram, catalamus, singulariter, nominativo haec Musa ...

6. The Limousin patois was a good source for comic effect as was Gascony in Molière's time; also one remembers that Monsieur de Pourceaugnac is a provincial man from the province of Limousin.

Some Reflections on Problems of Language in Corneille

Gwyneth Castor

The problems of language which I shall be discussing are those that arise from the gap between words and reality, between experience and expression — a gap pin-pointed by Constant in a memorable sentence:

> Les sentiments de l'homme sont confus et mélangés; ils se composent d'une multitude d'impressions variées qui échappent à l'observation; et la parole, toujours trop grossière et trop générale, peut bien servir à les désigner, mais ne sert jamais à les définir.[1]

Every writer must grapple with these problems and in particular with the paradoxical problem which is central to literary endeavour: how to render in words the complexities of feeling, behaviour and judgment which it lies beyond the power of words to express or define. And some writers, as well as grappling with problems of language, also reflect upon them in their works and incorporate them as a theme.

LANGUAGE IN CORNEILLE

In what follows I shall first look briefly at Corneille's treatment of problems of language as a theme in his comedies (taking *La Veuve* as an example), and then examine the less apparent but still central role played by problems of language in the tragedies, where they do not form an explicit theme.

Several of Corneille's comedies are centred on the unreliability of language. The most obvious case is *Le Menteur*; but since Dorante, *le menteur*, responds to this unreliability by exploiting it for his own ends, the fundamental problems of verbal communication are less directly confronted in this play than they are in earlier comedies. I take *La Veuve* as an example because it is a play which both dramatises and discusses the complexities of the language of love.

The play's discussion of the theme focuses on the problems of an inexperienced suitor, Florange, who never appears on stage. In his wooing of Doris, Florange is made to seem ridiculous, but the difficulties he has in finding a language suitable for his suitor's role are nonetheless real ones. Since all language depends on convention, love, which professes a special and individual commitment, struggles with the banality of a common currency. Moreover, the language of love has become doubly conventional: its own hyperbolic phrases and images have in themselves become a conventional language within a language. As Winifred Nowottny writes of love poetry:

> One may be driven to a new extreme in hyperbolic compliment in the endeavour to assert that what one feels is not the same as what lots of other people have already said on a similar subject. One of the poet's great problems is how to lay claim in words to intensity of feeling. ('If it be love indeed, tell me how much,' was Cleopatra's command to Antony.)[2]

Florange's language is packed with the familiar hyperbolic images of love poetry, and since he never appears in person, his reported speech, in its disembodied state, becomes even

more ridiculous: Géron, acting as Florange's spokesman, addresses Doris's mother, Chrysante:

> Ah! madame, il l'adore!
> Il n'a point encor vu de miracles pareils:
> Ses yeux, à son avis, sont autant de soleils;
> L'enflure de son sein un double petit monde;
> C'est le seul ornement de la machine ronde.
> L'Amour à ses regards allume son flambeau,
> Et souvent pour la voir il ôte son bandeau;
> Diane n'eut jamais une si belle taille;
> Auprès d'elle Vénus ne serait rien qui vaille;
> Ce ne sont rien que lis et roses que son teint;
> Enfin de ses beautés il est si fort atteint...[3]

At this point Géron is interrupted by Chrysante, for this language, full of what Shakespeare's Berowne calls 'taffeta phrases', leads her to assume that Florange is not serious, and her blunt insistence on money matters as the real subject of negotiation in this courtship brings comic *dégonflage*. However, Géron reminds us that though the exaggerated language is comic Florange's problem is a genuine one: ' ...s'il savait mieux dire, il dirait autrement. / C'est un homme tout neuf: que voulez-vous qu'il fasse? / Il dit ce qu'il a lu.' (lines 263-5)

Corneille also directly dramatises in *La Veuve* the unreliability of the language of love by contrasting two couples — Alcidon and Doris, Philiste and Clarice. The first couple do not love each other but pretend to each other that they do; the second couple do love each other but avoid saying so directly because loving words are so readily used by false lovers. As Corneille explained in his *Examen*, he used the encounters between these couples in such a way that 'l'amour a paru entre ceux qui n'en parlent point, et le mépris a été visible entre ceux qui se font des protestations d'amour.'[4] Alcidon and Doris, in their false protestations of love, go so far as to claim with comic irony that language cannot match their feelings (Alcidon: Ce que je ne puis dire est plus que je n'ai dit (662); Doris: Ton amour et le mien ont faute de paroles (675)). Philiste, in contrast, would rather rely on other 'languages':

> Mes soupirs et les siens font un secret langage
> Par où son coeur au mien à tous moments s'engage. (69-70)

For one couple language is a deliberate disguise; for the other it is a mistrusted instrument. In both cases the dramatic action drawn from the encounters and exchanges between the 'lovers' extends well beyond the surface-level of the spoken dialogue, and the spectator/reader is frequently invited to interpret what is said as only part of the drama which is being enacted on the stage.

When we turn to the tragedies, the picture is at first sight a very different one. Here a surface-level simplicity tempts us to see Corneille's language as a transparent (though stylised) vehicle for the thoughts and feelings of his characters. They appear to encounter no problems of self-expression, but on the contrary to rely on debate with others and with themselves to clarify issues and decisions. Their statements are often bold and simple formulations, frequently antithetical in form, which seem confidently to sum up firmly-held views or equally firm decisions. *Le Cid* alone can provide a number of examples:

> Contre mon propre honneur mon amour s'intéresse
>
> (Rodrigue, 302)

> ...qui peut vivre infâme est indigne du jour
>
> (Don Diègue, 284)

> Je ne consulte point pour suivre mon devoir;
> Je cours sans balancer où mon honneur m'oblige
>
> (Chimène, 820-1)

> Je le ferais encor, si j'avais à le faire   (Rodrigue, 878)

LANGUAGE IN CORNEILLE

Nous n'avons qu'un honneur, il est tant de maîtresses!
L'amour n'est qu'un plaisir, l'honneur est un devoir.

(Don Diègue, 1058-9)

However, although problems of language are rarely an explicit theme in the tragedies, they inevitably remain as problems to be confronted both by Corneille and (on a different level) by his characters. I shall argue later that it is, paradoxically perhaps, in the rhetorical simplicity of language which is so characteristic of Corneille's tragedies that we can see problems of language contributing to the tensions and conflicts at the centre of the drama.

First, though, let us pick up the most obvious signs of the presence of problems of verbal expression in the tragedies. There are moments when Corneille's characters, and even the dramatist himself, hesitate over the *naming* of actions and motives. In the case of the characters, hesitations or disagreements are occasionally marked by their use of the verbs *nommer* and *appeler*:

Maxime: Il appelle remords l'amour de la patrie!

(Cinna, 465)

Antiochus: Mais si la dureté de votre aversion
Nomme encor notre amour une rébellion...

(Rodogune, 1345-6)

Don Diègue: Qu'on nomme crime, ou non, ce qui fait nos débats... (Le Cid, 723)

Rodogune: Appelez ce devoir haine, rigueur, colère;
Pour gagner Rodogune, il faut venger un père.

(1043-4)

Rodogune may be happy to exploit the difficulties of labelling in order to bring about the action she wants, but what all of these examples point to is the possibility of the very same action or attitude being given markedly different names. This problem of naming has wide-ranging implications in the tragedies, especially in those plays which focus on the theme of commitment to moral and social codes of behaviour. Verbal labels which express evaluation are essential to such codes; yet they are also disconcertingly unstable. In the middle of Act III of *Cinna*, when Cinna has come to realise how far his own views are from those of Emilie, he accuses her of defining virtuous action in accordance with her own desires: 'Vous faites des vertus au gré de votre haine' (977). Emilie has clung to a single idea — that of avenging her father's death — and her commitment to this duty is fuelled by her hatred of Auguste. But by the end of the play, she has re-labelled her 'duty' as a 'crime': 'Je connais mon forfait qui me semblait justice' (1717).

The fact that Corneille himself sometimes hesitates over labelling — and thereby judging — is interestingly revealed in variants. Rodrigue's words to Chimène: 'Assurez-vous l'honneur de m'empêcher de vivre' (850) were in an earlier version[5] the very different: 'Soûlez-vous du plaisir de m'empêcher de vivre.' And another striking instance occurs in the King's speech at the end of *Horace*; in passing judgment on Horace, he has to weigh up the moral, psychological, and political implications of the case before him, and he explains his decision in these words:

> Vis donc, Horace, vis, guerrier trop magnanime:
> Ta vertu met ta gloire au-dessus de ton crime;
> Sa chaleur généreuse a produit ton forfait;
> D'une cause si belle il faut souffrir l'effet.   (1759-1762)

But the 1656 version has, not 'sa chaleur généreuse', but 'sa chaleur dangereuse'. The judgments made by these two sharply contrasting adjectives are both part of a single, complex evaluation of Horace's behaviour. We may guess that Corneille would have liked to use a word carrying both meanings simultaneously, but having to choose, he hesitated between the two.

Such hesitations, whether they are Corneille's in variant lines or those directly expressed to the audience by his characters, are responses to a central problem: how to determine what is the right application of abstract terms such as *honneur, vertu, devoir, crime, générosité, gloire* to possible courses of action in complex, concrete situations. This problem has two distinct aspects. First, the protagonists who face it need clarity of thought in the handling of language: they need to be lucid as they try to express (to themselves or to others) their own motives, and they also need to be lucid in their analysis of the implications of the possible courses of action which lie before them. For those characters who commit themselves to choosing the 'right' course of action, lucidity becomes not merely an intellectual value but also a moral one, since only through lucid analysis can they avoid misapplication of moral labels and the self-deception that would follow. They must probe beneath broad general labels, rather as La Rochefoucauld does in his *Maximes* ('Ce qu'on nomme libéralité n'est le plus souvent que la vanité de donner...'; 'Ce que le monde nomme vertu n'est d'ordinaire qu'un fantôme formé par nos passions...'[6]), and they must strive to achieve a clear and honest perception of the choices facing them. What their moral code most shuns, as Péguy noted, is self-deception:

> Avant tout, que rien ne soit faussé. Que ce grand combat constant se livre en pleine égalité. Que nulles chances ne soient favorisées. Que nulles chances aussi ne soient frauduleusement diminuées. Le contraire de Corneille et ce qu'il combat et vise et atteint diamétralement, ce n'est pas la faiblesse, c'est la fraude.[7]

The second aspect of the problem is the difficulty of bridging the gap between motivation and action. Concepts such as honour and *vertu* are abstract, general, and absolute;

in the real world, particular situations are concrete, individual, and often confused. As Cinna discovers, it is perfectly possible to commit oneself to doing the 'right' thing and yet be uncertain as to which of all the possible courses of action is the right one. Is it his duty to kill Auguste? He must consider whether it would be right in pragmatic political terms, right in terms of political principle, right in personal terms, both in the context of his duty to Emilie and in the context of his loyalty to Auguste. When Maxime has accused him of 'faiblesse' (862), Cinna says:

> Donne un plus digne nom au glorieux empire
> Du noble sentiment que la vertu m'inspire,
> Et que l'honneur oppose au coup précipité
> De mon ingratitude et de ma lâcheté;
> Mais plutôt continue à le nommer faiblesse,
> Puisqu'il devient si faible auprès d'une maîtresse,
> Qu'il respecte un amour qu'il devrait étouffer,
> Ou que, s'il le combat, il n'ose en triompher.   (865-872)

He sees with anguish the irony of the fact that both drawing back and pressing on could be interpreted as weak and dishonourable; both courses could also be labelled his 'duty'.

Furthermore, what should one do when two 'right' courses of action, two duties and two loyalties, are in conflict with each other? Upon what moral principle can one make a choice if both commitments are seen as absolute?[8] In an impasse of this kind, the process of lucid formulation plays a part in the dilemma itself because the more clearly and honestly the incompatible commitments are seen the greater the dilemma becomes, and also the greater is the anguish caused by the obligation to choose.

Certain problems of language, then, — problems of definition and of clear formulation, problems in the linking of principles with actions — are a fundamental feature of the kinds of tragic conflict which Corneille has created in his major tragedies. To these we must now add those problems of language which are more directly concerned with communication: with the expression to others or to oneself of feelings, thoughts or attitudes which may not readily fit into words, and which words may therefore tend to distort or to simplify.

Two contrasting scenes from *Le Cid* will serve to illustrate different aspects of these problems. The first is the meeting between Rodrigue and Chimène in Act III, scene IV, when Rodrigue appears unexpectedly in Chimène's house after he has killed her father. When Corneille was defending in his *Examen* the two visits Rodrigue makes to Chimène (which offended against the *bienséances*) he wrote:

> presque tous ont souhaité que ces entretiens se fissent; et j'ai remarqué aux premières représentations qu'alors que ce malheureux amant se présentait devant elle, il s'élevait un certain frémissement dans l'assemblée, qui marquait une curiosité merveilleuse, et un redoublement d'attention pour ce qu'ils avaient à se dire dans un état si pitoyable.[9]

' ...pour ce qu'ils avaient à se dire...' What *can* they say in such an exceptional situation? Whatever they may say, however much they may say, the tension and emotion of the meeting is felt by the audience in advance of their words, and seems to be beyond words. Yet there is a paradox here, for the audience is curious and eager precisely to hear inexpressible feelings being expressed, since they know that Rodrigue and Chimène will not remain silent. The dramatic convention of articulacy permits them to speak — and indeed demands that they speak — even in circumstances in which it might seem possible only to weep or to scream. But clearly, the convention cannot enable them to say what cannot be put into words. The audience will measure what they do say against the momentousness of the encounter itself, of which the audience is already aware as the scene begins.

So what is left unsaid becomes as important a part of this scene as the words which are spoken. In the lovers' discussion of their situation, the surface-level clarity becomes in itself a source of dramatic tension. Were the situation not so extreme and so desperate, many of the exchanges might appear to be merely verbal sparring:

> Rodrigue: Ne diffère donc plus ce que l'honneur t'ordonne:
> Il demande ma tête, et je te l'abandonne...
> (933-4)

> Chimène: ...C'est d'un autre que toi qu'il me faut l'obtenir,
> Et je dois te poursuivre, et non pas te punir.
> (943-4)

> Rodrigue: ...pour venger un père emprunter d'autres bras,
> Ma Chimène, crois-moi, c'est n'y répondre pas...
> (947-8)

> Chimène: Cruel! à quel propos sur ce point t'obstiner?
> Tu t'es vengé sans aide et tu m'en veux donner!
> (951-2)

But the discussion does not express, so much as mark, the dilemmas being enacted in this scene. The symmetrical language-patterns both in speeches and within individual lines seem to imply on the part of the two speakers a continuing confidence in reasoned argument as a means of coming to terms with their new situation and of determining the next step to take. Chimène accepts Rodrigue's explanation (and reaffirmation) of his duty to act as he did, and argues that she must by the same logic affirm the values they share and seek *his* death:

> Tu n'as fait le devoir que d'un homme de bien;
> Mais aussi, le faisant, tu m'as appris le mien.   (911-2)

The parallelism of the two characters, each caught up in a paradoxical situation, has a pattern which in its balancing and counter-balancing movement seems almost reassuring:

> Tu t'es, en m'offensant, montré digne de moi;
> Je me dois, par ta mort, montrer digne de toi.   (931-2)

In fact the dialogue is structuring the characters' predicament in two ways: not only are the speakers selecting arguments which form symmetrical and often mutually supportive patterns, but also at the same time the stylisation of the language they use is reinforcing those patterns and the coherence they imply. However, this coherence remains superficial in that it remains at the level of the language only; and it is through the tension between the insistent patterning of the dialogue and the underlying incoherence of an unresolvable situation that the presence of inexpressible feelings is conveyed. We become aware that the debate about what 'ought' to be done next is, in a sense, constantly beside the point, for it focuses on the future in order to avoid facing the present moment. Even Rodrigue's wish to die *now* is part of the same process: a dramatic gesture to fill the silence and to provide a pretext for discussion.

Certainly the discussion itself is far from cool and unemotional. Rodrigue's *plaidoyer* is, as Nadal has pointed out, also 'un aveu d'amour déguisé',[10] and Chimène's constant parrying of his arguments culminates suddenly in the simplicity and directness of what she can no longer hide: 'Va, je ne te hais point' (963). Earlier, too, she had lamented the irony of the fact that in any other circumstances it would have been to Rodrigue that she would have turned for consolation and support:

> Si quelque autre malheur m'avait ravi mon père,
> Mon âme aurait trouvé dans le bien de te voir
> L'unique allégement qu'elle eût pu recevoir;
> Et contre ma douleur j'aurais senti des charmes,
> Quand une main si chère eût essuyé mes larmes.   (918-22)

Throughout the scene, love finds direct or indirect expression. But what remains unexpressed within the dialogue is the disorderedness of the complex, interpenetrating, and conflicting emotions, feelings, and attitudes which have been provoked by their strange situation. The audience already knows from preceding scenes that the predicament of the lovers — their 'état pitoyable' — is one in which love, horror, respect, loss pride, and grief are inextricably intertwined. Moreover, we are aware that their plight is not merely that of star-crossed lovers about to be parted by fate: their fate has always been in large measure in their own hands; yet, by a tragic irony, the same web of emotions, ideals, and shared values which binds them together also now seems to stand irremovably between them.

The sheer force of the unexpressed feelings is felt at the end of the scene when the lament breaks through — a lament which, though inevitably powerless to describe indefinable feelings, can at least release them through sighs and exclamations: 'O miracle d'amour!' 'O comble de misères!...' (985). Rhetorical questions and exclamations echo and complement each other in a passage which is almost a duet —

Rodrigue, qui l'eût cru?

                          Chimène, qui l'eût dit?
Que notre heur fût si proche, et sitôt se perdît?   (987-8)

reflecting in its high degree of stylisation the strength of the tensions which have built up during the earlier more controlled dialogue and which are now released at the climax of the scene.

The second example I am taking is the last scene in Act I — Rodrigue's *Stances*. In the previous scene, Rodrigue has said nothing since hearing that Chimène's father is the man he must fight; Don Diègue had cut him off rapidly as he tried to speak ('Ne réplique point, je connais ton amour' (283)). Now that he is alone we witness the first expression of his thoughts and feelings, as he absorbs the shock of the news and the implications of the choice facing him.

Rodrigue tells us in the opening lines of his anguish ('Percé jusques au fond du coeur / D'une atteinte imprévue aussi bien que mortelle') and, later, that he sees no way out ('Des deux côtés mon mal est infini' (307)). At such a moment, it would not be surprising if he had difficulty in finding words to define his conflicting feelings and to encompass the full complexity of his dilemma. But he seems aware of no such difficulty, and his debate with himself seems to unfold in a controlled and logical way. A first response of stunned amazement and dismay —

> Je demeure immobile, et mon âme abattue
> > Cède au coup qui me tue   (295-6)

— rapidly gives way to a weighing up of his commitments both to his father and to Chimène. At first, analysis based on abstract values leads to an impasse: 'Je dois à ma maîtresse aussi bien qu'à mon père' (322); how can his code of values help him to choose? But when the debate shifts to a practical assessment of outcome, the choices are no longer evenly balanced:

> Allons, mon bras, sauvons du moins l'honneur,
> Puisqu'après tout il faut perdre Chimène,   (339-340)

and the monologue ends with a firm decision as he urges himself on ('Courons à la vengeance... Ne soyons plus en peine... ').

There may seem to be a strange incompatibility between Rodrigue's professed anguish and his careful assessment of the situation, and between the clarity of his presentation of the issues and the complexity of the problems he faces. What seems strange is that he appears to have no difficulty in formulating, and bringing order to, his feelings and the dilemma which faces him. And if indeed he has no problems of this kind, then we might, with Stendhal, regard this as a weakness of the play:

> Il y a plusieurs choses à corriger dans *le Cid*; les stances de la fin du premier acte ne sont que l'expression du jugement de la tête d'un homme sur les mouvements de son coeur, cela montre qu'il n'est pas entièrement troublé.[11]

However, the *Stances* are surely not as simple as this view implies. They show Rodrigue not, it is true, consciously reflecting upon problems of verbal expression, but nevertheless grappling with them as he tries to use language as a tool to clarify his dilemma and to help him to choose. On one level he succeeds in this aim; the practical issues are clarified and he is able to make a firm decision. But when he tries to formulate the complex emotional and moral conflicts, he over-simplifies them. Love is set against honour in a manner which implies that they are polarised alternatives:

> Que je sens de rudes combats!
> Contre mon propre honneur mon amour s'intéresse:
> Il faut venger un père, et perdre une maîtresse.
> L'un m'anime le coeur, l'autre retient mon bras.   (301-4)

The formulations suggest that Rodrigue's emotions are all ranged on one side in this opposition, pulling against nobler commitments:

> Père, maîtresse, honneur, amour,
> Noble et dure contrainte, aimable tyrannie,
> Tous mes plaisirs sont morts, ou ma gloire ternie.
> L'un me rend malheureux, l'autre indigne du jour.   (311-4)

Such a clear-cut opposition is obviously an over-simple one, for his emotions are engaged in his commitment to his duty and the love he shares with Chimène is based on mutual esteem. And indeed the polarisation collapses in line 322: 'Je dois à ma maîtresse aussi bien qu'à mon père' (though a binary pattern, albeit non-antithetical, persists even here). As the argument shifts ground, new binary relationships are created:

> J'attire en me vengeant sa haine et sa colère;
> J'attire ses mépris en ne me vengeant pas   (323-4)

and later:

> Que je meure au combat, ou meure de tristesse...   (343)

It is this insistence on order and patterning, on the establishing of relationships and the clarifying of choices, which suggests the firm dominance of reasoned debate in this scene, of 'le jugement de la tête', but its dominance is undermined by the fact that the patterns created by the verbal formulations are themselves too simple to bring any real clarification to the issues involved.

Thus there is a tension in this monologue between clarity and complexity, between control and distress — a tension which, beneath reason's apparent dominance, quietly underlines Rodrigue's anguish. If we compare for a moment this speech with Hermione's monologue in Racine's *Andromaque* which begins 'Où suis-je? Qu'ai-je fait? Que dois-je faire encore?', an interesting contrast emerges. Hermione is expressing her bewilderment and confusion in the face both of her situation and of her own feelings, yet the speech makes her confusion very clear. Through the conventions of articulacy and poetic diction, Racine has been able to use rhythm (e.g. displaced caesuras, brief almost staccato phrases) and structure (shifts of tone and argument irregularly spaced), as well as meaning, to convey very clearly a confused state of mind. From this point of view Hermione's language could be called transparent. With Rodrigue the opposite is the case. The speech seems to convey clarity of mind, but the symmetrical language-patterns here are opaque[12]: there are moments when we become conscious that they are superimposed upon intertwined, inter-related values and feelings which refuse to fit into polarised opposition. Rodrigue is not able to use language as a simple analytical tool.

One further point must be added. Rodrigue's insistence on establishing binary patterns expresses another important aspect of his response to the crisis, for these patterns are in themselves meaning-bearing. What they embody is choice: not the content of the choice but the fact of having to choose. So what happens in the *Stances* is not that the language-patterns reflect the range of options being faced or that they echo the patterns of the conflict, but that they express the pattern of choice itself, of the act of choosing. For Rodrigue, choice is both impossible (on the level of abstract values) and at the same time inevitable. In practical terms, in terms of action, the matter is starkly simple: either he will fight or he will not fight. Even not choosing is a choice, since refusing to make a choice is, in terms of action alone, the same as choosing not to fight. The binary patterns which are so insistently present in these *Stances* are a reminder — like an *ostinato* — of the straightforward either/or opposition into which action drastically simplifies Rodrigue's emotional and moral dilemma.

So the simplifying patterns are far from arbitrary; they demonstrate the pressure exerted by concrete situations on intractable theoretical problems.

Here is the tragic *impasse* at its most fundamental level: in practice, impossible choices must be made, yet making them does not alter their nature. As Chimène says of the fathers' quarrel, "Si l'on guérit le mal, ce n'est qu'en apparence" (470). After the heady excitement of exceptional challenges, everyday life will constantly expose continuing unresolved conflicts.[13] Corneille's characters must struggle not only with the gap between words and reality — with problems of definition, of labelling, of expression, and of communication — but also with the gap between values, motives, and intentions on the one hand, and on the other the crude physical reality of

the action to be taken (something which, despite the sometimes lofty language of discussion and debate, Corneille never minimises[14]).

Finally, of course, it remains true that the language of Corneille's tragedies is forceful and emphatic. I have argued that qualities such as these do not imply that the perennial problems of verbal expression have been either solved or by-passed, but rather that they have been built upon and turned to positive effect. And indeed it would be misleading to end without mentioning the supportive strength which Cornelian characters are able to find in language.

The language of firm action can almost become an action in itself. Take, for example, Chimène's words: "Je cours sans balancer où mon honneur m'oblige" (821). Lines such as this one are often quoted as evidence of an "inhuman" adherence to duty. Yet, though the statement could be taken as a descriptive one, summing up Chimène's attitude, its untroubled singlemindedness stands in contradiction to her hesitations at other times; only a moment later, she cries out almost in disbelief at her own resolve:

...cruelle poursuite où je me vois forcée!
Je demande sa tête, et crains de l'obtenir:
Ma mort suivra la sienne, et je le veux punir!   (826-8)

So perhaps line 821 is more appropriately read as what J.L. Austin[15] called a "performative utterance" or "speech act" — an action performed by the uttering of words, in this case the action of making a resolution. She is urging herself on, making a commitment about her future action. Horace's famous line: "Albe vous a nommé, je ne vous connais plus" can similarly be seen as a speech act; it does not describe present reality so much as perform the action of making a break with the past and making a resolution for the future. In both cases, the act of resolving for the future is expressed in the present tense, underlining the fact that it is a present action. As Jean Starobinski has argued, for Corneille's characters it is often

language which makes possible a movement forward:

> L'invention d'abord verbale du moi glorieux fait en sorte
> que le paraître précède l'être, lui propose d'avance une
> forme à accomplir, l'appelle à l'effort et à l'existence. En
> insistant sur la valeur des préfixes, l'on peut dire que l'être
> cornélien s'*anticipe*, qu'il se *prétend*.[16]

I have argued that very often in Corneille language has to
strive to match reality; but sometimes it is reality which must
strive to match language.

NOTES

1. *Adolphe*, ed. J.-H. Bornecque (Paris, 1955), p.30.

2. *The Language Poets Use* (London, 1968), p.101.

3. Act I, scene IV, lines 250-260. All quotations from Corneille refer to
   the Garnier edition: *Théâtre complet*, vol. I, ed. G. Couton (Paris,
   1971); and vol. II, ed. M. Rat (Paris, 1942).

4. Vol. I, p.240.

5. 1637 text and all subsequent editions before that of 1660.

6. Nos. 263 and (in *Maximes supprimées*) 34 in the Garnier edition, ed.
   J. Truchet (Paris, 1967).

7. *Note conjointe sur M. Descartes et la philosophie cartésienne*
   (p.1441 in the Bibliothèque de la Pléiade edition, *Oeuvres en prose
   de Charles Péguy 1909-1914*, ed. M. Péguy (Paris, 1961)).

8. Cf. the passage in *L'Existentialisme est un humanisme* where Sartre
   discusses what could be called a "Cornelian" dilemma and
   comments: "Qui peut en décider *a priori?* Personne. Aucune morale
   inscrite ne peut le dire" (p.42 in the Nagel "Collection Pensées"
   edition (Paris, 1963)).

9. Vol. I, p.730.

10. *Le Sentiment de l'amour dans l'oeuvre de Pierre Corneille* (Paris,
    1948), p.168.

11. *Journal*, le 10 juin, 1804 (p.471 in the Bibliothèque de la Pléiade edition, *Œuvres intimes*, ed. H. Martineau (Paris, 1960)).

12. This point is made, and interpreted rather differently, by Milorad Margitíc in his article "Texte et sous-texte chez Corneille. Une lecture des stances de Rodrigue" (*Saggi e ricerche di letteratura francese*, XVI (1977), pp.197-212).

13. See, for example, in *Horace*, Sabine's words to the King in her last speech:

> Sire, voyez l'excès de mes tristes ennuis,
> Et l'effroyable état où mes jours sont réduits.
> Quelle horreur d'embrasser un homme dont l'épée
> De toute ma famille a la trame coupée!
> Et quelle impiété de haïr un époux
> Pour avoir bien servi les siens, l'État et vous! (1613-8)

14. See, for example, Chimène's description of finding her father's dead body (act II, scene VIII) and her reiteration of the monosyllabic phrase "mon père est mort" (659, 689). Also the account of Horace's victory in *Horace*, act IV, scene II, where the realities of battle are not glossed over: Horace resorts to trickery in order to separate the Curiace brothers and kill each one in turn.

15. In his William James lectures at Harvard in 1955, published posthumously under the title *How to do things with words* (Oxford, 1962).

16. *L'Oeil vivant* (Paris, 1961), p.52.

Verga's *Il Marito di Elena* and the Art of the Inexplicit

Judith Davies

'Detesto il marito di Elena, ma troppo tardi', Verga wrote in August 1881.[1] The negative verdict which he passed repeatedly on the novel has been generally endorsed by his commentators. But that is only one reason for the cursory readings and swift dismissals which, on the whole, have been *Il Marito di Elena*'s critical lot. It was published at the end of 1881 (though bearing the date 1882) only months after Verga's Sicilian masterpiece, *I Malavoglia*, which had appeared in the February. The proximity of two publications so profoundly dissimilar has naturally raised acute critical difficulties. A meagre tale of failed middle-class marriage with obvious debts to *Madame Bovary*, *Il Marito di Elena* has posed problems particularly for those anxious to discover a coherent ideological development in Verga as he makes the transition from urban to rustic society — from *Eros* through *Nedda* to *Vita dei campi*, *I Malavoglia* and *Mastro-don Gesualdo*.

Now, however, an unpublished letter to his publisher, Treves, comes to the rescue. As Carmelo Musumarra reveals, Verga was already working on *Il Marito di Elena* in January 1879, and describing it moreover as a work which 'mostra un uomo il quale, per amore, scende a uno a uno tutti i gradini della scala morale e "si abitua a tutte le viltà, per un sentimento generoso, in fondo"'.[2] This revelation considerably diminishes the problem of reconciling the achievement of *I Malavoglia* with the mediocrity of *Il Marito di Elena*; and the problematic task — so often undertaken — of assimilating an *histoire intime* to the ethos of the *Vinti* cycle becomes needless. The book can now be legitimately read (as in any case critics have been inclined to do) as a late contribution to the series of novels that began with *Una peccatrice* and ended with *Eros*, and in which Verga probed over and over again the possibility of a lasting relationship between the two sexes.

Elena's husband was to be characterised by his *viltà*; and some form of moral degradation or coarsening was what lay in store for the heroes of those early novels, torn as they were between the lure of sexual passion and their sense of duty towards home and family, between mistress and mother. If Giorgio La Ferlita in *Tigre reale* escapes the common destiny of defeat, it is because the object of his passion, Narcisa, dies a timely death. For the hero of *Eva* in particular there had been another fundamental tension: for while the ideal of absolute Romantic passion was incarnated in the symbolically-named heroine, it was contradicted by the uncongenial notion of the female sex as a commodity commanding its price in the marketplace like other merchandise; and in Verga's Preface to *Eva* — 'la *sfuriata* posta in capo a *Eva*', he called it later[3] — the *provinciale inurbato* who lived on in him decried the 'febbre di piaceri' and the materialism that accompanied the industrial expansion of Italy's great cities.[4] Eva the ballerina is the product of that society. In reality she attains dignity by her frank admission of economic dependence on her admirers; nor does that dependence prevent her from sacrificing the career which is her means of survival because of Lanti's jealousy. Yet the dying hero, in Verga's name, will castigate himself for his continuing passion, and curse Eva for failing to embody his pure ideal. Among other characteristics of the early novels, this intimate connection between sexual passion and self-disgust is carried forward to *Il Marito di Elena*, where *amore* and *viltà* are inseparable. Here, it is true, the once contradictory ideals of passion and family are fused: Elena the lover is also Elena the wife. But like Verga's other early heroines she will prove an unworthy repository for the hero's ideals.

Before he completed the story of Cesare and Elena, however, Verga wrote the final draft of *I Malavoglia*. So it is that *Il Marito di Elena* came to stand astride a masterpiece, revealing in every aspect its composite, transitional nature. After *I Malavoglia* the burden of completing, or perhaps re-writing, the manuscript was so wearisome that work proceeded only 'a furia di volontà e di perseveranza'. In all probability it was the subject-matter itself that constituted the major inhibition — 'non ti pare che certi argomenti abbiano la jettatura?', asks a letter to Luigi Capuana, fellow novelist, Sicilian and habitual confidant of Verga's frustrations.[5] The novel indeed seems conceived according to a scheme which, while it might have appealed to Verga in '78 or '79, must have appeared irrelevant after the mature self-discoveries of *I Malavoglia*. For it incorporates, as I shall be suggesting, an essay in morbid psychology. This was not a path Verga would tread again.

The plain fact of the matter — and it needs some emphasis — is that *Il Marito di Elena* is not entirely a story of 'mortale gelosia'.[6] It is not, as it were, a more arduous and moralised *Madame Bovary* with a less negligible husband and a final 'punishment' which re-establishes, however melodramatically, the wholesome values of conjugal fidelity. For Cesare remains devoted to Elena *despite* her adulteries. Verga is absolutely clear that he kills her not from jealousy (although certainly he feels it) but because she finally reveals a total indifference to him. It is a story about a persistent abnormality of response. Verga is engaged precisely by the absence of the 'proper' vindictive jealousy, by the paradox *amore-viltà*. To some readers, like Portinari and Musumarra, the real protagonist seems to be Elena.[7] But almost certainly that was not Verga's intention. Eventually the name of Verga's adulteress reveals the secret of its selection. The rejected poet Fiandura in his avenging satire refers to the name as 'dolce al pare di quello della tua greca sorella', and the narrator follows up with 'Il marito della *greca donna* seppe in tal modo ... lo scempio turpe che si era fatto del suo onore' (pp.274, 275 — Verga's emphasis). But Verga was evidently less interested in Helen than in her Menelaus, for *Don Menelao* was the original, over-ironic title of the novel;[8] nor was the final title *Elena Dorello*, as it might well have been by analogy with other respected realist texts like *Madame Bovary* or *Thérèse Raquin*, but precisely *Il Marito di Elena* — with Cesare's anonymous, 'shadow' status in the title perhaps hinting that his centrality will not be obvious.

Shortly after *Il Marito di Elena*, Verga's interest in the psycho-pathological was to re-emerge in another 'opera sbagliata' — as critics have tended to see it:[9] the stories of *Drammi intimi*, published in 1884, and notably in 'I drammi ignoti' and 'L'ultima visita'. But there exists evidence of an interest in purely psychological matters which is contemporary with the conception of *Il Marito di Elena*. It comes in the letter to Farina which prefaces the short story 'L'Amante de Gramigna', a story eventually included in the Sicilian tales of *Vita dei campi* (1880). Rather ·unexpectedly,in view of the dramatic, terse nature of 'L'Amante di Gramigna' and other stories from the collection, Verga insists in his letter to Farina on the fascination of the psyche for the modern, analytic writer. For the foreseeable future, he writes, the 'fenomeno psicologico' will provide the major creative stimulus for contemporary narrative, inviting it to trace with scientific scrupulousness the 'sviluppo logico, necessario' of 'mysterious' passions.[10] He then passes on, in a far more widely discussed passage, to talk of the 'mystery' of artistic creations where the author remains invisible. But for a moment a devotee of positivistic psychology has surfaced (and, certainly, in the description given by Musumarra of the overall design of *Il Marito di Elena* there is something positivistically demonstrative about the undertaking to show the *progressive* degradation of the hero). The psychologist imbued with the 'scientism' of his age never in fact fully materialises in Verga's creative work; but one can catch a sight of him in *Il Marito di Elena*.

A purely psychological reading cannot, admittedly, account for all the material in the text: alongside the psycho-pathological vein run concerns and episodes which anticipate, or borrow from, *I Malavoglia*, and to these justice has been done elsewhere. Nor, more importantly, is the psycho-pathological focus immediately obvious. But to fail to show his hand is extremely characteristic of Verga. The incidence in his mature texts of omitted information, or misinformation, his use of an 'unreliable' narrator, and the concept of the *racconto che si fa da sé* are indicative enough. Besides, *Il Marito di Elena* benefits from the drafting of the stories of *Vita dei campi* and *I Malavoglia*, in which these strategies are embodied; and the introductory part of 'L'Amante di Gramigna' may again serve us as a species of preface to *Il Marito di Elena*. For while Verga asserted that it was the 'fenomeno psicologico' that attracted the modern analytic writer, he dissociated himself from overt analysis: 'tu veramente preferirai di trovarti faccia a faccia col fatto nudo', he told Farina; and: 'ti dirò soltanto il punto di partenza e quello d'arrivo', adding with a touch of oracularity, 'e per te basterà, e un giorno forse basterà per tutti'.[11] For *I Malavoglia* a special kind of reading was required. Verga insisted on the intense mnemonic collaboration demanded of the reader. The writing of *I Malavoglia* involved 'blurring' and 'dissembling': to Capuana he wrote of 'quella tal cura di smussare gli angoli, di dissimulare quasi il dramma' [story-line].[12] Even Felice Cameroni, devoted to the cause of Naturalism though he was, complained of Verga's 'tiring the reader' by depriving himself of 'mezzi parimenti oggettivi' and 'essenzialmente conformi alle teorie naturaliste' (sic).[13] In fact it is necessary to read all Verga's mature texts inductively. Meaning can very often be approached *only* via the perception of patterns, repetitions and hints, through a sorting and collating of evidence. And Verga saw himself ever afterwards as the artist of ellipsis, of the *sottinteso*. To Guido Mazzoni in 1890, for instance, he wrote that there was never any need to 'scoprire il movente interiore': 'uomini e cose devono parlare da sé'.[14] In conversation with Ugo Ojetti a few years later he said: 'gli psicologi in fondo non fanno che ostentare un lavoro che per noi è solo preliminare e *non entra nell'opera finale*'.[15]

Even more pertinent to *Il Marito di Elena* was Verga's response to Capuana's novel *Giacinta*, for its subject was a *caso patologico* and it was published in 1879, the year when Verga apparently began his own novel. 'Troppo coscienzioso', Verga diplomatically called it in a letter to Capuana. After dutifully admiring its 'rigore di analisi psicologica' he goes on to confess a preference for the first part of the novel 'perché l'azione è più viva, o almeno è presentata con maggiore *messa in scena*'. The analysis of the second half may be, he says, 'più perfetta', but for him it lacks 'quell'efficacia che nasce dalla rappresentazione viva, del fatto'.[16]

We should not be surprised then that the text is reluctant to speak openly of its conceptual substructure. The author's reticence is what makes *Il Marito di Elena*, in spite of everything, a truly Verghian text. In the context of Verga's reserve on precisely what concerns him most it is at any rate curious to note, by contrast, how explicit he proves on parallel, more 'Malavoglian' concerns in the novel, as though they were present in a merely *automatic* way. Cesare, for instance, is casually dubbed the 'Figliol Prodigo' (p.132) — in a mere proverbial formula Verga dismisses a theme that touches him profoundly from *I Carbonari della montagna* to *Mastro-don Gesualdo*; out in the open too is the vision of life as a current or tide (*La Marea* was the early collective title of the novels of the *Vinti* cycle), which sweeps onwards, obliterating landmarks and separating individuals (pp.75, 289).

Before testing the 'pathological' hypothesis against the text, it will be as well to mention a small piece of external evidence which tends to suggest that Verga saw his novel, essentially, as a dissertation on an aberrant psyche. Complaining to Capuana about his 'cornuto' *Marito di Elena* just then — in July 1881 — nearing completion, Verga continues: 'ho comprato il *Fanfulla* ultimo per la tua Mostruosità. La Mostruosità me l'hai fatta a me, ché m'hai fottuto *d'avance* quel *marito* ecc. ... Nondimeno è la più bella cosa dell'anno *Fanfullesco*.' In view of the similarities between the works, Verga's comment can hardly be dismissed merely as a back-handed way of paying a compliment. Capuana's story represents, once again, his psycho-pathological vein. His Giovanni (not unlike Verga's Cesare) remains abjectly fascinated by a wife who is openly indulging in sexual adventures. The truly 'monstrous' part of the tale, however, comes in a rapid twist of plot. Once the husband has unexpectedly proved a capacity for aggression the wife, ever perverse, begins to turn her attentions to him. But in her new submissive guise all she provokes is a sense of revulsion. The husband will end up trying to strangle her and regretting — and here is the final reversal — the days of his enslavement. This sado-masochistic pirouette of Capuana's, one guesses, was a shade too confidently symmetrical for Verga's taste (though, as usual, he was tactful, speaking of the second half as too 'precipitata' simply for 'ragioni dello spazio');[17] but the spirit of Giovanni's regrets is not too far removed from Cesare's masochistic reflection just before the murder that 'finché (Elena) fosse stata viva, lo avesse tradito cento volte, egli sarebbe tornato cento volte a leccarle i piedi!' (p.305).

Verga, then, refuses to make Cesare's stabbing of Elena a 'normal' crime of honour; and it is Cesare himself who at the book's climax calls himself ill, doing so precisely as he contemplates his inability to detach himself from Elena, whatever she does: 'Era malato, era pazzo! Quella era la sua malattia, quella era la sua pazzia! Finché ella vivrebbe!... Finché vivrebbe!... Di altri!...' (p.305). So that it is his own 'malattia' that Cesare destroys in Elena; and if this is so we have a rationale, at least, for the rapid transformation of suicide into homicide. But that final self-definition by Cesare is a culmination of a series of hints, none perhaps conclusive in itself, but having a cumulative force. Repeatedly there is evidence of what we may call regressive, infantile or unrealistic thinking. Cesare will return mentally to the emotional security of the elopement or to the honeymoon (pp.148, 149, 232); or indeed to childhood and to its modes of thinking (he experiences 'strane superstizioni', furtively he will pray before his mother's portrait, or cross himself 'come faceva lo zio canonico' before leaving home (p.171)). Immature thinking leads to a repeated expression of his determination to keep Elena in ignorance of their financial plight. The touches of fanaticism in the following sample should not be missed:

Avrebbe voluto risparmiarle *a qualunque costo* le sorde angosce che lo tormentavano   (p.154)

Suo marito *avrebbe sofferto la tortura* per risparmiare a sua moglie coteste scene [scenes of clamouring creditors]
(p.180)

Egli doveva tirarli [i creditori] ad uno ad uno nel vano di una finestra... perché nessun altri udisse, e *sopratutto* l'Elena   (p.181)

Ei sarebbe *morto dieci volte di fame*, piuttosto che andare a domandare del denaro in prestito, *se non fosse stato per* l'Elena   (p.188)

The reality of the situation, however, has not escaped Elena. In his absence she has sold her piano (p.183). Cesare's immaturity is borne out too in the first passage which accords us extended intimate knowledge of his attitudes to Elena:

Piangeva per quella contraddizione vergognosa, per quella tirannia della corruzione mondana che costringeva lui, il marito, a lasciare la moglie adorata senza difesa, in mezzo alle insidie velate, e alle brame incessanti dei seduttori, sola, perché gli altri fossero più liberi di confessarle col frasario ipocrita tutte le brame oscene che accendeva la sua casta bellezza nella loro fantasia viziosa, coi complimenti sfacciati, cogli sguardi impudichi che la ricercavano sotto le stoffe trasparenti. E andarsene lontano per non sembrare di voler ascoltare... Ecco cos'era ridotto a fare lui, il marito, il tutore, l'amante, lui che *avrebbe dato tutto il sangue delle vene* per lasciarle ignorare l'esistenza del male. (pp.162-3)

There would be some excuse for seeing all this as an anticipation of those later pages in which the novel mounts its attack on the hypocrisies and false values of polite society. But the passage, with its sexual obsessiveness and its immature vision of Elena, makes more sense when read in the pathological key. Besides, the unrealistic view of the relationship fits Cesare's perpetual tendency to regard Elena as a mere child (pp.89, 244, 245, 246). Against that view we are no doubt required to set the 'hard' evidence, carefully provided at the very outset, that Elena is older than Cesare and far more capable of taking the initiative. The 'femininity' of Cesare's nature — 'Egli era la donna' (p.245) — and his maternal fixation, frequently touched on in the text, also suggest some inadequate psychological development in Cesare. The passage in Chapter 11 which presents Cesare in close-up after the interception of Elena's letter to Cataldi presents some psychological curiosities. Cesare's tendency is always to ignore the evidence of his own eyes. Perhaps the letter is innocent (p.219); if it is not, she is perhaps only guilty of a 'leggerezza' (p.222); and even supposing that it contains a declaration of love, what after all is a letter but mere words (p.224)? Cesare is neurotically incapable of removing his idol from her pedestal, so that it is easier to inculpate himself than Elena. The real question of whether he can forgive *her* becomes one of her willingness to forgive *him* ('S'ella fosse innocente? ... Ella non gli avrebbe perdonato giammai!' (p.225)); the question of his own ability to live with the knowledge of Elena's betrayal becomes one of *her* ability to live down her bad conscience ('A lei non sarebbe rimasta in fondo al cuore la spina di quel torto che aveva dovuto farsi perdonare da lui?' (p.226)). It is *he* who envisages the constantly delayed confrontation as a 'prova terribile', who dreads being alone with her (p.226) and the possibility of her questioning him (p.227). Eventually even the fact that he has delayed speaking becomes an excuse for not doing so, something that almost puts him in the wrong or, at least, seems to him to diminish 'la sua parte di diritto' (p.228). Self-citation and repetition — which, as Annamaria Andreoli rightly maintains, are a fundamental, structuring device of the text — are also its primary vehicles of meaning.[18] This perpetual urge in Cesare to invert the situation cannot be casual, if it is picked up and 'concluded' a little later, where he reflects: 'Ella cercava l'amore. *La colpa era di lui* che non aveva saputo darglielo' (p.282). And this in itself is an echo of the page where Elena's self-appointed 'tutore' takes on the moral responsibility for her errors: 'Se pure un momento ella si era smarrita per correre dietro il suo cervellino romantico, la colpa era di lui che non era stato abbastanza prudente, né abbastanza forte' (p.245).

The text, far from being unmethodically or casually put together, is full of presages and unobtrusive connections. It seems to me that Verga, for example, rehearses in the text the pattern of psychic control and release that will finally and suddenly produce the murder. The preparatory episode is the one in which Cesare warns Cataldi to keep away from Elena. It is *lack* of authorial comment that in Verga tends to be a sign of his engagement; and none is offered on Cesare's uncharacteristic self-possession and apparent mastery of the situation. The strangeness of the situation is merely reflected in the fact that Elena and Cataldi are unnerved by it; and the psychological repercussion is not long in coming. It takes the form of an uncontrolled outburst of anger and despair, with Cesare weeping, not insignificantly, 'come un ragazzo' (p.161).

The attentive reader can discover other tiny preparations being made for the final suicide-murder. Cesare masochistically contemplates his own death from time to time; but he also contemplates Elena's — as a sort of alternative: 'Aveva invocata la morte, la morte per sé o per lei, *non sapeva per chi* ' (p.239). These last thoughts come to mind at Elena's bedside, while she lies silently sleeping, only the mass of her dark hair clearly visible — accompanying details which anticipate the moment before the denouement, when Cesare contemplates the 'otherness' of Elena, sleeping 'serena, quasi sorridente' 'coi capelli neri sul guanciale' (p.304). The logic of cause and effect which another writer might have been happy to evince through passages of analysis Verga tends to entrust to the self-citing narrative discourse.

There are, however, indications of a different kind — both structural and stylistic — that Verga is influenced by the idea of a positivistic 'studio dell'uomo interiore'. The backward look of Chapter 3 at what Verga calls Cesare's 'educazione quasi claustrale' (p.34), distorting as it does the natural order of the narrative material, is a pointer to the kind of novel that — in part — we are dealing with. To describe that monotonous, methodical life prior to marriage is to introduce an essential ingredient into the potentially explosive mixture which Verga is about to create when the headstrong, sensual Elena crosses the path of the mild-mannered, dutiful Cesare. Manzoni too had repeatedly glanced backwards to explain the personalities of *I Promessi Sposi*; but for an immediate precedent we need look no further than Capuana's 'pathological' *Giacinta*, far closer in its narrower psychological compass to Verga's linear story of a marriage. In *Giacinta* the curious refusal of the enamoured heroine in Chapter 1 to accept Andrea's marriage proposal triggers a long explanatory investigation of her past; eventually in Chapter 5 the reader is returned, armed by now with the knowledge to understand it, to the occasion of the refusal. In both *Giacinta* and *Il Marito di Elena* the retrospective sections are sparked off by a puzzling verbal formula (in *Il Marito di Elena* by Cesare's recollection of

Elena's enigmatic 'Ho paura' (p.26)), uttered in inhibiting circumstances, to which the text at length makes a precise return (*Il Marito di Elena*, p.59). This early section of *Giacinta* was what Verga most admired in the novel; and, as in the case of Capuana's work, the intelligibility of *Il Marito di Elena* depends crucially on the laying bare of a psychological *antefatto*.

It is in this section that Verga comes closest to the jargon of positivistic determinism, concluding his treatment of Cesare's boyhood with the comment: 'L'influenza di siffatta adolescenza in quel temperamento delicato aveva sviluppata una sensibilità inquieta, una delicatezza di sentimenti affinati dalle abitudini contemplative' (pp.37-8). For Elena, whom Verga intended primarily as catalyst in Cesare's psychological drama, there is no explanatory section on the formation of her temperament. But she is conceived in terms of Zolian 'temperament' nonetheless; Elena is all sensuality and self-indulgence, 'naturally' immoral — a 'bestia malefica, inconscia ed irresponsabile' (p.239), as Cesare reflects. The 'data' on Cesare and Elena will not change much in the course of the novel; the story is from the start orientated towards a fatal outcome. The primary, 'positivistic' challenge is to arrive 'naturally' at an unnatural act; and as it turns out psychological development is not as strong as psychological *process*.

Whether this is the result of a simplifying deterministic intention (rather in the spirit of Capuana's round declaration in *Giacinta* that 'Le conseguenze di una falsa premessa non si sfuggono mai; nemmeno quando ci si è accorti di aver commesso uno sbaglio ... Precipitano ruinose alla loro trista catastrofe'[19]); or whether it is the inevitable consequence of Verga's disinclination for analysis it is hard to tell. Certainly he seeks to avoid the kind of *extended* analysis that tends to draw attention to the controlling presence of the narrator; though, as we shall see, the idea of the total 'eclipse' of the author, already confided to Farina, is apparently not even a goal in *Il Marito di Elena*. Perhaps the failed impersonality of

Giacinta had warned him that the procedure was too arduous where a 'hidden', psychological subject was concerned. At all events his reading of *Giacinta* was not without its considerable influence, for he clearly attempts to put into practice his own recommendations from the letter on *Giacinta* to Capuana, replacing prolonged analysis by 'rappresentazione viva' and what he had called 'messa in scena'.

This preference for 'rappresentazione viva' is responsible for the novel's tendency to present itself in 'scenes'. It is also responsible, I think, for the curious nature of its free indirect speech. Cesare is naturally the main beneficiary of the device. But Verga seems reluctant to mediate between his hero and the reader. He is 'troppo immediatamente partecipe', as Spinazzola notes, for Cesare's outpourings to be transformed into a 'sondaggio in profondità delle zone più labirintiche della psiche'.[20] The opportunity for collaboration between narrator and character is passed over in the interests of dramatic immediacy, and what is technically *erlebte Rede* becomes nothing much more than highly organised reported speech. The problems that these abstentions create are perhaps even more evident in the case of Elena. In contact with the adulteress the text seems to bristle with moral uncertainty. Before the adultery she *seems* as innocent as Cesare would like to believe: 'Aveva bisogno di quella vita ... se ne inebriava spensieratamente, senza sospettare il male' (p.151), 'Elena in fondo non si sentiva cattiva' (p.157), 'al vederlo [Cataldi] così sottomesso ... s'irritava che non le permettessero quel trastullo innocente' (p.159). But these statements, which seem to aim at a 'neutral' diagnosis, in reality provoke a sense of disquiet about their 'reliability': what they exhibit is an uneasy absorption of the voice of the narrator by the voice of the character, with the narrator therefore secretly committed to apologia. Even after the adultery, Elena is still exonerated (with an adverb) and allowed a say in matters: 'Ella non era perversa, no! Si credeva *sinceramente* disgraziata, faceva il possibile per riannodare il passato' (p.205); but she will be pursued by Verga's stern denunciations of her 'bisogno irrequieto di emozioni vietate', her 'sentimentalismo isterico' (p.252), and by phraseology that curiously combines the collusive and the accusatory: 'Ella si creava *ingenuamente* delle sofferenze ideali ... nel tempo stesso che godeva il frutto di quei sacrifici ignorati' (p.252). These oscillations depend on the absence of an intermediate area of collaboration between narrator and character through which a more finely shaded moral portrait could have emerged. As matters stand, Verga is either over-identified with his character (so that, in the passage already quoted, it is impossible to attribute an expression like 'trastullo innocente' to one 'speaker' rather than the other); or his detachment is so complete that he sounds moralistic. What we are dealing with here, however, is not a problem of expressing moral judgment, but rather a problem of expression *tout court.*

In the same effort to avoid analysis, Verga opens up oblique channels of communication with the reader. He relies on the technique of the 'messa in scena' which he approved in *Giacinta.* The natural description of the countryside near Rosamarina for instance has a species of function within the narrative, acting as a sort of intermediary between the dreamy, sensual Elena and the provincial baron, owner of vast, fertile tracts of adjacent territory. That nature, Verga writes at one point, is composed of things 'che lasciano germi misteriosi nella mente o nel cuore' — a phrase which seems anxious to fudge a positivistic hint on causes and effects with the old-fashioned rhetoric of the 'curioso del cuore umano'. His description at all events will become significant in its perpetual return to a particular feature of the Rosamarina landscape, La Rocca, a soaring granite slab on terrain favoured by local hunters. La Rocca will gradually become associated with the notion of the *uomo-cacciatore*, with Elena's dreams of sexual self-fulfilment, reposing very soon in the figure of Baron Peppino. La Rocca is energetic aspiration ('senza un'ombra, senza un filo d'erba ... ritta contro il cielo turchino' (p.84)); it is associated with infinite longing ('nella viottola che correva sulla cornice della Rocca, si udiva il corno ... Elena ...

ascoltava ... quei suoni di corno lontani, vagava cogli occhi
sull'aspetto indeciso del podere' (p.87)). But this focus will
soon sharpen. It is Cesare, jealously intuiting her discontent,
who first connects it with La Rocca. 'Sarebbe morto di
vergogna prima di confessarle la sua strana gelosia', writes
Verga, and then (with a highly significant, apparently illogical
'anzi'): 'Anzi, allorché udiva l'abbaiare dei cani della Rocca, o lo
sparo dei fucili, la chiamava, le indicava la leggera fumata che
si dileguava'. Whereupon Elena will take to asking 'Perché non
sei cacciatore anche tu?' (p.95), and once 'Se ci assalissero i
ladri, mi difenderesti?' (p.98) (Verghian adaptations perhaps
of Emma Bovary's 'As-tu tes pistolets?').

When he first appears one night Peppino presents himself
as feudal lord and hunter, patterned seemingly on some
academic painting of the 'romantic' Middle Ages: 'Comparve ...
Don Peppino, nell'ombra, sull'alto cavallo pugliese come un
fantasma nero, seguito da due campieri di cui luccicavano le
borchie d'ottone, e le carabine ad armacollo' (p.111). And
Elena, beneath the 'nugolone minaccioso' of La Rocca, keeps
thinking 'a quel ragazzo che non aveva paura di andare solo al
buio' (p.113). After this, the narrative will adopt a more
contemporary slyness: 'Il barone tornò spesso alla Rosamarina,
a far visita alla Signora Elena, ... a cacciare la beccaccia nel
vallone' (p.119); 'era sempre a ronzare lì intorno, colla
cacciatora di velluto o lo schioppo in spalla. Ella lo vedeva da
lontano, fra i cespugli della Rocca' (pp.122-3). Finally, to help
Elena out of her financial difficulties, he will offer an
extravagant sum for the *podere*, excusing himself to his
mother with the words 'Alla Rosamarina v'è la caccia più
abbondante del territorio' (p.142). In reality, however, this art
of scattering hints — essential to the mature Verga — is
tautologous in a novel where the author is also perfectly
prepared to proceed by plain statement of fact. It is evidence
of that stratification referred to earlier.

The same 'doubling' of techniques is used in the
presentation of Elena's disappointed girlhood aspirations. They
figure frequently in the text in the synthetic formula of

'castelli in aria', but are also often 'translated' into a looking at immensity — the 'movente interiore' is transmuted into a physical act: Elena 'vagava con gli occhi sull'aspetto indeciso del podere' (p.87); she is 'assorta nella contemplazione della Rocca che si levava come un'ombra gigantesca e minacciosa' (p.123). But her eyes do not really see: they are 'occhi vaghi' (p.152), 'occhi fissi e astratti' (p.195), 'occhi pieni di visioni' (p.221), 'vaghi e erranti' (p.253), 'ardenti e vaghi' (p.259), eyes which search out 'larve che creava elle stessa' (p.253). All this looking, in fact, turns out to have been a purely narcissistic exercise, the outside world a mere projection of her desires. It is with a mere reflection of Cesare that she is in the habit of conversing as she watches herself 'seminuda' in the mirror (p.153) while slowly divesting herself of her finery: her smile 'finiva allo specchio, in una contemplazione astratta di sé stessa' (p.154). It is the symbolic mirror that sees her 'discingendosi con arte', posturing with her child as a Madonna figure (p.243); or composing rustic 'quadretti del genere', with a shawl and a brightly coloured head-scarf, and her child at her breast (p.247). And the verdict of incorrigible narcissism, superfluous as it is by now, comes from a carefully peripheral source, Cataldi, who declares that 'Ella non amerà mai altri che sé stessa' (p.156).

The visit, in his absence, to the Baron's flourishing estate is another *messa in scena*. It is a lengthy and richly descriptive passage which seems designed chiefly to show Elena exposed to the material attractions of the *rentier* class. Verga no doubt discovered in the course of writing that the *messa in scena* is an intensely uneconomic procedure. So it proves, once again, in Chapters 10 and 11 where an impertinent servant, absent from the rest of the narrative, rises to temporary and lively prominence, doing so in order to display, apparently, the mortification of the male and the *piccolo borghese* in Cesare. The unpunishable insolence of her repeated, sly 'povera ma onorata' (pp.213, 215, 216) is a model of its kind. She alone — with her 'manaccie unte' (p.199) as they seem to the obsessive mind of Cesare — can calm the mistress's nerves, excluding him from what becomes the female stronghold of the bedroom. But it is Donna Anna (by this stage — almost nothing in Verga is casual — the victim of Don Liborio's philandering, and therefore somehow caught up in the prevalent atmosphere of man-hatred) who completes Cesare's emasculation. She sends him to market in place of the allegedly pilfering maid, and this gives the maid an excuse, which she plainly relishes, for bothering him mock-deferentially over every domestic trifle. The antagonism betwen master and servant is Verga's opportunity to explore Cesare's moral degradation. In the long tortured hours after intercepting the letter to Cataldi Cesare will strain his ears to register the continued inhibiting presence nearby of the servant as she goes about her tasks. His *idée fixe* is that she, his social inferior, is enjoying his predicament: 'L'idea prima, sola, implacabile, era che la serva indugiasse apposta' (p.218); the servant, he is convinced, 'assaporava ipocritamente le sue angosce' (p.219). For her sake he walks on tiptoe, stifles his sobs and reflects: 'Perché mi tormenta così? Come gode del mio supplizio! ... Ella andrà a dirlo alla fruttivendola e al calzolaio. ... Andrà a ridere con loro delle mie smanie. Bisogna fingere ... Bisognerebbe mostrarmi al vicinato insieme all'Elena, uniti come prima!' (pp.223-4). Through her Verga can expose 'naturally' a near-paranoia born of, among other perhaps more important things, *piccolo borghese* snobbishness. But he would never again use to the same degree the elaborate technique of the *messa in scena.*

The indirect or unobtrusive supplying of psychological data which the technique could achieve did not, in any case, as we saw, remove the need for a guiding presence within the text. Nor, it must be conceded, do Verga's intrusions — either by wit or insight — dispel the impression of a 'monotonia d'ordine psicologico' which Russo noted.[21] But the nature of these intrusions, parsimoniously measured out and 'culturally' limited as they are, is, I suggest, the result of deliberate intent. In the preface to *I Malavoglia* — guided in this by the preface to *Les Frères Zemganno* — Verga had been clear that, as he mounted the rungs of the social ladder to create the projected *Vinti* cycle, the language of his various narratives would subtly alter. To Treves in July 1880 he wrote: 'Lo stile, il colore, il disegno, tutte le proporzioni del quadro devono modificarsi gradatamente in questa scala ascendente, e avere ad ogni fermata un carattere proprio. Questa è l'idea che mi investe e mi tormenta'.[22] The trick to be worked if the author was to be eclipsed — and his disappearance was not only the expected result, but also perhaps a passionate *raison d'être* of the system of 'modified styles' — was the creation of a language that would be felt as the emanation and the expression of a particular *ambiente*. This method of by-passing the author — realised with astonishing originality in *I Malavoglia* — was to be a lasting torment and obsession. Evidence of the long struggle lies in many letters, notably in one to Rod of 1899 where he writes of the deliberate suppression of his own self, equating it with a linguistic act: 'Ho cercato di mettermi nella pelle dei miei personaggi, vedere le cose coi loro occhi ed esprimerle colle loro parole'. The method is unchanged and unchanging: 'Questo ho cercato di fare nei *Malavoglia* e questo cerco di fare nella *Duchessa*, in altro tono, con altri colori, in diverso ambiente.'[23]

Il Marito di Elena plainly makes some attempt to match language to *ambiente*, drawing for this on the experience of *I Malavoglia*. As in *I Malavoglia* Verga uses a narrating 'voice' — sometimes a lightly sarcastic one which looks forward to *Mastro-don Gesualdo* — which is 'internal' to the ambience it purveys. Cesare for instance is seen departing for legal training in Naples 'dietro il carro che gli portava il letto e il tavolino *colle gambe in aria, e* le sorelle *si erano cavati gli occhi* a cucirgli il corredo' (p.39); or the provincial ladies, in emulation of Elena, are said to have placed on their heads 'tutti i fiori del giardino' (p.94). But this is not the world of *I Malavoglia* where a shared cultural code means a homogeneous language, and the narration, though passed surreptitiously from mouth to mouth, remains linguistically unified. In *Il Marito di Elena* Verga is confronting a diversified world: Cesare belongs to minor landowning countryfolk, while Elena's father has been part of the Bourbon bureaucracy, and that diversity, as Annamaria Andreoli has noted, has already left its mark on the text.[24] But in a psychological study there is the world 'within' as well as the world 'without'. And if *Il Marito di Elena* involves aberrant psychology — is the study of what deviates from a norm — it is hard to see how a language primarily conceived as mimicry or reflection of *ambiente* — apparently generated by that *ambiente* — can possibly decipher it adequately. Here, I think, was a further cause of Verga's frustration. It was this impossibility no doubt that precluded any autonomy of the text. But if the 'eclipse' of the author had to be forgone, there remained the idea of 'modified styles'. It follows that as a last resort — or so it seems to me — Verga matches his interventions, culturally and linguistically, to the *piccolo borghese ambiente* in which Cesare and Elena move.

Though they push the narrative forward, the glosses on their behaviour provide little in the way of privileged or rare insight. We are told, for instance, that Cesare is 'vittima della propria bontà' (p.89), that Elena quite simply 'aveva bisogno di quella vita, di quel lusso' (p.151), that, as far as their financial difficulties are concerned, Elena's is a 'crudele indifferenza' (p.154), that she is 'una di quelle fragili donnine che hanno una gran forza di dissimulazione' (p.160), that Cesare has 'il povero orgoglio mascolino di nasconderle le sue angosce' (p.170), that the temptation lying in wait for Elena 'la colse, se non pel cuore, per la mente guasta e fuorviata, nello spirito inquieto e bramoso' (p.186), that Cesare understands Elena 'colla divinazione penetrante di chi ama davvero' (p.207), and so forth. Positivistic psychological know-how is carefully adulterated, as we saw; and the synthesising authorial judgments on the couple are both superficial and repetitive. These insights offer no more than the wisdom of the *piccola borghesia*, its own often stereotyping self-awareness, in its own language. They are consonant with Verga's obvious preference for the unexceptional and even the prefabricated phrase in much of the text, consonant with the notion of a language that shall not appear to 'invent' but to mimic. The impression of a slipshod style is in reality the effect of a calculation.

Verga's language, then, seeks to match his *ambiente*. To be experienced as doing so it must keep within parameters which the reader recognises, precisely, as *piccolo borghese*. But where mimicry is so central an aim, an added touch of stylisation can produce parody. Verga can maintain his equilibrium very effectively where he is dealing with a Don Liborio or a Donna Anna, for their function in the text can be fully expressed in his 'stile piccolo borghese'. Problems are more likely to arise when a more intimately psychological approach seems required, especially since Verga's willingness to undertake analysis is of the limited kind we have indicated. So it is that the text is often poised on the brink of convention. The preliminary exchanges between the lovers as they prepare for their gesture of social defiance have a citational air: 'Ho paura!', 'La mamma sa tutto!', 'Cosa faremo?', 'Fuggire?'. They end with the inevitable, furtively delivered note: 'Domani sera, alle undici ... aspettami nella scala' (pp.26-31).

The socially acceptable alternative, the long official courtship of Roberto and Camilla verges on caricature. The pair also fall victim to the repetitive, self-citing nature of the narration (which in Annamaria Andreoli's view 'ritorna tanto rigorosamente su se stessa da finire per negare la "verità" dei personaggi e degli oggetti, sempre convertite nella serie e nel documento'[25]). The text returns perpetually to the idea of a marriage endlessly postponed pending 'better prospects', and to an unkind vignette of the couple: the fastidiously dressed 'giovanotto maturo' mutely sitting out the evenings by Camilla's side, and Camilla, equally taciturn, forever busy with her embroidery. Nor is it an accident that Elena's actions (rather like Emma Bovary's) are explicitly related to the models of behaviour offered by 'letture romanzesche' (the letter to Cataldi, for instance, is the 'episodio di un romanzetto da educanda' (p.255) — and perhaps even that mock-Medieval Peppino was the result of Verga's impulse to *mettersi nella pelle del personaggio).* Even the reckless Elena, in fact, feels the need to 'fare come fanno gli altri' (p.151). Her adulteries (which are viewed so obliquely — from a point-of-view identifiable with Cesare — that not all critics have noticed all of them, and one at least has not noticed any) take on the air of a conditioned reflex, and her lovers are more or less stereotyped. Cataldi successfully 'recites' (p.155) the part of the world-weary Don Juan; and the Duca d'Aragna will 'triumph' 'colla sua scuderia, col suo sarto, col suo gran nome' (p.273) — tautologously, that is to say, precisely in as far as he is ducal; while the rustic Baron Peppino (who long before has approached Elena with 'intenzioni conquistatrici veramente *baronali*' (p.114), and who has somehow had the impression of being 'al teatro' (p.115)) seduces her only in a later, more sophisticated incarnation when he is armed with the 'frasario convenziale dei saloni' (p.290).

Perhaps it is understandable that it is the literary suitor, the *poeta da salotto* Fiandura, who, as it were, bears the brunt of the writer's frustrations — the need not to say, or not to say too clearly (so that language and *ambiente* are matched), the effort to scatter an 'alternative' trail of clues; the problems raised in general by Verga's 'psicologismo senza psicologia'[26] (one is reminded by *Il Marito di Elena* that for Verga the psychological Bourget was to seem a 'famoso scocciatore').

For once Elena will fail to succumb. All Fiandura's rhetoric — an angry pastiche from Verga of the language of Romantic eroticism — proves useless. During the scene in the inevitable garret, despite his linguistic proficiency, Fiandura repeatedly blunders into self-betraying indelicacies. The whole episode is marked by the couple's efforts to restore the flagging encounter to its appointed course and by their embarrassed search for 'una parola adatta' (p.265). It is as though Verga, suffering from the constraints of his own demanding technique, were finally taking revenge on established, conventional literary languages in general; and one remembers his remark, contemporaneous with the second, post-*Malavoglia* period of drafting *Il Marito di Elena*, on an Italian readership over-fond of 'il pepe della scena drammatica' and the resulting temptation he experiences to 'ammannire i manicaretti che piacciono al pubblico per poter ridergli poi in faccia'.[27]

At this stage the novel is too uncontrolled merely to punish the consumers of novelettes with their taste for piquant scenes. It ends up by punishing itself. The irritation that produced the encounter in the garret creates its own momentum, so that the spirit of satire spills over into a testy indictment of high society, which directly exhorts and involves the reader:

> E questa gente che si stringe nelle spalle allorché vi sentite spezzare il cuore pel tradimento di lei ... la quale vi dice ... Perdonami! perdonami come Dio! ... Ebbene, questa gente, se voi fate come Dio, si stringe egualmente nelle spalle, ma di sprezzo.   (p.276)

The following chapter, in which that 'voi' continues in evidence, creates a hectoring collusive relationship between reader, writer and character as it fluctuates between generalisation — 'Quando il marito offeso non schiaccia la donna sotto il tacco, al primo momento, non ha altro di meglio da fare che prendere il cappello e andarsene' (p.279) — and specific probability — 'Elena sarà caduta ai piedi di lui ... O si sarà arrestata sull'uscio, ritta, immobile, pallida, fiera ... egli rimaneva pur sempre lo stesso uomo' (pp.279-80). The moralistic emphasis of the *feuilleton* is there — that impulse to derive a general teaching from individual example — as well as its violence of expression: the Fiandura chapter will end with a morally edifying tableau: the betrayed husband weeping over his child and the entry of that figure of vice, the adulterous wife: 'Tutt'a un tratto entrò l'Elena, coll'occhio impietrato, le labbra convulse e cascanti...' (p.227). It is as though the novel for the moment has despaired of its own diagnostic capacity.

In the final two chapters Verga is back in control. But the fundamental ambiguity of the text persists, poised as it is between the pathological and the socio-economic, 'Malavoglian', decodification of a failed marriage. On the one hand Cesare is seen in positivistic terms. He is the product of a family and a class background which require ambition in their children — 'avvocato' for them is the 'grosso titolo ch'empie la bocca' (p.38) — and which yet require them to curb that ambition with the prudent calculations which have ensured their own survival in the contradictory state of 'miseria decente' (p.41) (nor is Elena, with her inappropriate 'educazione da principessa', any less the victim of the contradictions of her class). On the other hand Cesare is also a close relation of 'Ntoni Malavoglia. He is the young man who makes fatal contact with the great world of the city, and comes in part to represent a longing for the lost integrity of the country-dwelling family. So it is that in the final episodes, which take place in Cesare's native village, Elena is seen by his sisters as the 'forestiera' who can never be assimilated, but brings with her the sense of a 'minaccia che maturava e s'accostava lentamente' (pp.296, 295).

The ambiguity of the ideological *impostazione* is matched by the unresolved nature of the narrative discourse. The formal experiments which belong to the positivistic and psychological Verga of 1879 sit uneasily alongside the techniques learnt from *I Malavoglia*. To dwell on the former enables us, if nothing else, to locate a 'missing' Verga, the Verga who so enthusiastically embraces the positivistic message in the preface to 'L'Amante di Gramigna' and who elaborates narrative strategies — in concert, as it were, with Capuana — which he hopes will give it fitting expression.

The techniques for representing the psyche which Verga deployed in *Il Marito di Elena* were never systematically used again, being perceived, one presumes, as too unwieldy even where the psychological information imparted was adequate. But in this sense the book was a preparation for the steps that lay ahead, on higher rungs of the social ladder, where the 'mezze tinte dei mezzi sentimenti'[28] awaited Verga. It is interesting in this connection to note that the most debatable of the scenes from *Il Marito di Elena*, the scene of Elena's assignation with Fiandura, is reworked in the story 'Né mai, né sempre!', first published in 1889. What has changed are not so much the morals of the narrative as its tone and control. In *Il Marito di Elena* one reads:

> Ella ... saliva trepida a guardinga le rampe del Vasto ... chiusa nella mantiglia, pallida. Il ciabattino lercio che faceva da portinaio si fece ripetere due volte il nome del suo inquilino, guardandola sfacciatamente, canticchiandole dietro una canzonaccia oscena ... mentre ella saliva rapidamente la scala sudicia e nera, premendosi la mantiglia sul seno ansante. (p.261)

By 'Né mai, né sempre!' the 'head-on', emphatic confrontation with reality has given way to knowing irony, a slanted angle of vision:

> Prese a due mani il suo coraggio e le sue sottane, e salì in punta di piedi quella scaletta sudicia, sfidando alteramente gli sguardi avidi e indiscreti del servatore bisunto, appena velata da un pezzetto di trina che si era cacciata in tasca.[29]

But neither stance, apparently, could call into being *La Duchesse di Leyra* — third novel of the *Vinti* cycle, but the earliest to aspire to the condition of a *roman réaliste de l'élégance*. And it was perhaps with *Il Marito di Elena* that Verga first confronted the difficulties he shared with other impersonal *veristi*: the problem of investigating complex psyches without appearing to do so, the problem of not saying what was sayable.

VERGA'S *IL MARITO DI ELENA*

NOTES

1. See Carmelo Musumarra, *Verga e la sua eredità novecentesca* (Brescia, 1981), p.153. All page references given in the text are to *Il Marito di Elena* (Milan, 1897); all emphases, except where otherwise indicated, are mine.

2. See Note 1; also Aurelio Navarria, *Annotazioni verghiane e pagine staccate* (Caltanissetta-Rome, 1976), who cites a letter — previously published in *Letteratura* in 1968 — from Luigi Capuana to Edouard Rod in 1884 claiming that *'Il Marito di Elena* era già scritto, in gran parte, prima che Verga mettesse mano ai *Malavoglia'* (p.170).

3. See Nino Cappellani, *Vita di Giovanni Verga* (Florence, 1940) p.225.

4. See *Una peccatrice e altri romanzi* (Milan, 1965) p.225.

5. See *Lettere a Luigi Capuana* (Florence, 1975) pp.190, 191.

6. The description is Folco Portinari's. See *Le parabole del reale* (Turin, 1976) p.172.

7. See Carmelo Musumarra, *Verga e la sua eredità novecentesca*, p.158; and Folco Portinari, *Le parabole del reale*, p.163.

8. See Matilde Dillon Wanke, *'Il Marito di Elena*, ovvero dell'ambiguità' in *Verga inedito, Sigma* (1-2), 1977), pp.116-7.

9. See Carlo A. Madrignani, 'L'altro Verga' (introduction to *Drammi intimi* (1884), Palermo, 1979), p.ix.

10. See *Vita dei campi* (Second Edition, Milan, 1881), pp.156-7.

11. See *Vita dei campi*, pp.155,156.

12. See *Lettere a Luigi Capuana*, p.162.

13. See Felice Cameroni, *'I Malavoglia'* (article of 1881) in *Interventi critici sulla letteratura italiana*, (Naples, 1974), p.104.

14. See Giovanni Verga, *Lettere sparse* (Rome, 1979) p.243.

15. See *Alla scoperta dei letterati* (1895) (Florence, 1946) p.119.

16. See *Lettere a Luigi Capuana*, pp.124, 125, 126.

17. See *Lettere a Luigi Capuana*, pp.189, 191.

18. See Annamaria Andreoli, 'Circolarità metonimica del Verga "borghese"' (in *Verga inedito, Sigma* (1-2), 1977, pp.177-204).

19. See *Giacinta* (reprint of first edition of 1879, Sesto S. Giovanni, 1914) p.96.

20. See Vittorio Spinazzola, *Verismo e positivismo* (Milan, 1977) p.236.

21. Luigi Russo, *Giovanni Verga* (1920) (new edition, Bari, 1969) p.213.

22. See *Lettere sparse*, p.94.

23. *Lettere al suo traduttore* (Florence, 1954) pp.130-1.

24. See 'Circolarità metonimica del Verga "borghese"', pp.183-4.

25. 'Circolarità metonimica del Verga "borghese"', p.203.

26. The phrase is Vittorio Spinazzola's (see *Verismo e positivismo*, p.33).

27. *Lettere a Luigi Capuana*, p.168.

28. Preface to *I Malavoglia*, in *Opere* (edited by Luigi Russo, Milan-Naples, 1968) p.177.

29. See *I ricordi del capitano d'Arce* (1891), in *Le Novelle* (edited by Gino Tellini, 2 vols., Rome, 1980) p.262.

'*Zut, zut, zut, zut...*': Novels where consciousness of language is a fictional theme (Proust, Constant, Flaubert, Stendhal, Gide)

Christine M. Crow

> 'Il faut chercher, chercher
> indéfiniment ce de quoi
> tout ce que nous disons
> n'est que traduction'
> (Valéry, *Cahiers*)[1]

The experience of speech can be fraught with ambivalence: on the one hand a sense of frustration that words are only words or that they lag behind the complexity of inner feelings and thoughts; on the other hand a sense of relief in what words alone make possible, not the least their power to signal and modify what we feel cannot be said. However much it may structure our mental make-up in the first place, language can still be the object of self-conscious awareness, the sensation of discrepancy between expression and experience transforming itself from joyful challenge to burden or anxiety in the twinkling of a tongue. For Valéry — mentioned here since he reflected on the 'duologue' of the mind with itself perhaps more far-rangingly than any other writer of the modern period — consciousness is the capacity to 'hear oneself speak', and the natural duty of the imagination is the task of listening interpretatively both to others and to ourselves.[2] Literature — itself a thing of language — is accordingly an art of effects, a dancing provisionality set against the general linguistic tide and designed to increase the expressive and suggestive powers of individual utterance, 'la parole'.[3]

Compared with the poem, the novel may seem — and for Valéry not only at first sight — a very different story of fish. Even the late nineteenth-century and early twentieth-century novel in France — the novel of self-consciousness — chooses the mimetic illusion of character and plot rather than exploiting the materiality of language in the way Valéry preferred. Yet is a novel necessarily so far from a poem or less effectively poetic when, unlike certain more recent examples, it veils its linguistic origins and uses mimetic illusion to allow us to listen to experience outside words? What if self-consciousness in relation to language, sometimes even an analytic understanding of language, is embodied within the novel's own fictional frame? This study is an attempt to bring together from a group of major novels of the earlier part of the 'language-conscious' modern period certain key scenes — mainly occurring when two characters meet in moments of emotional strain or plenitude — when consciousness of language has become a visible literary theme. Setting these scenes side by side will enable us to reflect in our turn on the nature of at least one form of literary reflexivity.[4] What relation between art and reality is implied by the novel which uses reference to words, often to the inadequacy of words and to the banality of literary discourse, as an integral part of its own discourse? Surely the work which disguises itself as a true story of the fiction of words is no less aware of the nature of language than the 'Nouveau' or 'Nouveau Nouveau Roman' epitomised by Robbe-Grillet which presents *itself* as fiction, and fiction, that of the 'self' included, as linguistic in kind? I shall treat the Proustian passage first and with the greatest reference to its context since, by making visible the urge towards expression involved not only in spoken language but also in literature, Proust might be thought to be employing a self-referential form. Is this really the case, however, and if so, how far or in what sense is his novel made to appear to designate itself? Does it proffer a knowledge which pierces or preserves the literary illusion involved?[5]

* * *

> '...je fus frappé pour la première fois de ce désaccord entre nos impressions et leur expression habituelle.' (Proust, *Du Côté de chez Swann*)[6]

'Zut, zut, zut, zut ...', Proust's self-listening narrator tells us he once shouted, brandishing his umbrella enthusiastically on one of his Rimbaud-like Autumn 'promenades'. The sense of a 'privileged moment' of perception, its outer ingredients the unifying freshness and movement of wind and sunshine in a landscape after rain, is evoked by Proust through a series of half-stated analogies which allow us imaginatively to recognise and to interpret in the form of general laws — difference and identity, familiarity and newness — the basis of individual delight. The wild grasses growing in the wall of the gardener's shed, and the downy feathers of a chicken walking on the roof, were drawn out sideways by the breeze, 'avec l'abandon de choses inertes et légères'; the red-tiled roof appeared mirrored in the pond — once more now a smoothly reflecting surface after the rain — as a pink marbling previously unnoticed, and the walls and water seemed to

reply with a 'pâle sourire' to the smile of the sky with its
newly washed rays of the sun. Proust chooses to make the
walks which give rise to these formative relationships with
the outer world take place after long sessions of reading[7] —
walks in which, his body full of pent-up energy like a spinning
top, Marcel would find himself rushing about in all directions,
banging the walls, trees and bushes with his umbrella or
walking-stick and uttering as he did so the most joyful of
cries. The very choice of expletive — 'Zut, zut, zut, zut'
(preceded by the grammatically reflexive 'je m'écriai') —
implies frustration and elation in near-equilibrium. The
impression of beauty seems somehow inseparable from the
need to understand, to record and to share, while running the
parallel risk that the sheer ebullience of the sensation will
thereby be lost. Indeed, the mental experience we recognise
here is a complex one not confined to the inadequacy of
language. Its stimulus seems to derive from the inner
perception that there is just as much danger in using as in not
using words. (The passage ends accordingly with Marcel's
realisation, thanks to the surly villager who barely responds
to his rapturous 'What a fine day!', that we cannot rely on
people to feel things in the same way or at the same time. It is
from precisely this solitude that art will be felt to originate:
words called upon to convey and understand, not to obliterate,
the vital contradictions of the individual mind).

The role of the 'Zut' episode is both intricate and clear. It
allows Proust to provide us with an example of the
impressions of joy — as strong as the experience of
involuntary memory to which they will later contribute —
from which his 'personnage narrateur' builds up a sense of the
inadequacy of immediate expression and the need to probe
further into the nature of sensation itself. From his position of
mature hindsight into the 'humble discoveries' of the 'côté de
Méséglise' Marcel introduced the resurrected anecdote by
stating that most of our so-called 'translations' of feeling — the
term was also Valéry's — are simply a means of unburdening
ourselves of the expressive pressure within us, while doing

nothing to help us elucidate their true sense. ' ... je m'écriai dans tout mon enthousiasme ... : "Zut, zut, zut, zut". Mais en même temps je sentis que mon devoir eût été de ne pas m'en tenir à ces mots opaques...'. We do not have to wait until the last pages of *Le Temps Retrouvé*, where the already reported incident is picked up again,[8] to detect the sense of vocation which Marcel now considers his own. Proust's whole paragraph is structured in such a way as to suggest a germinating link in identity between that comically intermittent yet intensely receptive creature of yore and the enlightenment which comes from the reflexive intelligence itself, picking up and accentuating its own rôle in creating long-term rewards.

A great writer has no need to invent the essential book, we read in these same final pages where the 'Zut' episode comes to 'rest in the light' it helped to form: 'Le devoir et la tâche d'un écrivain sont ceux d'un traducteur'.[9] The joyful but fleeting and incomplete sense of certainty felt by Marcel on that day by the Montjouvain pond — now, more loftily, the bridge over the Vivonne — has played, we learn, a major part in the revelation of the nature of art which is prepared and justified all along. Experience itself is the radiant metaphor which the novelist must 'translate' through the medium of style, allowing the reader access to other individual worlds. In a sense this is the very subversion of concept and literary stereotype which takes place in *A la Recherche...* too. Yet given that no work can contain a total image of itself, how far does Proust choose to make his work *appear* self-referential?

When the narrative finally folds back on itself, the novel form passionately proposed by Marcel is certainly reminiscent of *this* novel in very obvious ways: individual experience as material, the primacy of metaphor, the essential ingredient of time, in fact the potential joy of life itself, this life, consciously and expressively re-lived. Yet, leaving aside the ontological differences between created work of art and inset image of art — Proust has to create in words the mime of experience from which we feel Marcel's 'theory' to grow, and so on — it is surely significant that the image of an actual author-figure is never allowed to control the central narrative focus at all, leaving only the image of the potential novelist or of the writer failed or obliquely perceived. Marcel may be 'porteur d'une œuvre' whose expression is urgent, but its verbal execution remains decidedly hypothetical and remote. In fact Proust makes his character's inward conviction of the work to be accomplished grow in proportion to an almost Baudelairean fear of weakness regarding actual production.[10] The narrative moment is kept to a shadowy region unspecified[11] — nor, for all its consciousness of self is this narrative self-conscious in the sense that *Tristram Shandy* is, where telling becomes itself the subject of the tale. References to language and fiction in the textual sense are likewise totally absent from the work.

Why should this be so, and why, having interlaced the beginning and end of his novel — in fact virtually every element within its thematic architecture — should Proust not continue the 'mise en abyme' that last crucial step?

One of the reasons why *A la Recherche...* stops short of fully recursive reflexivity could be said truistically to lie with the first-person narrator device. Marcel cannot tell us he completed his novel *and* that it is this one, if psychological realism is to be maintained. Yet this is to forget the very relationship between experience, language and literature which the first-person narrator 'Marcel' is invented to explore in the first place.[12] A sense that revelation is pre-linguistic — 'la vérité n'a pas besoin d'être dite pour être manifestée' (II, 66) — is a vital factor in the conception of reality as a subjective construction, which Proust conveys artistically at every possible turn, the inner work of joy which the artist must 'translate' in language if its legacy is to be able to enrich other minds. It was of a creature of pure inner joy, not of language, that he wrote 'Il n'y a que lui qui devait écrire mes livres', a creature capable of perceiving relationships between things.[13] Of course we can pierce the illusion; of course we *know* that literature is made not of joy but of language. Yet the fiction which allows Proust to keep his own novel linguistically transparent is the same as that which Marcel makes the conscious basis of experience. Joy, like fiction, like the 'magic' of metaphor,[14] does not, through knowledge, cease to exist.

If, then, there is self-referentiality in *A la Recherche...*, it is of a kind we are led to imagine for ourselves in relation not to the novel itself as a finite creation of language, but to the desire for expression which the novel represents as a constant presence over and above its necessary closure of form. It is not only to the richness of his own wordless experience that Marcel's 'Zut' acts as the pointer — that myth of prior unity which is nonetheless operative for being mythical — but to the structure of the whole novel as a provisional utterance: a novel which expresses its own urge to transcend words, making us imagine not language, but art, and, through art, the forever unwritten novel of life itself.

* * *

'Les sentiments de l'homme sont confus et mélangés; ils se composent d'une multitude d'impressions variées qui échappent à l'observation; et la parole, toujours trop grossière et trop générale, peut bien servir à les désigner, mais ne sert jamais à les définir'. (Constant, *Adolphe*)[15]

Proust's preoccupation with the creative imagination and the sources of illusion and reality means that his narrator is more likely to be concerned with the fabulous, redemptive possibilities of language as style than with language in its own right.[16] A novelist who frequently concentrates on the existential problem of language itself is Constant, writing almost a century before. The discourse of *Adolphe* is interwoven on the level of both characterisation and plot with epigrammatic attentiveness to the paradox involved in the very nature of speech. ' "Chère amie", lui dis-je', confides the narrator of his own spoken words, ' "On lutte quelque temps contre sa destinée, mais on finit toujours par céder..."'. In the well-known passage where Adolphe attempts to end his longstanding relationship with Ellénore, the language he reports using is straightforward in itself but pompous and clichéd in effect, suggesting to the reader — placed *partly* with Ellénore as listener outside words — a form of inner conflict. Adolphe is drawn both to mitigate and to justify his behaviour, proposing that the rational action of leaving is the one he most suffers to wish. Yet is not the 'bad faith' we detect here of linguistic rather than of directly psychological origin, the simple statement of an attitude imposing a spurious unity on feelings diverse and contradictory in kind?[17] With characteristic urge to understand the truth of his feelings, it is the narrator himself who now confides to the reader the false ring of his words: 'A mesure que je parlais sans regarder Ellénore, je sentais mes idées devenir plus vagues et ma résolution faiblir', a comment which conveys succinctly both the necessity of language and its power to transform the experience it helps to reveal. The purpose Adolphe communicates is undermined by the very form necessary for its transmission to another person (at whom, significantly, he cannot look as he speaks). Hoping to regain strength, Adolphe tells us, he now continued in a 'voix précipitée', and we find him enveloping his message in protestations of friendship and affection, eventually resorting to a form of analysis where the general concept is broken down into further compartments as if infinitely to chase a prey finally discovered in absence alone: 'Mais l'amour, ce transport des sens, cette ivresse involontaire, cet oubli de tous les intérêts, de tous les devoirs, Ellénore, je ne l'ai plus'.

'J'attendis longtemps sa réponse sans lever les yeux sur

elle': Ellénore's silence has become a source of dramatic concern to Adolphe and reader alike. She is found gazing at the objects in the room as if they are strange to her — the exact counterpart of that state of self-identifying attentiveness in which Proust's Marcel projected his enthusiasm onto the material world. Her hand is cold (from which we infer that Adolphe took it in his, yet how different in perspective would be such a statement), her whole body is immobile, and, after her own words of painfully destructive honesty — 'Qu'avez-vous encore à me dire? ne m'avez-vous pas tout dit? ...' — she loses consciousness, a gesture to be used by Flaubert in *Madame Bovary* to suggest the problematic interplay of the authentic and conventional, but which Constant endows with poignant simplicity and pain. Yet if words can kill, they can also return to life again:

Crédulités du cœur, vous êtes inexplicables! Ces simples paroles, démenties par tant de paroles précédentes, rendirent Ellénore à la vie et à la confiance; elle me les fit répéter plusieurs fois; elle semblait respirer avec avidité. Elle me crut: elle s'enivra de son amour, qu'elle prenait pour le nôtre; elle confirma sa réponse au comte de P***, et je me vis plus engagé que jamais.

The scene is remarkable not least for its power to convey the double nature of words, both incomplete and necessary, means of access and instruments of closure, potentially the instruments of both seduction and truth. We are made to feel the almost physical drama involved in the human transaction of speaking, the living 'space' in which speech operates, as consciousness flows towards and away from its own supplement and source.[18] Nor is it simply the narrator's general comments on language which draw us in this direction. Constant has used the resources of literary indirectness — inner monologue, rhythm, gesture and so on — in such a way that the reader enters the gap between expression and experience from which we imagine individual consciousness to be formed, and in so doing — for of course we are intensely aware at the same time of the fictionality of the character whose thoughts we share — appreciates the communicative intention of the work as a whole, what Valéry would call the 'poids probable d'origine' of its own created 'Voice'.

Language itself is necessary to the expression of a sense of discrepancy between word and experience, just as literature alone can confirm the 'illusion' of shared experience as real. It is *this* value — carried over in this case into the notion, but still not the self-referential image, of writing (the manuscript of Adolphe's confessional 'novel' is discovered by an *éditeur*)[19] — which enables us to relate the narrator's discovery of the alienating effects of language as the expression of individual feelings to his equally important sense of language as the instrument for analysing the limits of definition and for conveying the silence beyond speech.[20] 'Crédulités du cœur, vous êtes inexplicables!' — its lyrical tone suggesting as much mastery as mystery — becomes, like Marcel's 'Zut', an expressive rhetorical figure, pointing in this case not to a work in the future but — and here the refusal to conceive of language as absolute is the same as Proust's — to the image of a mind present to itself dialectically in the search for rational truth. Constant's critique of language is not allowed to erode with the irony of infinite regression the essentially verbal victory of the literary *moraliste* in conveying the limits and longings of speech.[21]

* * *

> 'Frédéric, se grisant par ses paroles, arrivait à croire ce qu'il disait.' (Flaubert, *L'Education sentimentale*)[22]

Constant and Proust employ a first-person speaker as an essential part of their linguistic symbolism, extending the subjective significance of moments of external speech or inner monologue by placing them within a narrative permeated with awareness in time: 'later I understood', 'how I felt as I spoke or thought then' and 'what I know of that feeling now'.[23] Arch-investigator of the cliché, of experience as well as of expression, Flaubert in *L'Education sentimentale* uses no such first-person perspective, leaving us, as we follow the experience of Frédéric, to make for ourselves the reflections of an absent Adolphe or Marcel.[24] Led to these discoveries we still are, however, and perhaps even more inescapably by virtue of that famous impersonal voice through which is built up by every possible means, direct analysis not excluded, a vision of human reality, of a complexity which the categorisations of language help shape in their turn.

In the famous last scene between Frédéric and Madame Arnoux it is negatively, through the impossibility of speech, that language first enters the novel as a conscious theme. After their first startled exchange of names (' — Madame Arnoux! / — Frédéric!') and her half private 'C'est lui! C'est donc lui!', they are *unable* to speak, we are told: 'Tous deux restèrent sans pouvoir parler, se souriant l'un à l'autre'. Is this narratively-revealed silence due to the inadequacy of language or to the inadequcy of those particular people, unable to express themselves? What, in such moments, might one really wish to say? It is, of course, typical of the precisely controlled ambivalence of Flaubert's style that it can handle simultaneously the genuine and the inadequate. The phrase 'sans pouvoir parler' (silence specifically designated in relation to speech) acts as the literary pointer to a fusion of cause and effect far more complex than the linear sequence of 'plot' and any judgment of character which it might seem to involve.

The ensuing verbal exchange (no longer presented in direct speech) is purely conventional in itself: he asks after her husband and the details of her life since they last met. In its context, however, it is charged with the curiosity and empathy which the questions allow us to attribute to Frédéric himself as the partial interpreter of language, and, beyond this, with a form of stylistic imagination through which we are led to speculate on the potential ambivalence of emotion itself. It is partly the speed and positioning of the narrative comments which gives rise to such suggestions, making the tiniest remarks of the two characters reveal — as language itself reveals — far more than what is actually said. Her '— Mais je vous revois! Je suis heureuse!' conveys an attempt to adjust words back to the immediate personal feeling which each new conversational direction appears to leave unsatisfied, conveying at one and the same time an immense feeling of solitude and yet the recognition of a common human source. Closely based on observation of the colloquial — but serving a different stylistic purpose from Proust's similar observations — remarks like 'C'est lui, c'est donc lui', 'Mais je vous revois' serve, together with reference to voice and physical gesture, the continuous flow of expressive intention through which Flaubert makes his novel 'speak'. Nor is the narration external to identifying involvement even at the novel's most critically detached: where Ellénore looks at objects as if she had never seen them before, Madame Arnoux looks 'avidement, pour les emporter dans sa mémoire'. There is no need for a 'comme si'.

'— Quelquefois, vos paroles me reviennent comme un écho lointain, comme le son d'une cloche apporté par le vent; et il me semble que vous êtes là, quand je lis des passages d'amour dans les livres'. Where the shared excitement of talking after a long period of absence can blot out the presence of the surroundings,[25] words recalled and the imagery of the written word can convey the presence of an absent person, but convey it, one supposes, in idealised form. Speculative judgements on the part of the reader — in this case on the nature of authentic emotion and, indirectly, of literature — are constantly called forth by the 'absent present' point of view. Yet *how* has Flaubert handled the notion of literary stereotype so relevant to our concern with consciousness of language as a theme? Frédéric's protestation that he has felt for Madame Arnoux 'all that is blamed as exaggeration in literature' conveys a complex attitude to the power of language which fails to resolve itself into sympathy or criticism as we tease out the ironies and half-truths on which it rests. Is Frédéric not superior in his imaginative vulnerability, perhaps even in the mediocrity of his passion, to the philistine who protects himself by the sanction of impoverished 'taste'? The subsequent statement that Frédéric grew intoxicated by his own words to the point of believing in what he was saying is undoubtedly more *openly* mocking, but only in a context where the interference of words and experience has already been presented as a general truth. It is significantly 'quelque chose d'inexprimable' — a revulsion related to the fear of degrading his ideal and not totally unrelated to tenderness — which finally draws Frédéric to recoil from gesture, the silence between them based now on parallel solitude rather than on an emotion identically overwhelming the ability to speak. 'Et ce fut tout': after the famous generality on the moment before parting, its 'nous' form indicting narrator, reader and character alike, plot and narrative emotion finally converge.

What of the 'poids probable d'origine' of words in this passage? In allowing us to dream of the difficulties and dangers of language, Flaubert critically separates the voice of the novel from the values of his protagonists while still making us sympathise with the fully human problems they represent. As we read of failure to communicate, a sense of shared experience is paradoxically increased. To Proust's 'Zut' and Constant's 'Crédulités du cœur' can be added Flaubert's 'La bêtise consiste à vouloir conclure', equally valid as satirical utterance and as disclaimer of pretensions to definitive judgement in the novel itself.[26] Once more, even in a highly 'modern' work which some would regard as more transitional than Proust's, language is made to seem more the culprit than life. No image of the novel-form itself is brought to bear on communication this time (other than through a sense of the literary as ambivalently false). Instead, the mirror has acquired a reality of its own and the power of the critical imagination makes silence and emptiness speak.

* * *

'... si l'on se fût parlé, de
combien de façons
différentes n'eût-elle pas
pu chercher à deviner
quelle était précisément la
nature des sentiments que
Fabrice avait pour la
duchesse.' (Stendhal, *La
Chartreuse de Parme*)[27]

The novel using a scene based on the emotional tension
between two people does not always invent dialogue
(reported in *Adolphe*, narrated as if direct in *L'Education
sentimentale*) to convey the relation between expression and
experience necessary to its own intentions. As Stendhal builds
up the relationship between Clélia and Fabrice in the prison
sequence of *La Chartreuse de Parme* (1839), verbal language
is present as a theme only by its absence as a possible
communication channel. Imprisoned in the 'tour de Farnèse'
high above the city, Fabrice attempts to initiate his
relationship with the prison officer's daughter by signs:
piercing a hole in the window shutter, for instance, as she
feeds her caged birds on the terrace below. From the most
rudimentary 'Je suis là et je vous vois', we feel the message
pass to more elaborate forms of 'I know you know I know you
know I know'. For Fabrice at least, communication and
seduction are synonymous. The need to break down imposed
restrictions on his natural right of speech humorously
coincides with the need to break down resistance to his
assumed personal appeal.

'C'est à dire de parler, par signes du moins, de ce qui se
passait dans son âme';[28] in what sense, in fact, does that small
qualification relativise our attitude to Fabrice's inner self or
'soul'? Like Flaubert, Stendhal eschews first-person narrative,
yet the result, different again from Flaubert's 'style indirect

libre', is a visible narrative presence operating through comment and tone. The phrase 'par signes du moins' is a signal to us too: a lightly ironic throw-away on the part of the narrator, and yet the opposite of a throw-away on the part of the implied author. What *is*, after all, that secret part of the self we feel we must communicate at all costs? Can Fabrice be sure of anything other than the desire to express the desire to express — the kind of tautology which music takes for granted? Is that which can be communicated in the purely 'digital' language of non-verbal signs anything Clélia will find sufficiently individual to wish? Indeed, from her reticence in the face of such rapturous gestures we conclude, long before it is stated directly, that she longs for *verbal* language, '... si l'on se fût parlé...'. Can words really make plain the nature of our feelings? — if so, it is through the *image* of such a possibility that Stendhal communicates with us here. The shape of desire available only in the harmony of style, with its equivalent in love and in the emotion of song,[29] the moment which affords Fabrice the most joy is one where words are notably absent (their impossibility caused this time by external circumstance). As he watches Clélia tending her plants in the courtyard below, he sees her spill water, a movement he interprets as the outward betrayal of inner emotion, and the narrator, with an elation of his own which could never have been felt for Frédéric, confides affectionately 'Ce moment fut le plus beau moment de la vie de Fabrice, sans aucune comparaison'. The 'prison-house' of Farnèse sets the perfect limits to words and resurrects in so doing the 'illusion' of joy.

* * *

'Voici l'instant, pensai-je, l'instant le plus délicieux peut-être, quand il précéderait le bonheur même, et que le bonheur même ne vaudra pas...' (Gide, *La Porte étroite*)[30]

Where the relationship between Fabrice and Clélia strains *towards* verbal communication, Gide's Alissa and Jérôme deliberately hold back the verbal — 'ne pas trop chercher à parler d'abord' — even going so far as to plan a language of gesture for words deemed too painful to use at the time. Hedged with joyful anticipation and Spring flowers — the symbolically charged precision of the piece encourages zeugma and allegory — the path along which Jérôme slowly advances offers a zone of being where the mind is intensely conscious of equilibrium with its surroundings — 'le ciel était comme ma joie, délicatement pur' — yet where the privileged moment is far more vulnerable to the disruption of the inner world by change of outer circumstance than it is for Proust's Marcel, avidly learning from each new interruption and dependent only on himself.

There *is* no dialogue in this passage, direct or reported. Jérôme's narration — 'Voici l'instant, pensai-je' — proffers his thoughts and feelings retrospectively in the form of inner monologue, while including, as did his close companion figure, Adolphe, description of the sensations of speech felt at the time ('N'ayant point préparé mes phrases, je parlais plus aisément'). The fear that words will destroy the moment by over-defining feelings or revealing what cannot be admitted is reinforced by the plan that when the time comes for departure, Alissa will wear round her neck the little, in this case doubly symbolic cross which will act as the signal for Jérôme to depart. She may not be able to *tell* him to go. Where Clélia in *La Chartreuse de Parme* required the extra precision of words to clarify feelings, Alissa hides from the banality of words as from loss of individuality, yet only to risk further suffering, intensified by the choice. Silence has now become equated masochistically with the pain of departure and loss.

But where does Gide appear to 'speak' himself through *La Porte étroite*? In that Jérôme is his own narrator — concerned in any case with conveying the absence of mental distance which was his experience at the time — there is no extra dimension to play against subjectivity as in Stendhal, none of the multiple viewpoints adopted by Flaubert. Nor, if irony is the answer, is it an irony which works directly against the characters[31] — the kind of perspective which suggests that all Alissa had to do was to recognise a fear of her own 'natural' desires, Jérôme taking meanwhile a more forceful hand. Irony in *La Porte étroite* is directed as much against reductive views of this nature as against intransigence itself, posing the problem of how to protect potentially valuable drives from themselves. It is through style alone that we hear what Valéry would call 'l'auteur que l'œuvre fait supposer', the perfect balance of the work in all its devices, character and plot included in an always further signifying net. We are not *told* anywhere in the work that provisionality is the essence of judgement and utterance. No 'Zut' is necessary when style itself has become self-conscious without losing self-confidence, inviting us to 'listen' to the qualities required by literary form.

* * *

Narrative structures in the five chosen works have been richly varied, and, on the level of character fiction at least, responses to the theme of language have seemed to differ to the point of contradicting one another. Where Clélia longs for the possibility of words with which to ascertain the precise nature of Fabrice's feelings towards her, Adolphe asserts that words can never pin down the variety of what we feel; where Frédéric is seduced by his own words to the point of believing the emotions he is describing, Adolphe feels his belief falter the more he speaks, and so on. Yet these differences disappear when we respond to the full contextual implications of the episodes concerned. In Stendhal's novel a warm irony suggests that Clélia appeals to verbal analysis partly as a protection against the emotion her eyes have already spontaneously signalled, thus bringing our perception of language closer to that of Adolphe with its belief in pre-verbal awareness (his own sense of the need for language to point to its own incompleteness and, indeed, the deluded nature of his emotive 'edenism', bringing us back closer to Clélia's rationalism in turn). Or, again, the beam of light directed by Flaubert on Frédéric's inadequately self-perceived experience allows us to reflect on the same problem of authenticity which Adolphe attempts to use language to elucidate and which Constant demonstrates, by this particular narrative fiction, to be contingent upon social exchange with the world. The common denominator in all these 'character' reactions is the sharp sense of incommensurability between expression and experience — in turn a stimulus to conscious being — which the activity of speaking is used to reveal. That language itself — the suggestive framework provided by the novel — is still the source of this effect, is a secret kept closely guarded. More often than not it is through their treatment of the theme of *failure* to communicate in language that these novelists achieve the transformation of lack to presence which ensures the 'victory' of the book as a whole.

It could be argued that a form of reflexivity is present in all the passages recalled here, then: not only in the most obvious sense in that reference to language is made *in* language, but because, less obviously, the theme of the limits and possibilities of language has become, in inverted form, an integral part of the novel's own creatively achieved ideology of meaning and form. Perhaps for language to affirm itself victoriously as creation, some form of *dédoublement* must always occur.[32] Yet before subsuming this particularly versatile contribution to language-conscious literature under the general banner of reflexivity, it would seem important to emphasise that the process is never presented as fully self-referential in the 'scriptural' or textual sense. The illusion of a narrating character or third-person narrative voice conscious of the linguistic dimension of experience is a very different matter from those narrative strategies which place the image of a writer within the fiction in such a way as to draw attention to the language of the work itself, the linguistic codes involved in story-telling, or, a further degree of reflexivity still, which take as their subject the generative processes which govern the work as a text. It is the concept of *listener* rather than writer — reader rather than author — which these five novels might be said to have set as their central metaphor on the level of form and when we translate their created intentions back through written language to speech. It is a choice which makes their own discourse appear constantly to open onto a rich, unmediated reality beyond the confines of their enabling medium, yet without denying the value of language as a vital part of the relationship between the mind and the world.

Is the literature of 'blasted words' really less conscious of language, in particular its own source in language, than later novels which appear to deconstruct their own techniques? All literature is aware of its nature as fiction, visibly or invisibly so,[33] and the choice of what might be called expressive mimesis involves in these novels a highly conscious use of the reflexive powers of language when its fictional resources are released in a non-self-referential way. If there is a lesson to be learned from the 'ethic of listening' such works encourage, it would seem to be one which equates critical knowledge as much with the preservation as with the destruction of fictive illusion. Novels which imagine a 'self' independent of language are still as highly conscious of the provisional nature of their art.[34] The power of words *and* words of power.

NOTES

1. VI, 762 (Paris, 1957-61).

2. 'Le "devoir" de ne pas croire — c.à.d de n'attacher aux *paroles* venant des autres ou *de soi* (en Soi) qu'une "valeur" provisoire — laquelle, d'ailleurs, est vraie valeur; de ne donner ou consentir aux mots que leur poids probable d'origine ... . Rien n'enseigne plus cette nature provisoire que le travail littéraire' (*Cahiers*, XV, 179). A volume in honour of Alison Fairlie as both teacher and critic seems a particularly appropriate place to remind ourselves of this art of creative 'listening' and its implications for literary criticism.

3. In *Paul Valéry and the Poetry of Voice* (Cambridge, 1982) I suggest that Valéry's notion of poetic form is both expressive and communicative, while remaining self-consciously fabricated, and that literary intentionality is defined accordingly as creative discovery through form.

4. Many important aspects are only loosely touched on here, in particular the relationship between self-conscious literature and 'deconstruction' and the question of where a work may or may not accept or display the linguistic values which occasion its own power (see notes 16 and 29, images of style).

5. This article is concerned not with revealing unconscious metaphors of language, but with the 'myths' of language consciously created within a work. It would seem to me that the tasks of critical appreciation and of literary theory invite different perspectives on the relation of knowledge to literary illusion, almost a different theory of truth.

6. *A la recherche du temps perdu*, édition établie et présentée par Pierre Clarac et André Ferré, Bibliothèque de la Pléiade (Paris, 1954), vol. I, p.155 (the paragraph studied begins 'Mes promenades...', pp.154-5).

7. Proust's treatment of reading as a means to recuperate 'all that inner contemplation has discarded' is discussed by Paul de Man in *Allegories of Reading, Figural Language in Rousseau, Rilke and Proust* (New Haven and London, 1979), p.60.

8. *ARTP*, vol. III, p.890. Where Gérard Genette uses the term 'iterative' and 'singulative' for two different types of Proustian construction (see J.M. Cocking's comment in *Proust, Collected Essays on the Writer and his Art* (Cambridge, 1982), p.253), it seems important to note that 'iterative' forms are still part of narrative and distinct from the 'generative' repetitions used by Robbe-Grillet in, say, *Dans le labyrinthe*.

9. Valéry appears to use the term 'traduction' and 'devoir' in a different way from Proust (see epigraph and n.2), yet both statements imply a sense of pre-verbal authenticity as the special goal of writing (something quite different from notions of 'pre-verbalism' in direct mental life).

10. E.g. *ARTP*, vol. III, pp.1041-5. The claims and strains on Baudelaire's creative imagination are evoked with insight in Alison Fairlie's 'The procrastinations of a poet', *TLS*, June 28, 1974.

11. Proust uses a conditional tense — 'du moins ne manquerais-je pas d'y décrire...' (p.1046) — and a 'maintenant' which belongs to

discourse rather than to 'récit' — '... cette notion du temps évaporé ... que j'avais maintenant l'intention de mettre si fort en relief' (ibid.).

12. Cf. Malcolm Bowie's comment in *Proust Jealousy Knowledge* (London, 1978): 'What is often overlooked is that all the narrator's theoretical pronouncements — including the celebrated "Une œuvre où il y a des théories est comme un objet sur lequel on laisse la marque du prix' (882) — are caught up in the fictional texture, infused with desire and intention, and subject to the same ironic action-at-a-distance from the remainder of the book as any other of its parts' (p.3).

13. *Contre Sainte-Beuve* (Paris, 1954), p.360.

14. Paul de Man (op.cit., pp.57-78) suggests that Proust's metaphorical world is involved in a form of self-destruction (i.e. that it reveals itself as chains of 'literal' or metonymic detail). In this sense the work is allowed a double relationship to the figurative, unravelling the 'magic' and knowing it to be rhetorically powerful at the same time. Knowledge of language is not allowed to destroy the goal of its enquiry.

15. Ed. P. Delbouille, 1977, p.1178 (whole passage pp.163-4). The reader is referred to Alison Fairlie's invaluable essays in *Imagination and Language* (pp.4-125) for many more suggestions about language than those taken up here.

16. 'La matière de nos livres, la substance de nos phrases, doit être immatérielle, non pas prise telle quelle dans la réalité, mais nos phrases elles-mêmes, et les épisodes aussi doivent être faits de la substance transparente de nos minutes les meilleures...' *Contre Sainte-Beuve*, p.368. Cf the passage in *Le Temps retrouvé* where Marcel expresses the desire to write the work which his fine days in nature have made him experience (p.1044).

17. See Godelièvre Mercken-Spaas, *Alienation in Constant's 'Adolphe', An Exercise in Structural Thematics* (Bern, 1977).

18. That the subject is divided by the processes of language which call it into being (see Lacan) is not necessarily to deny the illusion that subjectivity is extra-linguistic in kind. A novel which offers this double perspective might be said to offer us the means to 'deconstruct' its own ideology rather than appearing to do so itself as is the case in some later works.

19. Just as in Proust's novel, however, there is no stress on 'writing time'.

20. Godelièvre Mercken-Spaas suggests that language in *Adolphe* passes

from 'pre-linguistic' silence to the expression of silence through language (op.cit.).

21. Constant's implied vision of language as a limited but vital instrument of reason can be contrasted with the post-Symbolist view where the inner complexities of language can be tapped to approach the 'unsayable'.

22. Flaubert, *Œuvres*, II, texte établi et annoté par A. Thibaudet et R. Dumesnil, Bibliothèque de la Pléiade (Paris, 1968 (1952)), part III, Chapter IV, p.451 (whole passage, pp.448-53).

23. In Nathalie Sarraute's 'novels about language' there is no interior monologue in the sense of inner speech. The 'sous-conversation' is a metaphorical description of movements which are not linguistically articulated (see Celia Britton's article 'The Self and Language in the Novels of Nathalie Sarraute', *M.L.R.*, July 1982, vol. 77, part 3, p.577 and compare with Valerie Minogue, *Nathalie Sarraute and the War of the Words* (Edinburgh, 1981)).

24. See Alison Fairlie, op.cit., p.379.

25. Alison Fairlie draws attention to moments in Flaubert's novels when speech is silenced and the sensation of sound increased (op.cit., pp.430-2). Here, conversely, the two walk amidst the sounds of the city without hearing anything, as if — heavier irony — they were walking in the countryside on a bed of dead leaves.

26. The question of self-reference as utterance is briefly discussed by W.A. Bennett in 'Literature and the Liar Paradox: a Comment', *French Studies Bulletin*, Summer 1982, n.3, pp.11-13.

27. Bibliothèque de la Pléiade (Paris, 1952), p.322 (and Chapter XVIII).

28. For Gérard Genette, 'L'amour stendhalien est entre autres choses un système et un échange de signes ... . Le sentiment tend pour ainsi dire naturellement à la cryptographie...', 'Stendhal', *Figures*, 2 (Paris, 1969), p.165. However, the communication channel develops later to include music (Clélia's singing) and eventually the means of writing as well.

29. The equivalent image of verbal transcendence in *L'Education sentimentale* is when Frédéric hears the 'music' of Madame Arnoux's voice. Alsion Fairlie points out in relation to this work that 'Un livre qui refuse de représenter la réussite de l'artiste sera en lui-même l'éclatante preuve de la victoire de l'art', *Imagination and Language*, p.420.

30. André Gide, *Romans*, Bibliothèque de la Pléiade (Paris, 1975 (1958)), pp.561-2.

31. Frederic Jameson contrasts the 'baring of the device' type of formalism with the form of irony which reabsorbs conventional authorial interventions back into the text (see *The Prison-house of Language* (Princeton, 1972), p.78-9).

32. See Lucien Dällenbach, 'Les derniers avatars d'une forme: la mise en abyme', *Australian Journal for French Studies*, XIV (1977), p.202 (and *Le Récit spéculaire* (Paris, 1977).

33. Even the recursive 'mise en abyme' is still a fictional device. (For definition and discussion see Michael Tilby, *Gide, 'Les Faux-Monnayeurs'* (London, 1981).)

34. Cf. Valéry, 'Tout ce qui est verbal est provisoire. Le langage est moyen. La poésie essaie d'en faire une fin' (*Cahiers*, XII. 673).

Théophile Gautier's *Voyage en Italie*. The Description of Experience, or the Experience of Description.

Joan Driscoll

In its earliest version, Gautier's account of his travels in Italy appeared in instalments in *La Presse*, beginning in September 1850, while Gautier himself was still absent in Venice.[1] At first sight, the *Voyage en Italie* seems to represent a relatively simple literary enterprise: the author visits Italy and describes, for his readers at home in France, what he sees there.

It is evident, however, from the moment of Gautier's entry into Italy, that this simplicity is more apparent than real; and, throughout Gautier's *Voyage*, we find him reflecting, not only upon the character of Italian life and scenery, but also upon that of the language which he must use to represent them.

'Le caractère des montagnes, que l'on croirait devoir devenir plus doux et plus riant en approchant de l'Italie, prend au contraire une âpreté et une sauvagerie extraordinaires. On dirait que la nature s'est fait un jeu des prévisions... Ce renversement est très-curieux: c'est la Suisse qui est italienne et l'Italie qui est suisse dans cette étonnante route du Simplon' (pp.22-3).[2]

The fiction of a mischievous Nature who, by a paradoxical reversal of the faces of Switzerland and Italy, makes play with our normal expectations concerning the relationship between words and the things they represent, provides a fitting starting point for our own investigation. Following the author in his travels, we shall try, without too assiduously avoiding the temptation to share Gautier's own pleasure in the paradox and the *boutade*, to examine some of the ways in which the text encourages us to examine our own assumptions about the nature and purposes of description.

The notion that nature or 'reality' is the model, and that the value of descriptive language lies quite simply in its power to provide a faithful mirror-image of that model is, of course, naive; and the theory itself is not one to which Gautier himself would have subscribed. Nevertheless, the *Voyage en Italie* is, at least in its role as a work of popular journalism, a travelogue: and the reader who read it in the expectation that it would provide him with an accurate account of a series of places which had an objective existence in the external world, and which he could himself visit, would not be making an altogether unreasonable assumption.

Moreover, Gautier's own observations concerning the purpose and the character of the text suggest that we may at least begin from this premise. He states his intention of bringing to his reader a more complete account of Italian life and scenery than those which he had found in the works of his predecessors: 'en lisant les récits des voyageurs, il nous est arrivé de souhaiter des détails plus précis, plus familiers, plus tracés sur le vif, des remarques plus circonstanciées sur ces mille petites différences qui avertissent qu'on a changé de pays ... Nous avons fait notre butin de tout cela, et décrit des maisons, des cabarets, des rues, des traguets' (p.295). He suggests, indeed, that his concern for accuracy, even photographic accuracy, was greater than his concern for the formalities of literary composition: 'ce sont des croquis faits d'après nature, des plaques de daguerréotype, de petits morceaux de mosaïque recueillis sur place, que nous juxtaposons sans trop nous soucier d'une correction et d'une régularité qu'il n'est peut-être pas possible d'obtenir dans une chose aussi diffuse que le vagabondage à pied ou en gondole d'un feuilletoniste en vacance' (p.273).

However, Gautier himself stresses the fact that the *Voyage* is not a guide, but a series of impressions: in other words, it is not a work of reference, to be dipped into or consulted on occasion but, albeit within the limitations of the *feuilleton*, a literary text, where the detailed description which 'conviendrait plutôt à un guide spécial qu'à un recueil d'impressions de voyage' (p.120) has no proper place. Moreover, as he observes, the very act of writing such a text imposes conditions which conflict at times with the demands of accurate and faithful description. Indeed it is, paradoxically, the journalist's very desire to minimise the role of the writer and to relax the formality of literary composition, so that all the variety, and even the incoherence, of Italian life and scenery may be presented directly to the reader as it is experienced in reality, which leads Gautier to reintroduce into his text the figure of the author — the author who, if his account is to be readable at all, must first solve the problems of composition and give at least a minimum of coherence to his narrative. 'Nous ne sommes pas de ceux dont la joie ou la tristesse importe au monde, et, si nous usons quelquefois de notre personnalité dans ces notes de voyage, c'est comme moyen de transition et pour éviter des embarras de formes' (p.143).

The decision to broaden the scope of the existing *récit de voyage*, and to include not only the splendid and the monumental but also the detail of everyday life, is of course in itself the decision of a writer who is conscious of the literary framework within which he works, and of the limitations which existing conventions may place upon innovation or faithful representation.

The very nature of things, and our multiple experience of them, seems to defy the assumption that they can be represented without distortion within the bounds of a text which is coherent enough to be readable; and Gautier remains to the end of his *Voyage* uncertain of his ability to combine successfully the assessment of artistic treasures, the description of architectural monuments, the presentation of historical and geographical information, the notation of the details of everyday life, and the representation of the varied scenery through which he travels. 'L'architecture nous a souvent entraîné, et nous avons souvent abusé, en dépit du précepte de Boileau, du feston et de l'astragale... Les mœurs de la société vénitienne ne tiennent peut-être pas assez de place dans ces esquisses, et le tableau y a souvent le pas sur l'homme' (pp.295-6): the written text demands a polish, a unity, and a balance of its different elements which is at variance with the complexity and even the confusion of the things to be described.

Moreover, as Gautier more than once has cause to observe, the reader himself makes other demands which conflict at times with the avowed purpose of the text — to bring to the public at home a faithful description of the places which the author has visited.

In the description of the art treasures of Venice, Gautier finds himself confronted with a veritable *embarras de richesses*. Eager as he is to omit nothing of significance, and even to restore the reputation of some of the minor artists who are more usually overlooked, he remains mindful of his reader's limited endurance: 'nous sentons malgré nous s'allonger cette nomenclature; mais à chaque pas un chef-d'œuvre nous tire par le basque de notre habit quand nous passons, et nous demande une phrase. Le moyen d'y résister! nous allons, ne pouvant tout dire, laisser travailler votre imagination' (p.129).

It is in fact a weakness of Gautier's text that the distinction between the guide (in which comprehensiveness and accuracy of reference are of prime importance) and the more literary series of 'impressions de voyage' (where techniques of selection and suggestion might more successfully convey the quality of the author's own experience) is not always sufficiently respected. Aware though he is of his reader's limited patience, and of the greater potential of suggestion as opposed to statement, Gautier does not always resist the temptation of enumeration or accumulation, and offers, in his account of the splendours of the Doges' Palace for example, not a persuasive picture of the riches of the place as a whole, but a mere list of the names of the many artists whose works he has no space to describe: 'comme architectes, Palladio, Scamozzi, Sansovino, Antonio da Ponte, Pierre Lombard; comme peintres, Titien, Paul Véronèse, Tintoret, Carlo Cagliari, Bonifazio, Vivarini, J. Palma, Aliense, Contarini, Le Moro, le Vicentino...' (p.130). The catalogue continues.

The techniques of communication and persuasion themselves differ from those of accurate notation and description. As Gautier well knew, it is not enough that something should be real, it must seem to be real. Even with the object before us, we may remain unconvinced of its authenticity — like that of the famous porphyry columns of the 'palais Vendramin Calergi' which 'paraissent fausses, quoique de la vérité la plus incontestable' and disappoint because their appearance belies the reality of their great value: 'elles sont placées devant une porte, et font aussi peu d'effet que les lapis-lazuli du salon Serra à Gênes, qu'on croirait volontiers peints et vernis, et qui ressemblent, à faire peur, à du moiré métallique bleu' (p.278-9).

The persuasiveness of any representation, and the writer's descriptions are no exception, derives as often from art, or even artifice, as from accuracy or strict authenticity. Dürer's map of medieval Venice seems as real as the contemporary city itself to the author of the *Voyage*; and this impression is achieved, not by total fidelity to the detail of the city, but by a skilful combination of mathematical precision and free fantasy: 'ce grand artiste, à la fois si fantastique et si exact, qui introduisit la chimère dans les mathématiques, a retracé la ville d'or, la *città d'oro*, comme la nomme Pétrarque, telle qu'elle était à cette époque avec une minutie scrupuleuse et un caprice étrange' (p.125).

The ostensible purpose of Gautier's descriptions, if not the *raison d'être* of the *Voyage* itself, may lie in the accuracy with which they mirror the reality of Italian life and scenery. Nevertheless, there are numerous indications in the text of the fact that the real business of the writer lies just as much in the reinforcement of common preconceptions concerning the nature of that reality, and indeed in the flattery of the reader's own preference for the unreal or the artificial, rather than the real or the natural.

The interest of the travelogue might well be expected to lie in the fact that it creates for the Frenchman at home an impression of a country which is strange, exotic, and different from his own. It was, after all, Gautier's intention to bring to his reader 'tous les détails caractéristiques de ces mille et une différences presque imperceptibles, mais qui vous avertissent à chaque instant qu'on a changé de pays' (p.197).

However, Gautier's own text reveals the extent to which language, as a means of communication, remains inimical to the precise decription of things which are truly foreign or exotic. His account of his visit to the 'hôpital des fous' on the island of San Servolo demonstrates the degree to which the artist's powers of representation are limited by the necessity of using forms of expression which are familiar to both artist and spectator, to writer and reader alike. In short, the abnormal can only be represented by means of the conventional.

The fresco painted by the mad monk of San Servolo might be regarded as the counterpart of the frescoes of St Mark's, the latter with their 'monde d'anges, d'apôtres, d'évangélistes, de prophètes, de docteurs' (p.109), representing the triumph of reason and enlightenment, the former 'une ménagerie de l'extravagance la plus effrénée ... des bêtes sans forme et sans nom, dont l'équivalent ne se trouve guère que dans le monde microscopique ou les cavernes des dépôts diluviens' (pp.245-6), the triumph of unreason and obscurity. The madman's fresco is as empty of real significance for the spectator as the frescoes of St Mark's are rich in meaning. However, if the figures which the mad monk represents have no reality for the spectator, this is not because he is mistaken in his belief that they are copied faithfully from nature (many of the figures in the frescoes of St Mark's have themselves no equivalent in the world of everyday reality), but because of the absence, in the case of the monk's painting, of the shared cultural convention which permits both Gautier and his reader to recognise the figures depicted in the frescoes of St Mark's as elements of the languages of a number of different religions or creeds. The difficulty of describing works so rich and varied as the frescoes of St Mark's within the brief space of the *Voyage* is indeed great: but the difficulty of representing forms so strange and singular as those of the madman's imagination within the common currency of language is much greater. Gautier himself can only communicate the outlandish nature of the monsters of the madman's painting by referring his readers to a series of very well-known works and genres: 'les animaux héraldiques ... les monstres chinois ... la fantaisie des songes drôlatiques de Rabelais ... peuvent seules en donner une idée' (p.246). The very familiarity of these references, which were already part of the stock repertoire of the French writers of the 1830's, threatens to render the unknown commonplace.

In the *Voyage* as a whole, the description of landscape very often involves the transmutation of the strange or the exotic into a type of scenery which corresponds closely with the Frenchman's own preconceived ideas of the picturesque. The use of such points of reference as Canaletto's Venetian painting from the Louvre provides a compromise between the known and the unknown, lending an authentically Italian air to the description without disturbing that sense of familiarity which permits both writer and reader to 'recognise' a landscape with which they are not yet acquainted: 'nous reconnûmes sur-le-champ la Salute, d'après le beau tableau de Canaletto, qui est au Musée' (p.71). More often, however, Gautier describes the scenery of both Switzerland and Italy by using references to the paintings of his own countrymen or to works of other origin which were well known to them — creating in this way a series of picturesque impressions which belong, not so much to the Swiss or Italian countryside itself, as to the artistic repertoire of the French. The landscape of Lake Geneva is compared with those of Isabey, Wyld, Bonington and Decamps, those of Venice with the work of Bonington, Joyant and Wyld — repetition in these different contexts of similar patterns of references itself gives emphasis to the affinities between the landscapes of the different countries rather than to their exotic or unique character.[3]

Throughout his travels in Switzerland and Italy, Gautier rediscovers those picturesque or poignant scenes which he and his Romantic contemporaries had earlier discovered much closer to home; and the predominance of references in the text of the *Voyage* as a whole to works which enjoyed their greatest vogue in the Romantic 1830's itself seems to belie Gautier's expressed intention to bring a greater immediacy and realism to the description of Italian scenery. The settlement on the shores of the Rhône as it leaves Lake Geneva: 'tout cela, vermoulu, fendillé, noirci, verdi, culotté, chassieux, renfrogné, caduc, couvert de lèpres et de callosités à ravir un Bonnington ou un Decamps' (p.5), offers a picture of neglect and decay very similar to that which Gautier had evoked in his early poem, 'Pan de mur', a reminiscence of the house in the Marais district of Paris where he had spent his youth and which would, he observed, have provided Boulanger or Bonington with a characteristically picturesque motif.[4] The landscape of Fusina on the Venetian lagoon: 'sur le bord des canaux, le nénuphar déploie ses larges cœurs visqueux, et soulève ses fleurs jaunes, la sagittaire fait trembler son fer de lance au vent' (p.191), has much in common with those which the poets and painters of the 1830's discovered on the outskirts of Paris, and which Gautier himself evoked in 'Le Marais': 'C'est un marais dont l'eau dormante / Croupit, couverte d'une mante / Par les nénuphars et les joncs'.[5]

Even when, in order to discover the real Venice behind the magnificent façade, Gautier penetrates the mysterious Jewish quarter, less often pictured and described by previous travellers, we seem to find ourselves within the familiar territory of Victor Hugo's *Notre-Dame de Paris*: 'ce quartier fétide et purulent, cette Cour des Miracles aquatique' (p.284), or of the Dutch interiors whose popularity with Gautier's own countrymen dates again from the 1830's: 'nous remarquâmes, dans cette synagogue, un grand nombre de lustres en cuivre jaune avec des boules et des bras tortillés d'un goût hollandais, comme on en voit souvent dans les tableaux de Gérard-Dow ou de Mieris, notamment dans le tableau de la *Paralytique*, que la gravure a rendu populaire' (pp.284-5).[6]

The quest for an accurate exchange of information between writer and reader almost seems to preclude the exchange of accurate information, and leads at times to a mere repetition of the commonplaces and platitudes which render the foreign familiar and the exotic banal. Nor does this tendency appear simply as a weakness of descriptive language, in which the demands of communication conflict with those of faithful representation, but as a fundamental characteristic of our perception of things. The desire for the reinforcement of the familiar cliché is often stronger than the willingness to acknowledge the change and flux which is an essential part of our true experience. So much so, that what Gautier seeks to acclaim as the truly Italian style of dress survives in fact in the village of Sesto-Calende only on market days, and is only discovered by chance: 'c'était jour de marché. Circonstance favorable pour un voyageur; car un marché fait venir du fond des campagnes une foule de paysans caractéristiques qu'il serait fort difficile de voir sans cela' (p.39). The modern, urban Italian hastens to abandon his Italian dress in favour of a mode which is indistinguishable from that of his French neighbour: the characteristic Italian of the traveller's folklore survives in present reality only as an untypical exception.

Gautier observed, and the paradox certainly amused him, that the commonplaces of popular exoticism, far from being discredited by the real experience of the traveller, at times persuade reality itself to conform, so that the stereotype becomes more true than the living reality. The domination of the cliché is a little sinister in the décor of Venice: 'la Venise monumentale, espèce de décoration d'opéra féerique' (p.142), 'ce masque monumental que chaque cité se pose sur le visage pour dissimuler ses laideurs et ses misères' (p.281), more comical in the persons of its singers, the gondoliers, who preserve traditional local colour by reviving their forgotten songs for the tourist: 'comme les filles d'Ischia, qui ne revêtent leurs beaux costumes grecs que pour les Anglais, ils ne déploient leurs mélodies qu'à bon escient et avec accompagnement de guinées' (p.178).

Although the performance of the gondoliers is now self-conscious and artificial where once it was natural and spontaneous, the repetition of the platitude remains unavoidable for the author of the travelogue: 'c'est un de ces lieux communs de voyage qu'il est plus maniéré peut-être d'éviter que d'accepter' (p.178).

Far from being a simple enterprise, the writing of the travelogue reveals the complexity of the relationship between words and the things they represent, a relationship in which the word reflects the object, while the object, itself at least in part a creation of language, reflects or even seems to guy the word.

* * *

So far, we have considered the *Voyage en Italie* as a travelogue. However, Gautier was of course not only a journalist but also a poet; and the *Voyage* is, like much of his writing, the work of both the journalist and the poet.

In the preface to *Albertus* of 1832, Gautier deplored the

prevalent confusion between the poetic or aesthetic mode of language and its prosaic or practical mode, indicating the danger of the erosion of the former by the latter.[7] The dangers of this confusion are nowhere more apparent in Gautier's own work than in the series of *Voyages*, journeys which the poet makes only by courtesy of the journalist's copy.

Of the *Voyage en Italie* itself it might be said that the text contains, not one single homogeneous account, but two different versions of the same journey, recounted by two different narrators, playing two different roles and serving two very different ends. Gautier knew all too well the difficulties of combining the roles of the journalist and of the poet, difficulties which were no doubt responsible, to some extent, both for the richness of this text as a source of observations by the writer upon the practice of his craft, and for its characteristic weakness, which Gautier himself noted — imperfection in the balance and distribution of the material and a lack of coherence in the composition.

The overall shape of the *Voyage* itself suggests some uncertainty as to the role of the narrator and the character of the written text. The *Voyage en Italie* was based upon a real journey which took Gautier through Switzerland into Italy, to Milan, Venice, Padua, Ferrara and on to Florence, Rome and Naples, ending with the author's expulsion from Naples in the Autumn of 1850. As a journalist, Gautier apparently intended to follow the outline provided by this itinerary closely; and indeed the articles which appeared as regular *feuilletons* in Parisian newspapers contain accounts of the visits to Geneva, Milan, Venice, Padua, Ferrara and Florence.

However, the form of the *Voyage* as it was published first by Lecou in 1852 and subsequently in the augmented edition of Charpentier, sugests that its author was influenced by something other than the journalist's concern to bring to his public an accurate account of the principal stages of his journey. The text of the *Voyage* as we have it ends with the account of the visit to Florence: there is no mention of the visits to Rome and Naples. Moreover, the predominance of the

Venetian episode, to which twenty of the twenty-nine chapters of the *Voyage* are devoted, confirms the impression that the writer, if not the traveller, had reached his true destination in Venice and was reluctant to continue.[8] This, together with the richness and abundance of references to the works of the French writers and painters of the 1830's and to those of other periods and origins which enjoyed a particular vogue at that time, points to the dual nature of the text as, not merely a journalist's account of his own present travels, but also a more poetic recapitulation of the familiar artistic and literary theme of the 'voyage en Italie', in which the visit to Venice traditionally played a major part, as it does in the earlier versions which Gautier sketched in his own first Romantic works.[9]

Throughout the *Voyage*, the journalist and the poet (if we may continue to use these convenient labels to distinguish between the two voices of the narrator) display very different priorities and reveal very different attitudes to the use of language as a means of representation — and, indeed, to the nature of the subject to be represented.

The distinction between the two approaches is particularly apparent in the Venetian episode itself. The journalist, equating reality with realism, sets out to observe the characteristic details of Venetian life. The chapters devoted to such matters as 'la vie à Venise' (XII), 'détails familiers' (XIII) and 'détails de mœurs' (XXVI) testify to his intention. In this respect, the failure of language to embrace completely the reality of the traveller's experience may be seen as an involuntary failure, and the fiction of a mischievous Nature, who repeatedly defies the attempts of language to encapsulate her fickle moods within the confines of its conventional formulæ, holds good.

By contrast, in the poet's version, the failure to seize the realities of Italian life and scenery is not really failure at all, but the result of the writer's own deliberate refusal to identify truth with the detail of everyday life. In direct contravention of the principles on which the travelogue is ostensibly based,

Gautier observes more than once in his reflections on the works of fellow artists, both writers and painters, that realism in art is of little value in his eyes — a position to which he repeatedly returned, as the basis for both his criticism and his own creative writing. Although his task as the author of a travelogue took him into the backstreets of Venice, he found that the true atmosphere of the city was most perfectly captured in the magnificence of Veronese's vast architectural compositions which had, as he himself acknowledged, little to offer to 'les amateurs de la vérité vraie' (p.221). The sight of the marionettes which entertained him in Domo d'Ossola at the outset of his journey through Italy had already caused him to reflect that truth is more often to be found in the unreality of art than in the so-called realities of everyday life.[10]

The journalist seeks the reality of Venice in its present, and bases his account upon close, direct observation of the lives of its inhabitants and their immediate surroundings. The poet, on the other hand, prefers to view the city from the height, and the distance, of the campanile of St Mark's. From this aesthetic distance, characteristically represented in many of Gautier's works by the view of the city from the height of a tower, the poet discovers, or rediscovers, a landscape which is revealed by the intuition or the imagination of things distant in time and space.[11] The buildings of Venice, with their 'milliers de cheminées rondes, carrées, évasées en turban', their domes and roofs which offer 'l'effet de ces armures de chevaliers mystérieux dans les tournois du moyen-âge' (p.83) seem to be inhabited still by the Oriental potentates and the medieval knights who peopled the world of the Romantic past.

The journalist attempts, if he does not always succeed in his aims, to widen the scope of the existing *récit de voyage* by uncovering, behind the magnificent façade of conventional representation, the minutiæ and even the misery of contemporary Venetian life. The poetic vision on the other hand, free from the limitations imposed upon the journalist by the necessity for direct observation, gives to the travelogue its own new dimension by the very means of recollecting and even repeating the procedures and practices of its author's predecessors in the literary and artistic tradition to which this version of the *Voyage en Italie* belongs. Gautier's account of the ascent of the campanile and the view over the rooftops of Venice echoes Hugo's ascent of the cathedral of *Notre-Dame de Paris*, from whose towers the modern city appears transfigured by the memory of its more glorious past. Moreover, the Venice of the *Voyage* markedly resembles the half-medieval, half-oriental city which Gautier had himself evoked in the poem which he entitled 'Notre-Dame' and dedicated to the master.[12]

The contrast between observation and imagination is reinforced in the text of the *Voyage* by the opposition between daylight and darkness. Venice by day belongs to the journalist, Venice by night to the poet.

Arriving in Venice by night, the journalist strives in vain to find his bearings by means of the landmarks made familiar by the versions of previous travellers: 'des deux côtés, la lagune, avec ce noir mouillé plus sombre que l'obscurité même, s'étendait dans l'inconnu ... on ne pouvait distinguer ni le ciel, ni l'eau, ni le pont' (p.67). In the light of morning, he is reassured to recognise the church which Canaletto had represented with such meticulous accuracy: 'nous reconnûmes sur-le-champ la Salute, d'après le beau tableau ...'; and it is as though, despite all their apparent exoticism, his travels do not after all take him outside the formal galleries of the Louvre with its well-known masterpieces.

The darkness, which masked the familiarity of the Venetian scenery for the journalist, illuminates the links between the forms of the poet's own imagination and those created by the artists and writers whom he recognises as his precursors in the Romantic tradition: 'nous croyions circuler dans un roman de Maturin, de Lewis ou d'Anne Radcliff, illustré par Goya, Piranèse et Rembrandt' (p.69).[13] The poet accepts with pleasure the hazards of a journey in which darkness opens up perspectives almost beyond the reaches of the imagination, and where reality, in defiance of all preconception, apes unreality: 'certes, ce n'était pas ainsi que nous avions rêvé notre entrée à Venise; mais celle-ci dépassait en fantastique tout ce que l'imagination de Martynn eût trouvé de mystérieux' (p.67), 'jamais la réalité n'a moins ressemblé à elle-même que ce soir-là' (p.69).[14]

In the eyes of the journalist, the reality of Venetian life becomes most intelligible when the things which he describes conform most perfectly with the simple logic of cause and effect. The 'marchand de fritures', who peddles some of the most tempting morsels of Venetian local colour, lends himself obligingly to the demonstration of the principle of the influence of climate upon character: 'la sobriété est une vertu méridionale qui se complique aisément de paresse, et il se fait peu de cuisine dans les maisons. On envoie chercher à ces officines en plein vent des pâtes, des beignets, des bras de poulpe, des poissons frits' (p.155).

In the eyes of the poet, truth is more often glimpsed when Venice rediscovers the freedom of its imagination. In the hours of darkness, the Venetians are revealed in their true light, regaining a verve and a passion which serves the more mysterious purposes of melodrama: 'l'ombre lui rend le mystère dont le jour la dépouille, remet le masque et le domino antiques aux vulgaires habitants, et donne aux plus simples mouvements de la vie des allures d'intrigue ou de crime. Chaque porte qui s'entre-baille a l'air de laisser passer un amant ou un bravo' (p.70).

The journalist observes in the conduct of the present inhabitants of the city the sad realities of a life which is dominated by the consequences of their historical position. He remarks upon the response of the Venetians to the celebrations in honour of the Austrian emperor: 'ce peuple qui faisait le mort tandis que ses oppresseurs exultaient de joie, cette ville qui se supprimait pour ne pas assister à ce triomphe' (p.239).

The poet on the other hand discovers the true heritage of the Venetians in the survival of an artistic tradition which liberates them, under cover of darkness, both from subjection to an alien regime and from conformity to the conventions of realism: 'tout le mélodrame et la mise en scène romantique de l'ancienne Venise nous revenait malgré nous en mémoire ... cette impression, qui semblera peut-être exagérée, est de la vérité la plus exacte, et nous pensons qu'il serait difficile de s'en défendre, même au philistin le plus positif; nous allons même plus loin, c'est le vrai sens de Venise qui se dégage, la nuit, des transformations modernes' (p.69). Fantasy has its own strange truth; and human nature finds a more spontaneous expression in the contrived inventions of melodrama than in the apparently artless observations of the journalist.

In the poetic version of the *Voyage*, the Venetian episode is not a description of a real city but the evocation of an ideal place whose importance stems from the position which it occupies, not in geography or history, but among the states of the mind: 'chaque homme, poëte ou non, se choisit une ou deux villes, patries idéales qu'il fait habiter par ses rêves, dont il se figure les palais, les rues, les maisons, les aspects, d'après une architecture intérieure ... Pour notre part, trois villes nous ont toujours préoccupé: Grenade, Venise et le Caire' (pp.65-6). The landscape of Venice is defined here, not as the journalist had tried to define that of Italy, by opposition with that of Switzerland, but by analogy with the two other images of the ideal city which occupy a place of privilege in the poet's mind, representing the area where his imagination, finding itself at home, and not abroad, may freely move.

The poetic version brings about a reversal of the values on which that of the journalist was apparently based. Much of the humour of the travelogue arises from the author's observation of the ways in which direct experience banishes his preconceptions and illusions. With a smile, Gautier recalls the idea which he had formed of the city of Geneva: 'une idée enfantine ... nous fait toujours imaginer les villes d'après le produit qui les rend célèbres ... ainsi Bruxelles est un grand carré de choux ... Nuremberg une boîte de jouets, et Genève une montre avec quatre trous en rubis' (p.3). The imaginary city is picturesque, enchanting: 'nous nous imaginions une vaste complication d'horlogerie, roues dentées, cylindres, ressorts, échappements, tout cela faisant tic-tac et tournant perpétuellement' (p.3). The reality is drab, monotonous: 'Eh bien! ce rêve s'est envolé comme les autres. ... La courbe et l'ellipse sont proscrites comme trop sensuelles et trop voluptueuses: le gris est bien venu partout, sur les murailles et sur les vêtements (pp.3, 4). Accurate description is associated with the use of a language stripped bare of its colour and charm, whose questionable virtue lies in its power to banish the frail but fertile visions of the imagination in favour of the more robust but arid observations of the external eye.

The imaginary vision is denounced as false in this context because it upsets the logical basis of the realistic description, reversing cause and effect, taking the product of the city for the city which produced it, and allowing the character of the object to be determined by that of its representation.

In the Venetian episode, by contrast, the imaginative vision becomes powerful, legitimately, by virtue of its fidelity to the true character of the writer's experience, which is revealed to be more closely associated with the nature of his previous responsiveness to other forms of representation, both visual and verbal, than with that of the objects of the external world themselves: 'qui jette les fondations de cette ville intuitive? ... Les récits, les gravures, la vue d'une carte de géographie, quelquefois l'euphonie ou la singularité du nom, un conte lu quand on était tout jeune' (p.66). The preconception loses its comic naiveté now, to emerge, in place of the landscape of the external world, as the subject to be represented, or re-presented, to the mind's eye by means of a poetic evocation whose theme is, this time, not the dominance of present realities, but the continuing strength of the images of past experiences which the creative mind receives and builds upon: 'nous ne connaissons encore Venise que par cette image tracée dans la chambre noire du cerveau, image souvent si arrêtée que l'objet même l'efface à peine' (p.66).

However, the recognition of the poetic qualities of these images sometimes becomes so closely bound up with the familiar pattern of the writer's thinking that he is tempted to forget the real origins of their significance — to be found in the chance encounters which have left their indelible impressions upon his own imagination, with the forms of an engraving or the sound of a word. He tries to redefine their meaning by allowing himself to glimpse a promise of the authenticity of the image in the appearance, within external reality, of figures which closely reflect the forms of his ideal. Knowingly led astray in his pursuit, through the backstreets of Venice, of the young girl whose fate it is to represent the incarnation of the poet's ideal of feminine beauty — she is cast in this role because she possesses, naturally, all the elegance and dignity achieved by the art of the actress Mlle Rachel in the performance of classical tragedy — Gautier protests his innocence with less than perfect good faith: 'entre toutes les suppositions que put faire cette pauvre enfant, attaque galante, séduction, enlèvement, elle ne s'imagina certainement pas qu'elle était suivie par un poëte plastique qui donnait une fête à ses yeux' (p.164).

The poet's error, the converse of that denounced in the journalist's account of his attempt to impose the picturesque character of the preconceived image upon the drab reality of the city of Geneva, is revealed when the version of the artist is betrayed as a mere copy of a real model rather than an expression of the ideal of his imagination. The imperfection of the ideal vision is apparent, not when Gautier fails to find it realised in the person of the young girl whom he follows through the backstreets of Venice and who constantly eludes him, but when the paintings in which he thought he had glimpsed its perfection prove to be too perfectly matched, or indeed surpassed, by the beauties who parade in the public parks: 'après une promenade aux jardins publics, on ne s'étonne plus de la splendeur dorée de l'école vénitienne; ce qu'on croyait un rêve de l'art n'est que la traduction quelquefois inférieure de la réalité' (p.162).

* * *

Surprised to find blue hydrangeas growing on the shores of Lake Maggiore, Gautier had himself indicated that the culmination of artistic endeavour, if not of all human endeavour, lay not in the cultivation of the perfections of existing reality, but in the creation of those which were absent from it: 'ces hortensias bleus nous ont beaucoup frappé, car le bleu est la chimère des horticulteurs, qui cherchent sans les trouver la tulipe bleue, la rose bleue, le dahlia bleu' (p.36). The abundance of literary and pictorial references in the *Voyage*, as in Gautier's writing as a whole, itself indicates the extent of his own preoccupation with the processes of artistic creation and the perfection of artistic expression. The subject of the conflict between the interests of the journalist and those of the poet brings us naturally to that of the rivalry between the poet and the painter, and to a reinterpretation, proposed by Gautier himself in the *Voyage*, of the familiar theme, in which Gautier has so often been thought to give the upper hand to the painter. In his attempt to capture the splendours of the Piazzetta viewed from the sea: 'ce tableau sans rival au monde, et le seul peut-être que l'imagination ne puisse dépasser' (p.75), he himself seems to envy the painter and the musician their superiority in the representation of the landscapes of the external world: 'car le poëte, moins heureux que le peintre et le musicien, ne dispose que d'une seule ligne; le premier a toute une palette, le second tout un orchestre' (p.78).

Nevertheless, by another of the quirks of language, the expression of impotence may serve to mark what the consummate artist knows to be a *tour de force*; and Gautier himself offers a felicitous account of the failings of language in the representation of those things which language is apparently unable to represent: 'comment exprimer ces tons roses du palais ducal, qui semble vivre comme de la chair; ces blancheurs neigeuses des statues ...? Qui peindra cette atmosphère vague, lumineuse, pleine de rayons et de vapeurs, d'où le soleil n'exclut pas le nuage?' (p.77).

Moreover, in his account of the beauty of Lake Geneva, though he borrows the conventions of pictorial perspective or, to be more accurate, the terminology of the painter, to define the principal outlines of the scene, he indicates the superiority of language over pictorial means in the suggestion of those aspects of the subject which seem to lie beyond the scope of artistic representation:

> Voilà à peu près les linéaments grossiers du tableau; mais ce que le pinceau serait peut-être plus impuissant encore à rendre que la plume, c'est la couleur du lac ... le cobalt, l'outre-mer, le saphir, la turquoise, l'azur des plus beaux yeux bleus, ont des nuances terreuses en comparaison. Quelques reflets sur l'aile du martin-pêcheur, quelques iris sur la nacre de certaines coquilles peuvent seuls en donner une idée.   (pp.14-15)

Gautier's acknowledgement of his own impotence is no doubt well founded. The power of poetic evocation is not in direct proportion to the abundance of the imagery; and the apparent virtuosity of Gautier's writing does not always disguise an underlying sterility, which is betrayed by the repetition of stock patterns of images, recurring in different contexts, and indicating a preference for the well-tried formula rather than a perfect sensitivity to the most telling or the most appropriate form of expression. In the rehearsal of the different analogies, the immediacy of the impression of the colours of the lake is all too easily lost: the rarity of nature's gems is itself commonplace. Nevertheless, the fleeting aspects and the subtle hues are perhaps, as Gautier himself indicates, more easily captured by the writer's images, themselves no more than a series of suggestions, than by the substitution of another and possibly inferior colour from the painter's limited palette. If the scope of the artist's work is to be restricted to the direct representation of the visible aspects of the external world, the painter may just have the edge. However if, as Gautier's own reflections on the image of the ideal city of Venice suggest, the real aim of the artist is to recapture the impressions and associations with which the mind gives meaning to the things the eye perceives, then the poet may well regain the upper hand.[15]

Throughout the *Voyage* there is both confusion and distinction between statement and suggestion, description and evocation. These are, after all, different versions of the same journey, a journey in which the traveller addresses himself as much to the processes of literary creation as to the landscape of Italy itself. The voices of the different narrators belong to different modes of the same language, in which, through the constant shifting in the relationships between words and the things they represent, the pursuit of meaning is both frustrating and fertile. If the text of the *Voyage* speaks explicitly of the difficulties of adapting the existing forms of language to the description of the unfamiliar landscapes of the external world, it speaks implicitly, though none the less essentially, of the riches of the creative imagination which can be revealed in the patterns of poetic evocation.

NOTES

1. Twenty-eight articles appeared in *La Presse* between September 24, 1850 and November 15, 1851. The version published by Lecou in 1852, with the title *Italia*, contained in addition to these the text of one article devoted to Ferrara and previously published in *Le Pays* for January 11, 1852. The first Charpentier edition of 1875 took the title *Voyage en Italie* and included the text of one further article, devoted to Florence and first published in *Le Pays* for January 13, 1852.

2. Page references in the text indicate the Charpentier edition of the *Voyage en Italie* (Paris, 1876), reprint of the edition of 1875.

3. Eugène Isabey (1803-1886), Wiliam Wyld (1806-1889), Richard Parkes Bonington (1801-1828), Gabriel Decamps (1803-1860) and Jules Joyant (1803-1854) were influential in the development of the new school of French landscape painting which emerged in the early 1830's.

4. Théophile Gautier, *Poésies complètes*, ed. Nizet (Paris, 1970), I, 97.

5. Ibid., I, 9.

6. See *Notre-Dame de Paris* (first published 1831), Book II, chapter vi, 'La cruche cassée'. Gérard Dow (also known as Gerrit Dou), 1613-1675, and Franz van Mieris the Elder, 1635-1681, were among the Dutch painters of the seventeenth century whose influence was frequently acknowledged by the French writers and painters of the 1830's and whose works were popularised by engraving.

7. 'En général, dès qu'une chose devient utile, elle cesse d'être belle. — Elle rentre dans la vie positive, de poésie, elle devient prose, de libre, esclave.' *Poésies complètes*, I, 82.

8. As Jean Richer points out in his *Etudes et recherches sur Théophile Gautier*, ed. Nizet (Paris, 1981), Part II, ch. iv, 1, 'Venise imaginée', the chapters devoted to Venice represent 65% of the text as it stands and, had Gautier completed his itinerary, giving similar attention to Rome and Naples, the *Voyage* would have occupied several volumes.

9. See, for example, *Albertus* (*Poésies complètes*, I, 127), the Romantic poem to end all Romantic poems, in which, as my study of *Transposition d'art in the poetry of Théophile Gautier* (diss. Cambridge, 1972) has shown, Gautier makes abundant use of a range of pictorial and literary references which are very similar to those of the *Voyage en Italie*.

10. See p.32: 'C'est un spectacle étrange et qui prend bientôt une inquiétante réalité, qu'une représentation de marionnettes...'.

11. Pierre Citron discusses Gautier's preference for this aesthetic viewpoint in *La Poésie de Paris dans la littérature française* (Paris, 1961), II, 5.

12. See *Notre-Dame de Paris*, III, i, 'Notre-Dame', and ii, 'Paris à vol d'oiseau', and Gautier, *Poésies complètes*, II, 147.

13. These were again familiar references for the author of *Albertus* and for his contemporaries.

14. Christopher Thompson discusses the influence of the work of the English painter John Martin (1789-1854) upon Hugo's early poetic evocations of vast and fantastic architectural visions — see *Victor Hugo and the Graphic Arts* (Geneva, 1970), pp.74-95.

15. Sainte-Beuve's Joseph Delorme had already drawn a similar lesson from his own meditatation upon the relationship between poetry

and painting: 'les couleurs naturelles des choses sont des couleurs sans nom; mais, selon la disposition d'âme du spectateur, selon la saison de l'année, l'heure du jour, le jeu de la lumière, ses couleurs ondulent à l'infini, tout en paraissant copier. Les peintres vulgaires ne saisissent pas ces distinctions ... Mais, sous ces couleurs grossièrement superficielles, les Bonington, les Boulanger, devinent et reproduisent la couleur intime...', *Vie, poésies et pensées de Joseph Delorme*, ed. Gérald Antoine (Paris, 1957; first edition, 1830), p.148. See also Baudelaire: 'Si tel assemblage d'arbres, de montagnes, d'eaux et de maisons, que nous appelons un paysage, est beau, ce n'est pas par lui-même, mais par moi, par ma grâce propre, par l'idée ou le sentiment que j'y attache', "Salon de 1859, vii, Le Paysage", *Oeuvres complètes*, ed. de la Pléiade (Paris, 1976), II, 660.

Vallejo, Heidegger and Language

Lorna Close

'A cette question
nietzschéenne: qui parle?
Mallarmé répond, et ne
cesse de reprendre sa
réponse, en disant que ce
qui parle, c'est en sa
solitude, en sa vibration
facile, en son néant le mot
lui-même — non pas le
sens du mot, mais son être
énigmatique et précaire.'[1]

The reader coming to the poetry of César Vallejo, the
Peruvian poet who died in Paris in 1938 at the age of 44, is at
once confronted by and locked in struggle with linguistic
difficulty. Words appear as no mere symbols, but have the
density, timbre, impact, weight and opacity of physical objects,
recalling what Gerard Manley Hopkins said of language in his
essay on 'Rhythm and other Structural Parts of
Rhetoric-Verse': 'We may think of words as heavy bodies, as

indoor and out of door objects of nature and man's art'.[2] To Hopkins, as to Vallejo, language has a corporeal character, a substantiality that cannot be effaced by the formalities of meaning. In Vallejo's verse, one is made conscious of the anarchic associative drive and energy of words, and has a sensual, indeed sexual awareness of their independent identity — we are never allowed to forget, in Vallejo, that Spanish is a language particularly rich in obscene or comic double meanings that subvert the decorum of some of the commonest words in usage. Language in Vallejo is in rebellion. In his second collection of poems, *Trilce*, published in 1922, he says 'La creada voz rebélase y no quiere / ser malla ni amor.' (*Trilce*, V). It is rebelling unpredictably even here, because through phonetic identity in pronunciation between b and v in Spanish, what appears orthographically as 'rebélase' — *rebels*, with a b, is indistinguishable from 'revélase' — *reveals itself*, with a v. This single example is typical of a systematic and far-reaching habit of word-play of every kind in Vallejo's work. Writing in *El arte y la revolución*, the poet had claimed for himself considerable licence in the handling of language: 'La gramática, como norma colectiva en poesía, carece de razón de ser. Cada poeta forja su gramática personal e intransferible, su sintaxis, su ortografía, su analogía, su prosodia, su semántica... El poeta puede hasta cambiar, en cierto modo, la estructura literal y fonética de una misma palabra, según los casos'.[3]

Writing of *Trilce*, Jean Franco has said: 'a volcanic eruption has taken place, destroying the hierarchies of the past, leaving man to confront a universe in which he has no special purpose or importance'.[4] This 'volcanic eruption' expresses itself in a radical dislocation of the common procedures of language: Vallejo disrupts syntax, mingles different registers of discourse, abruptly shifting from the familiar trivia of meaningless colloquialism ('qué me importa', 'qué se va a hacer', 'anda', etc.) which are the daily currency of speech, to scientific, technical or musical terminology. Poetic archaisms rub shoulders with arcane number symbolism. The result of this idiosyncratic and incongruous mingling is to slow down our rate of reading, violently disturbing our comprehension, making each word starkly distinct, so that we are forced back to that childhood state of having to grapple with meaning half-understood, making us recapture the primal impact of the *strangeness* of words.[5] Unexpected departures from the familiar are also found in the coining of neologisms: 'tristura' for 'tristeza', sadness; 'dulcera' instead of 'dulce', sweet, or 'dulzura', sweetness; or in sudden shifts in orthography — often only affecting one letter — e.g. 'excrement*i*do' for 'excrementado (covered in excrement); 'toz' with a z for 'tos' (a cough). Further, Vallejo abandons formal verse-structures in most poems — each poem has its own organic form, as it were generated by its content.

In considering Vallejo's practice as a writer, and his ideas on language, I suggest that it is illuminating to compare these with the German philosopher Heidegger's conception of man's being and of language — especially poetic language. The latter are first explored in *Sein und Zeit* (1927), then in an essay on 'Hölderlin and the Essence of Poetry' (1935), to become an increasingly major preoccupation of the writings published in the 1940s and 1950s (such as *Über den Humanismus* (1949), and *Unterwegs zur Sprache* (1959)). In some senses it may be said that Vallejo wrestles with two conundrums that have equally concerned twentieth-century philosophers such as Heidegger or Sartre: the enigma of what Neruda termed man's 'Residencia en la tierra' (in Heideggerian terminology man's 'being-in-the-world') coupled with the enigma of language. I do not wish to suggest a direct influence of Heidegger's thought on Vallejo, rather to point to an interesting coincidence of attitude between philosopher and poet.

To Heidegger, man is defined not by essence or spirit but by his habitation on earth, and in this he sees three elements as intimately interrelated — dwelling, building and being. He bases this intuition etymologically on the association between Old High German *buan* — to dwell, to live in a place, with *bauen*, to build, which is in turn related to the first person singular of the verb to be — *ich bin*. In this context he says: 'to be a human being means to be on earth as a mortal, it means to dwell.'[6] Dwelling is the basic character of Being in keeping with which mortals exist, and 'building belongs to dwelling and receives its nature from it'.[7] In other words, the familiar trappings of human existence, houses, tools, etc. are the unselfconscious expression of human need, in function, and collectively arrived at. In the fullest sense these are extensions of man's being, in relation to which he defines the contours of self. Buildings — for example a bridge — are human constructs, but have autonomous reality, exist in themselves, not just as objects of perception. A bridge is not simply *placed* in a location, it *makes* or marks out a location, changes a landscape by 'gathering' together elements in a relationship that could not otherwise exist. Buildings are products of human activity that map out human topography, give a definition of the relevant space surrounding a human being. Space is not to be understood in terms of a void 'out there', it is comprehensible only in terms of a clearing within boundaries, in relation to what is given in terms of things and locations: 'When we speak of man and space it sounds as though man stood on one side, space on the other. Yet space is not something that faces man. It is neither an external object nor an inner experience.'[8] Space is no more than the medium of man's 'stay' in the world: 'The relationship between man and space is none other than dwelling, strictly thought and spoken.'[9] Things and locations are the expression and measure of the boundaries of man's being on earth, they at once contain and express him.

What has this to do with language? First, language is equally a human construct, but is the creation of no single individual. Language speaks *through* us because it is communal and pre-existent; it is therefore a perversion of the proper order of things to regard the individual as the master of language — language is the master of man, he is its vehicle. Secondly, for Heidegger there is a strict correlation between dwelling/building/being/speech. The relationship between man and space — his dwelling — *demands* to be spoken, hence Heidegger can say, in a famous aphorism: 'Language is the house of being' (*Über den Humanismus* (1949)). The interaction between humanity and the world is essentially linguistic: 'Only when there is language is there a world'.[10] Language is essentially speech, conversation: 'The being of man is founded in language, but this only becomes actual in conversation.'[11] Conversation 'gathers' people into communal existence, as a bridge or building may be said to 'gather' landscape. Communal existence is at the same time our experience of dwelling among a world of things. Paradoxically, it is in poetry that we find the most intense expression of speech. Common speech is 'dead' poetry that can be revivified in verse. Poetry is not to be thought of as a 'higher' form of diction, but as a 'presencing' of language, in the sense of showing, disclosure, revelation.[12] In his essay on the poetry of Georg Trakl, 'Language in the Poem', he says: 'The dialogue of thinking with poetry aims to call forth the *nature* of language, so that mortals may learn again to live within language.'[13] In poetry we encounter not the language of signs, but the *being* of language — language as an immediate presence that surrounds and incorporates us as our clothes or dwelling might: 'Poetry builds up the very nature of dwelling. Poetry and dwelling not only do not exclude each other; on the contrary, poetry and dwelling belong together, each calling for the other.'[14] Poetry is also a measuring of what it means to be human, and the first 'measure' of existence is the awareness that man is mortal.[15] In projecting a view of the language of speech and poetry as not primarily rational, Heidegger is reacting against those alienating habits of usage that treat language as a mere conceptual tool, a logical, categorising instrument which divorces linguistic signification from being, lived experience. Bruns sees Heidegger's own style as a 'calculated affront to such speech, and even more is it an affront to the tradition of philosophical utterance... For Heidegger is a philosopher who makes us aware of the presence of language. His speech is never transparent: it never proceeds according to the decorum of clarity that distinguishes logical discourse ... Like the poet ... Heidegger is concerned to transform language in a way that releases it from or opposes it to conventional usage'.[16]

To return to Vallejo: throughout his poetry, and especially in *Poemas humanos*, his posthumously published collection of verse, there is an acutely exacerbated consciousness of the body and bodily functions; a sense of the structure, the weight, mass and behaviour of the human body in relation to its daily environment, and in particular to the banality of its surroundings. As much as is the case in the poetry of Quevedo, the seventeenth-century poet with whom he had considerable affinity, house and body become interchangeable terms to express earthly existence.

Thus in 'Canciones del hogar' in his first published collection of poems, *Heraldos negros* (1919), recollections of childhood and family relationships are inseparable from the spatial context of the house that was their setting, with its pictures of saints on the walls, its ancient armchair, the corridors and rooms where the child played, the stone bench marking the boundary between indoors and outside. The loving warmth of his mother's body, and the expression of that love in the giving of sustenance are evoked by transforming that body into an oven: 'Tahona estuosa de aquellos mis bizcochos' (*Trilce*, XXIII). And in *Trilce* LXV his dead mother, immortalised by memory, takes on the monumental grandeur of a cathedral: 'Me esperará tu arco de sombra / las tonsuradas columnas de tus ansias / que se acaban la vida... Así, muerta immortal. / Entre la columnata de tus huesos / que no puede caer ni a lloros:' Life itself is defined by the spatial context in which it takes place, as in 'Santoral' (*Heraldos negros*): 'Llegué hasta la pared / de enfrente de la vida. // Y me parece que he tenido siempre / a la mano esta pared.' Environment and being are inseparable: 'Mi casa, por desgracia, es una casa, / un suelo por ventura, donde vive / con su inscripción mi cucharita amada, / mi querido esqueleto ya sin letras, / la navaja, un cigarro

permanente'.[17] It is significant that these lines with their ironic evocation of the familiar human dwelling-place as a fragile, if comforting refuge from the threat of the void should be the prelude to consideration of the nature of life, mortality and human suffering, expressed with the colloquial directness of speech. To Vallejo, a house is essentially a dwelling, inextricably associated with being, bearing the marks of human habitation and presence as intimately as shoes or the tomb wear the imprint of the human body: 'Una casa viene al mundo, no cuando la acaban de edificar, sino cuando empiezan a habitarla. Una casa vive únicamente de hombres, como una tumba. De aquí esa irresistible semejanza que hay entre una casa y une tumba'.[18] Here, as characteristically in Vallejo, man's dwelling on earth is measured with the yardstick of mortality. At times, too, the impossibility of escaping the constricting and delimiting confines of the given is a cause for despair: 'En el campo y en la ciudad, se está demasiado asistido de rutas, flechas y señales, para poder perderse. Uno está allí indefectiblemente limitado, al norte, al sur, al este, al oeste. Uno está allí irremediablemente situado... a mí me ocurre en la ciudad amanecer siempre rodeado de todo, del peine, de la pastilla de jabón, de todo. Amanezco en el mundo y con el mundo y conmigo mismo... Esto es desesperante'.[19]

To turn now to language: in her studies of Vallejo's use of language,[20] Jean Franco gives an extensive analysis of the poet's work, which she sees as typically modern in exemplifying a breakdown of faith in the power of the Word, showing the inoperability of traditional images and metaphors, the speciousness of 'harmony', in the Modernist sense.[21] Professor Franco sees in Vallejo's poetry in part a rebellion against the alienating power of language and logic, in part an expression of frustration over the impotent poverty of language to adequately express experience. So she says of *Trilce* 'Words and phrases suggest new images as if creation itself obeyed half-voluntary processes and as if the poet's apparent sense of direction were constantly being undermined by the ambiguity of words. Thus language does not so much

denote experiences or objects as show that a limited number
of words and expressions must cover a wide and even
contradictory range of experience'.[22] Of *Poemas humanos* she
writes: 'it is impossible to read the *Poemas humanos* and still
doubt that Vallejo was profoundly concerned with the failure
of both script and speech to replace the Christian Logos'.[23]
Only in such 'social' poems as 'Los mineros' and 'Gleba' in
Poemas humanos, and in the poems written about the Spanish
Civil War in *España, aparta de mí este cáliz* does she see
Vallejo showing confidence in the possibility of once again
restoring expressive power to speech. I would argue rather
that paradoxically it is in struggling with the very frustrations
and inadequacies of language that Vallejo both attempts to
project a more accurate and authentic view of the human
condition, of man's 'being-in-the-world', and offers a critique
of language which shows how the very nature of language
itself reveals that 'being' to us. I will analyse two of Vallejo's
best-known poems from *Poemas humanos* in support of my
argument.

intensidad y altura

Quiero escribir, pero me sale espuma,
quiero decir muchísimo y me atollo;
no hay cifra hablada que no sea suma,
no hay pirámide escrita, sin cogollo.

Quiero escribir, pero me siento puma;
quiero laurearme, pero me encebollo.
No hay toz hablada, que no llegue a bruma,
no hay dios ni hijo de dios, sin desarrollo.

Vámonos, pues, por eso, a comer yerba,
carne de llanto, fruta de gemido,
nuestra alma melancólica en conserva.

VALLEJO AND HEIDEGGER

Vámonos! Vámonos! Estoy herido;
Vámonos a beber lo ya bebido,
vámonos, cuervo, a fecundar tu cuerva.

A common theme of twentieth-century writing is a dialectic in which the compulsion to speak is set against the impossibility of expression. In Samuel Beckett's words: 'The expression that there is nothing to express, nothing with which to express, nothing from which to express, no power to express, no desire to express, together with the obligation to express'.[24] It is ironic that Vallejo's confession of inarticulacy should be couched in the strictly formal terms of the sonnet, with all its connotations of compression, concision and control of expressive means. Further, it is full of overt parallelism: 'Quiero — pero' and 'Quiero — y', four times repeated, are exactly balanced and negated by 'no hay — que' in the third and the seventh lines of the first and second quatrains, and 'no hay — sin' in the fourth and eighth lines. Terms evocative of writing: 'escribir' and 'escrita' alternate with or are balanced by those suggestive of speech: 'decir', 'hablada'. There is a strict rhyme scheme in '-uma' and '-ollo' in the quatrains and '-va' and '-ido' in the tercets, end-stopping every line and effectively putting a halt to forward movement or thought. However, if we look at the first eight lines of the sonnet, it becomes clear that there is no 'mot-thème' in Saussure's terms, from which the other words may be said to spring. The rhyming words certainly demonstrate high phonetic similitude — 'espuma — suma — puma — bruma', and 'atollo — cogollo — encebollo — desarrollo', but it would be difficult, not to say arbitrary, to designate one word of the respective chains a key-word. Each refers backwards and forwards in a circular pattern of resonances. The relentless dominance of the rhyme-scheme is strongly reminiscent of seventeenth-century satirical and burlesque sonnets — especially those of Quevedo — which show great ingenuity in rhyming words ending in unlovely sounds or with coarse associations — 'ajo', 'ujo', 'ote', 'azo', etc. In fact the sonnet is

both a poem about inarticulacy and a controlled ironic burlesque of literary form.

There is further apparent symmetry in the use of reflexive forms of the verb in the first two lines of each quatrain. Yet the apparent syntactic parallelism does not mask an incongruous distortion of syntax in line six. We begin with three true reflexives: 'me sale' (suggestive of action outside the control of the speaker — cf. 'me sale sangre' — 'blood pours out of me'); 'me atollo' — figuratively 'to be in a jam', 'to get stuck', has also very concrete associations, because the verb literally means 'to be blocked or clogged' (as of gutters); 'me siento' is straightforward and requires no comment. However, 'laurearme' in the next line is odd, since it does not exist as a reflexive verb. It is, in fact, an example of the so-called 'ethical dative', common in colloquial speech; the use of a reflexive form when not strictly necessary to give affective, emphatic or personal value to a statement (compare English use of 'up', 'down' with the verb in such constructions as to eat *up*, drink *down*, with, e.g. 'comer*se* una manzana' as distinct from 'comer una manzana'). If this construction is possible with 'laurear', it sounds highly incongruous with 'encebollar', a verb used only transitively meaning 'to cook something with a garnish of onion'. It is typical of Vallejo to exploit the possible confusions and ambiguities of the reflexive form, which in Spanish can be used to express the passive, to make impersonal statements, and is also found colloquially, in the 'ethical dative', as well as the true reflexive. By diverging from the norm, he makes us acutely aware of the unconsciously expected patterns of syntactical usage.

A similar disruption of linguistic norms occurs at the lexical level with the neologism 'toz' in the seventh line. As we read in the 'Advertencia' of *César Vallejo, Obra Poética Completa — Edición con facsímiles* (Lima, 1968), with reference to this word: 'Ante la imposibilidad de saber si quiso escribir *tos* o *voz*, se ha dejado como está el sétimo verso del soneto de la página 347'. S and z are pronounced identically by perhaps a majority of Latin-American speakers, but by removing the

orthographic distinction between them, the neologism conflating 'tos' and 'voz' suggests their intrinsic synonymity, that inarticulate cough and voice are one. Further, 'toz' brings to mind a variety of other terms: *tozo*, small, dwarfish, tubby; *tozudo*, stubborn; *tozar*, to come upon, to be stubborn; *tozuelo*, the back of the head; *tozotada*, a heavy blow on the nape of the neck. This may remind us of the fact that individual words may themselves evoke a succession of images independent of and even irrelevant to their context, as Sartre observes in *L'idiot de la famille*: 'le graphème, par sa configuration physique et *avant tout traitement* éveille des résonances.'[25] So 'le château d'Amboise' may suggest 'framboise', 'boisé', 'boiserie', 'Ambroisie', 'Ambroise' — not a private range of associations, but objective connotations that can be potentially apprehended by any reader, allowing him to range beyond the confines of the text.

Another term with confusing multiple meanings is 'cogollo' which may signify 1) vegetable heart; 2) cream, summit, choice part of something, e.g the 'cream' of society; 3) nucleus or centre of something. The fact that it is not immediately obvious to the reader from the context which is the appropriate sense of the word adds to the disorientating effect of the poem as a whole.

The major and central notion of the sonnet is the discrepancy and discontinuity between man's sentient, physical, animal nature, and his desire to achieve controlled expression through speech or writing — a desire always doomed to frustration. A dialectical tension is set up within the poem between two levels or sets of associations: on the one hand there are images and patterns of order — pyramid, cypher, sum, the controlled form of the sonnet and the verbal symmetries within it. On the other, animal and vegetable imagery, expressions of involuntary and innocent ejaculation — *espuma, llanto, toz, gemido* — together with a network of anarchically proliferating free associations. In this, language becomes a self-generative process, without beginning or end. As Michel Foucault puts it, referring to modern literature as a

whole: 'Car maintenant il n'y a plus cette parole première, absolument initiale par quoi se trouvait fondé et limité le mouvement infini du discours: désormais le langage va croître sans départ, sans terme et sans promesse. C'est le parcours de cet espace vain et fondamental que trace de jour en jour le texte de la littérature'.[26]

I have already suggested that the rigidity of the rhyme-scheme sets in train a causal pattern that is in part responsible for the apparently arbitrary and certainly arresting choice of terms — 'encebollo', cogollo', 'puma', etc. But the notion that association is by homophony or the independent meaning of words outside the line of strictly logical argument is far-reaching in the poem. The implicit analogy/contrast between a stately geometrical construct — a pyramid, empty within, and the clustering leaves of cabbage or lettuce, layer upon layer packed around nothing (suggesting perhaps that there can be no formal construct without vulnerable organic heart), gives rise to a chain reaction of unpredictably metamorphosing vegetable association. So the evocation of the poet's crowning 'laurearme' is appropriate within the context of the poem, but the onion garnish of 'me encebollo' brings aspiration mockingly down to earth, while also transposing to a vegetable the idea of layers clustering tightly on one another. The vegetable theme is continued in 'Vámonos, pues, por eso, a comer yerba' — become like the beasts cropping grass in the knowledge of one's impotence — but this also has biblical overtones of the story of Nebuchadnezzar, who in his madness gave way to eating grass; ' and he was driven from men, and did eat grass as oxen, and his body was wet with the dew of heaven, till his hairs were grown like eagles' feathers, and his nails like birds' claws.' (Daniel, 4, 33). The fleeting evocation of a once-proud king brought to the level of the beasts contrasts sharply with the preceding line's allusion to the son of God as the procession of God, the Verbum, or the Word made flesh. The biblical-vegetable theme continues with the expression of human sorrow and travail — man the fruit brought forth, like

the children of Eve in grief and lamentation. However, at this point the heightened language with its echoes of the Psalms, Ecclesiastes and the Book of Job is undermined and mocked by the anarchically mutating shift from fruit (figurative and metaphorical) to literal fruit in cans — 'en conserva'.

In much the same way, the allusions to animality mutate bizarrely from the suggestion of potent energy and latent menace of the puma, the Amerindian tribal sacred animal, to the subliminal echo of Christ, the bridegroom in the guise of the wounded hart seeking his beloved in St. John of the Cross's *Cántico espiritual* evoked by the urgency of 'Vámonos! Vámonos! Estoy herido;' an association which I suggest is sparked off by the preceding biblical allusions. In his commentary on the lines from the *Cántico espiritual* '...el ciervo vulnerado / por el otero asoma', St. John of the Cross writes: 'Y es de saber que la propiedad del ciervo es subirse a los lugares altos, y cuando está herido vase con gran priesa a buscar refrigerio a las aguas frías...' (Commentary to *Canción* XIII, 9). Here, however, it is not cool water brooks that the wounded lover will drink, but stale water, and the faint subliminal shadow of the 'ciervo' yields place by phonetic shift to 'cuervo', the crow, bird of ill-omen and death. It is possible too to see, in the last line, with its injunction to the crow to make his mate fecund, a sardonic reminder of the Spanish proverb which warns against misplaced, self-destructive and self-defeating generosity: 'Cría cuervos y te sacarán los ojos'.

While it is possible to trace a train of associations in this fashion, we do not have satisfyingly purposive exploration of extended metaphor, whose implications are exhaustively worked out, as in, say, a seventeenth-century 'metaphysical' sonnet, but rather, to pursue the train metaphor, a series of deflections into sidings that lead no further, save in indirect and haphazard fashion. Thus the mocking analogy in lines seven and eight: 'as soul is to body, so fruit is to the can, one contained within the other', appears to be merely a banal and unilluminating comparison, a parallel simply stated, whose appropriateness is not elucidated, as is, for example, Donne's

'spider love, which transubstantiates all, / And can convert manna to gall' ('Twickenham Garden'), a brilliantly illuminating conceit, which triumphantly succeeds in convincing the reader of the aptness of yoking together such opposites as 'spider' and 'love'. Relationships between images are not arbitrary, but function at the level of the fluid interaction of words, whose momentum seems self-generated, and whose associations appear haphazard and non-functional, not elucidated in terms of controlled metaphor, and therefore not predominantly rational.

The opacity of the images in the sonnet has much to do with their being banal, familiar, everyday, anti-poetic, — resistant to symbolisation; 'given' objects with no ready-made intrinsic meaning or point. A clogged drain, lettuce heart, onion garnish, cough, canned fruit, lack the dignity and resonance of assuagingly familiar literary allusion. Such terms pose the problem of the discrete existence of *things*, challenging the attempt to incorporate them by language or understanding. The incongruous mingling of the banality and trivia of existence defeats the aspiration that would attempt to transcend it, and this defeat is conveyed at the level of language, through the autonomy, the unpredictable twists and turns of words. The poem itself in all its use of expressive means is an exemplification of its theme of frustration: the impulse to act, to give definition to expression is negated, dissipated, absorbed in inertia or brute sentient, but irrational being. A series of impulses is generated, only to end in self-defeat, frustrating the reader to whom *feeling* is conveyed clearly enough, while individual elements of the poem remain opaque, resistant to comprehension. The poem's final paradox is that it eloquently succeeds in conveying the experience of inarticulacy, reminding us of Heidegger's view that 'in "poetical" discourse the communication of the existential possibilities of one's state-of-mind can become an aim in itself and this amounts to a disclosing of existence'.[27] Through language, Vallejo has achieved the exact mirroring of a state of mind, full of inconsistencies, waywardness and

contradiction.

considerando en frío, imparcialmente...

Considerando en frío, imparcialmente,
que el hombre es triste, tose y, sin embargo,
se complace en su pecho colorado;
que lo único que hace es componerse
de días;
que es lóbrego mamífero y se peina:

Considerando
que el hombre procede suavemente del trabajo
y repercute jefe, suena subordinado;
que el diagrama del tiempo
es constante diorama en sus medallas
y, a medio abrir, sus ojos estudiaron,
desde lejanos tiempos,
su fórmula famélica de masa...

Comprendiendo sin esfuerzo
que el hombre se queda, a veces, pensando,
como queriendo llorar,
y, sujeto a tenderse como objeto,
se hace buen carpintero, suda, mata
y luego canta, almuerza, se abotona...

Considerando también
que el hombre es en verdad un animal
y, no obstante, al voltear, me da con su tristeza en la
cabeza...

Examinando, en fin,
sus encontradas piezas, su retrete,
su desesperación, al terminar su día atroz, borrándolo...

Comprendiendo
que él sabe que le quiero,
que le odio con afecto y me es, en suma, indiferente...

Considerando sus documentos generales
y mirando con lentes aquel certificado
que prueba que nació muy pequeñito...

le hago una seña,
viene,
y le doy un abrazo, emocionado
¡Qué más da! Emocionado... Emocionado...

This poem enacts a dialectical debate between two attitudes to man, implicit in two different registers of language. The first is impartial, impersonal, conceptual, legal, scientific or pompously pedantic; the language of documents, of detached official modes of classification. Thus we have man defined as a lugubrious mammal — 'lóbrego mamífero' — a pedantic coupling of *esdrújulo* words, stressed on the antepenultimate syllable, uncommon in Spanish and found mostly in Classical or foreign loan-words (cf. also 'fórmula famélica'). Human time is charted by diagram, and man is measured in terms of formula and mass, his activities determined by the Cartesian subject-object relationship. Contrasting with this, we have a truly comprehensive view of man as a being in the pathos of his animal nature — inconsequential, lacking in self-awareness, yet darkened in his existence by the intermittent capacity for thought, as instinctive and uncontrollable as weeping. Vallejo's half-compassionate, half-mocking view of man as an animal condemned to suffer because of his consciousness is frequently expressed in *Poemas humanos*, as in 'El alma que sufrió de ser su cuerpo'[28]: 'Tú sufres, tú padeces y tú vuelves a sufrir horriblemente / desgraciado mono, / jovencito de Darwin... y a tu ombligo interrogas: ¿dónde? ¿cómo?' Man is a prisoner of existence, 'cautivo en tu enorme libertad'.

The poem here analysed ends with a touching abdication of the power of words in favour of the silent eloquence of behaviour and gesture, as the poet embraces his fellow-man, eliminating the distance between them, to stand as equals communicating and showing true comprehension, like animals, through touch. The poem is remarkable for the complex pattern of alliteration, assonance and harmony it contains: *triste — tose*; *complace — componerse — colorado*; *suavemente — suena subordinado*; *diagrama — diorama*; *fórmula famélica*. More important though than sound patterns set up independent of meaning are firstly, association of meaning through homophony; and secondly, a complex use of words with double, often unrelated meanings. Thus:

se complace = takes pleasure in, but also suggests complacency
componerse = (little used) to be made up of, to comprise; also to dress up, adorn oneself
suavemente = softly, gently; also meekly, weakly
fórmula = recipe/scientific formula/model
masa = mass (weight)/mass (number)/dough
voltear = to tumble; also to be tossed, thrown in the air as by a bull
encontradas = opposing or alternating, but also past participle of 'encontrar', to find
piezas = parts, pieces/theatrical plays/rooms
retrete = retreat, inner sanctuary, but primarily now used to signify 'lavatory'
sujeto = a person/to be subject to/ syntactical subject of a sentence.

So 'fórmula famélica de masa', for example, may be read as either 'famished formula of mass-man' or 'hungry recipe for dough', and 'sus encontradas piezas, su retrete' may be either 'his opposing parts, his retreat', or 'his discovered rooms, his lavatory', or a combination of either. Ambiguity of meaning is therefore far-reaching in the poem, encouraging a doubleness of vision in the reader, who must hold two equally significant meanings in focus. It is perhaps appropriate that the poem should speak of a diorama, for this form of scenic representation lighted from above and viewed through an aperture was made up usually of transparent canvases painted on both sides, and by varying the intensity of light on the canvases, it was possible to transform the same scene from dark to light, day to night, or to highlight different elements in the same scene, allowing for a variety of different perspectives of the same representation, in other words.

All the way through the poem, man's being, the poem's subject, is related to his habitation and his unselfconsciousness and revealing behaviour. Man's being is circumscribed by his dress, the tools and adornments of his daily routine of toilet and work. The very parts of his body are interchangeable with the rooms he inhabits; his place of intimate retreat is the lavatory, where he performs the most basic of animal bodily functions.

In his 'Apuntes para un estudio', notes for a study of contemporary literature that was never completed, under a series of headings such as Romanticism, Realism, Symbolism, etc., Vallejo classifies himself and the Chilean poet Pablo Neruda under the heading of 'Verdadismo'. We may remember in this context Neruda's manifesto in the first issue of *Caballo verde para la poesía* in 1935, where he announces his intention to write 'impure poetry' — 'une poesía sin pureza' — 'like a suit of clothes, like a human body, with food stains and shameful gestures, with wrinkles, observations, dreams, vigils, prophecies'. Neruda's stated aim was to record, as far as possible unselectively, all the traces and minutiae of human existence, convey its confused diversity in an intellectually 'impure', sensual, material form of verse that should have the physical consistency of wood, iron, flower, water, flesh. To Neruda, the poetic act is an act of constant mingling with the physical world, and he comes to be seen by his contemporaries as the prophet of unashamed acceptance of the body in all its animality, its ordinariness and even shabbiness. We have already seen how Vallejo's poetry conveys an equally intense awareness of the human body, but his 'verdadismo' goes further in compassionately recording the vulnerable inconsequentiality, the inconsistency of human behaviour. So, he can place conscious human activity, whether in work or in acts of violence ('se hace buen carpintero, suda, mata'), on the same plane as, and in the context of, the habitual daily routine of eating, dressing, singing a song ('y luego canta, almuerza, se abotona'), or can project a view of man as an absurd, clownish tumbling animal, yet one whose very tumbling is oppressively sad. Man's life is no more than the accumulation of days; existence, whose mere tool or object he is, and which he can neither control nor comprehend, fills him intermittently with despair and grief. In general terms, the poem can be seen as a progressive shedding of the position of detached, official observer, considering and examining the human condition, checking on latrines and documents like a government inspector to an *understanding* that is effortless — 'sin esfuerzo' — because it is emotional identification with the erratic vagaries of human feeling, expressed through direct physical contact that speaks for itself without need of words.

Vallejo's 'verdadismo', the capacity to capture 'un timbre humano, un latido vital y sincero, al cual debe propender el artista', as he wrote in an article in *Variedades*, 7th May (1937), is no less evident in his use of language in the poem, for here language may truly be said to speak *through* man, in Heideggerian terms, to be possessed of independent energy. The poem gives the impression that the forward unfolding of thought is generated by patterns of association sparked off by chance by the words themselves. So 'repercute' leads to 'suena', paralleling the symmetrical association between 'jefe' and 'subordinado'. 'Diagrama' by phonetic similitude suggests 'diorama'. The ambiguity of meaning of 'fórmula' anticipates and is linked with that of 'masa', and the punning word-play of 'encontradas *piezas*' provides the momentum that generates 'retrete'. That 'sujeto' should naturally bring to mind 'objeto' calls into play a whole series of relationships in which the syntactical categories are a mirror in philosophical terms of the Aristotelian/Cartesian distinction between perceiving self and perceived object, and in socio-political terms encapsulates the Marxist view of the capitalist relationship of employee to boss, already touched on in the poem. If, as Vallejo wrote in an article in *Mundial*, 11th March (1927) 'Cada cosa contiene en potencia a todas las energías y direcciones del universo. No sólo el hombre es un microcosmos, cada fenómeno de la naturaleza es también un microcosmos en marcha', then each word which is used to convey such a reality should also contain a protean associative energy. By forcing us to acknowledge the anarchic self-generative associative drive of words, Vallejo directs us to the nature and being of language as an immediate presence, like the world of 'given' material objects we find ourselves in. To use Heidegger's term, Vallejo 'presences' language in the sense that he reveals its true nature and function.

In this poem as elsewhere in his verse, Vallejo shows a grasp of the fluid dynamic potential of language and thought. Thus, though man and the poet himself can only avail themselves of an 'alfabeto gélido'[29] to answer the questions posed by 'el bimano, el muy bruto, el muy filósofo... saber por qué tiene la vida este perrazo, / por qué lloro, por qué, / cejón inhabil, veleidoso, hube nacido / gritando...'[30] we are left with the paradox that pessimistic awareness of the limitations of language can have a corrective and liberating effect, for as he wrote in 'Autopsia del superrealismo', pessimism and despair are mere stages in a quest, not its goal: 'El pesimismo y la desesperación deben ser siempre etapas y no metas. Para que ellos agiten y fecunden el espíritu, deben desenvolverse hasta transformarse en afirmaciones constructivas'.[31]

Having recognised the extent of language's power to alienate and to schematise, he intensifies sensitivity to the way the writer can succeed in overcoming this alienation, finding a register of poetic discourse that will more authentically convey the nature of the human condition, true to his own injunction in his 1936/37 notebook: 'Cuidado con la substancia humana de la poesía'.[32] The independent associative logic of words through which is heard the voice of the community, the 'gathering' power of language, in Heidegger's phrase, reflects the form of the human mind, either in expressing dialectical opposition between contraries or in sequential, self-generative, unpredictable evolution of terms. Like the material objects that map out the terrain of human dwelling — shoes, clothes, articles of toilet, eating implements; like human habitations, whether house or tomb; like the awareness of death against which life is measured, language gives evidence of human weakness, poverty and imperfection, but at the same time testifies to its energy and indomitable creative persistence. Vallejo's language, full of inconsistencies, paradox and contradiction faithfully reflects the confused inconsequentiality of human animal behaviour, as it also succeeds in conveying the inflections of speech. As Jean Franco says, '[the] counterpoint between the solitude of print and the immediacy of the spoken word provides the *Poemas humanos* with much of their energy... his "Sermon upon death" and many others of the *Poemas humanos* represent astonishing efforts to make print translate the presence of the human voice'.[33] In this, Vallejo's practice would appear to bear out Heidegger's paradox that it is in poetry that we find the most intense expression of speech. Further, if Heidegger could say, as we have already seen, that 'the dialogue of thinking with poetry aims to call forth the *nature* of language, so that mortals may learn again to live within language',[34] it is paradoxically by demonstrating the autonomy of language that Vallejo achieves a reconciliation between man and the word — not the Christian Logos, the divinely uttered Word made flesh — but the word as it emerges from its essentially human context, for as he says, 'El intelectual revolucionario desplaza la fórmula mesiánica, diciendo "mi reino es de este mundo"'.[35] By using language to testify to the mundane truth of human behaviour and thought processes which are ignored by systems of thought — whether

VALLEJO AND HEIDEGGER

philosophical, psychological, scientific or aesthetic, as he suggests in 'Un hombre pasa con un pan al hombro' in *Poemas humanos* — Vallejo restores the word to its human function, true to the spirit of his own dictum: 'Hacedores de imágenes, devolved las palabras a los hombres'.[36] The punning 'rebélase' of *Trilce* has proved to be prophetic, for in rebelling, words have truly revealed themselves as they are.

NOTES

1. Michel Foucault, *Les mots et les choses* (Paris, 1966) p.317.

2. Gerard Manley Hopkins, *The Papers and Journals of Gerard Manley Hopkins*, ed. Humphrey House and Graham Storey (London, 1959) p.269.

3. *El arte de la revolución, Obras completas*, vol. II (Lima, Perú, 1973) p.64.

4. Jean Franco, *César Vallejo. The Dialectics of Poetry and Silence* (Cambridge University Press, 1976) p.80.

5. See, for example, such poems as 'La paz, la abispa, el taco, las vertientes' or 'Transido, salomónico, decente' from *Poemas humanos*, with their strangely incantatory catalogue of words unrelated save in that they fall under the heading of different parts of speech: nouns, adjectives, verbs, adverbs.

6. 'Building Dwelling Thinking' in *Poetry, Language, Thought*, trans. Albert Hofstadter, (New York,1975), p.147.

7. Op. cit., p.151.

8. Op. cit., p. 156.

9. Op. cit., p.157.

10. 'Hölderlin and the Essence of Poetry', in *Existence and Being*, trans. Douglas Scott (Chicago, 1949) p.276.

11. Op. cit., p.277.

12. 'Language' in *Poetry, Language, Thought*, ed. cit., p.208.

13. Quoted by Gerard L. Bruns, *Modern Poetry and the Idea of Language*, (New Haven/London, 1974) p.205.

14. '...Poetically Man Dwells...' in *Poetry, Language, Thought*, ed. cit., p.227.

15. Op. cit., p.221.

16. Bruns, op. cit., p.203.

17. 'Ello es que el lugar donde me pongo', *Poemas humanos*, in *Obra Poetica Completa, Obras completas*, vol. III (Lima, Perú, 1974) p.316. (This edition referred to hereafter as *OPC*.

18. *OPC*, p.200.

19. *Contra el secreto profesional, Obras completas*, vol. I (Lima, Perú, 1973) p.37.

20. *Poetry and Silence. César Vallejo's 'Sermon upon Death'* (London, 1973) and *César Vallejo. The Dialectics of Poetry and Silence* (Cambridge University Press, 1976).

21. *César Vallejo. The Dialectics of Poetry and Silence*, p.83.

22. Op. cit., p.131.

23. Op. cit., p.222.

24. 'Dialogue between Samuel Beckett and Georges Duthuit' in *Transition*, no.5 (1949), p.98.

25. *L'idiot de la famille*, I (Paris, 1971) p.25.

26. Foucault, op. cit., p.59.

27. *Being and Time*, trans. John Macquarrie and Edward Robinson (Oxford, 1967) p.205.

28. *OPC*, pp.306-7.

29. 'Traspié entre dos estrellas', *Poemas humanos, OPC*, pp.296-7.

30. 'Quiere y no quiere su color mi pecho', *Poemas humanos, OPC*, p.288.

31. *El arte de la revolución*, p.75.

32. Op. cit., p.97.

33. *César Vallejo. The Dialectics of Poetry and Silence*, p.191.

34. Already cit., note 13.

35. *El arte de la revolución*, p.14.

36. *Favorables — Paris — Poema*, 2 Oct. (1926), p.14.

Definition as the Enemy of Self-Definition: A Commentary on the Role of Language in Unamuno's *Niebla*

Alison Sinclair

In discussing Unamuno's attitude to the phenomenon of language, and to the question of how useful or otherwise words may be to us, I intend to leave on one side an issue which to many will seem central, that is, Unamuno's own apparent display of bad faith in using a medium he does not trust in order to say something in which he believes. In the context of the novel *Niebla* there is undoubtedly a strong querying of the business of language and literature, and the whole novel is designed to imply their relative inadequacy for the tasks they are intended to perform. Other critics have touched on this.[1] I propose instead to look at the simpler and in some ways more central and communicable issue of what language actually means to Unamuno's fictional characters in their attempts to define themselves.

One of the most striking consistencies in Unamuno's writings is his emphasis on the need for inconsistency, for flexibility of response, for individuality and quirkiness as opposed to lucidly organised and sterile system. So if it is the case that language represents a system, which by being a system is at odds with the shifting and elusive nature of life itself, then it is hardly surprising that he should at times have had such a declared lack of faith in the validity of individual words *per se*, or in groups of them forming a system. That language for Unamuno as a man and a writer was a problem is evidenced by the prominence that it has as an area of discussion in the philosophical essays, and in two early novels, *Amor y pedagogía* (1902) and *Niebla* (1914).

While Unamuno has always provoked dissent and argument among those who read his works, and who come to establish an anguished love-hate relationship with the man and his text, there is at least one area that seems to have remained free from dispute, and that is the estimation of *Niebla* as the most complex and fascinating work in his literary output.

Apparently his most formless novel,[2] *Niebla* is not as it is through mere youthful ingenuousness or lack of novelistic expertise. It comes nearly two decades after the massive novelistic apprenticeship of *Paz en la guerra* (1897), which despite its outward concern with the externals of life, and in particular, war, was the clear forerunner of Unamuno's existential preoccupations. It also came after *Amor y pedagogía*, a novel often berated for its over-schematic and parody-ridden view of life, but which has important similarities with *Niebla*. On a conceptual level, it provided another type of literary apprenticeship.[3] Unamuno, in his prologue to the third edition of *Niebla*, ponders on why it should be that of all his works, this novel was the most widely translated. He concludes that it is the work which speaks most directly to the individual man. As a result it becomes universal.[4] That this is the case may be accounted for by two factors: firstly, of all Unamuno's novels it is the least static and

openly schematic, and secondly, one of the main problems of
the central character, Augusto Pérez, is the impossibility of
expressing for himself or others the various states of emotion
in which he finds himself, and consequently the apparent
impossibility of coming to terms with the nature of his
experiences. What grips us about the insignificant figure of
Augusto Pérez, whether we see him as man-in-the-street or
fin-de-siècle dandy,[5] is that since we observe him in the
process of trying to become himself, and to understand what
that process entails, we become involved with him in a way
that is denied to us by the cut-and-dried character shells that
dominate the fiction of Unamuno's middle period.

Pérez, before the action of *Niebla* opens, was no more than
a child cossetted by his mother, deprived of the chance of
developing his own personality.[6] The novel is therefore able to
show us his development from a starting point much earlier
than his chronological age would make appropriate. This
inevitably carries with it all the intense questioning of
childhood and adolescence. By contrast, the characters of the
novels that follow after *Niebla* are 'en general tensas,
concentradas en la individualidad de sus personajes,
exponentes ya no del desarrollo de la personalidad, sino de la
afirmación de ésta, una vez formada'.[7] Questions are usually
more interesting than answers, and in the case of Unamuno's
fiction, the questioning in *Niebla* comes closer to the nature of
the human condition than does the more vociferous
questioning that comes in the middle-period novels. Although
this vociferous questioning that we find, for example, in *La tía
Tula* and *Abel Sánchez* is indicative of human frailty and
uncertainty, the manner of posing the questions comes close to
constituting an affirmation, albeit the affirmation of
Unamuno's colossal doubt. The questions in *Niebla* are ones
which involve the reader. They receive no answer in the text,
or at least, none that will satisfy Augusto Pérez. Moreover, by
questioning not only life, but also the novel form which has
been chosen to portray it, they anticipate the deep-seated
querying of the validity of our perceptions that is

characteristic of the *San Manuel bueno, mártir* collection and *Cómo se hace una novela*.[8] Before looking at how uncertain Unamuno shows himself to be about the ultimate value of language, it may be best to give an initial focus to that uncertainty by referring to those parts of his work where the role of language is of prime importance, a necessary tool for the exploration and understanding of our environment. Within his poetry, for instance, one can find examples of a simple expression of faith in the power of words, as in 'La palabra', which makes no reservations about the New Testament (and neo-Platonic) faith in the power of the Word:

Juan I.1, Mat. VI.9.

Llave del ser, fue en un principio el verbo
por el que se hizo todo cuanto muda
y el verbo es la cadena con que anuda
Dios los dispersos granos de su acervo.

Por él el hombre deja de ser siervo,
se vale de él en la batalla ruda
y en él la apaga cuando su alma suda
come en la fuente tras de acoso el ciervo.

Sea de Dios santificado el nombre
que es Dios también, pues fue con la palabra
como creara el mundo en un principio.

Con la palabra, como Dios, el hombre
su realidad de ideas forja y labra:
nunca la profanéis a huero ripio.[9]

Or again, if we look at *Del sentimiento trágico de la vida* (1913), we find a philosophical approach which claims equal importance in man's life for the 'hombre de carne y hueso' on the one hand, and reason on the other. Here language surfaces

190

as the mainstay, and the tool of reason. It is what makes reason capable of functioning:

> La rázon, lo que llamamos tal, el conocimiento reflejo y reflexivo, el que distingue al hombre, es un producto social. Debe su origen acaso al lenguaje. Pensamos articulada, o sea reflexivamente, gracias al lenguaje articulado, y este lenguaje brotó de la necesidad de trasmitir nuestro pensamiento a nuestros prójimos. Pensar es hablar consigo mismo, y hablamos cada uno consigo mismo gracias a haber tenido que hablar los unos con los otros, y en la vida ordinaria acontece con frecuencia que llega uno a encontrar una idea que buscaba, llega a darle forma, es decir, a obtenerla, sacándola de la nebulosa de percepciones oscuras a que representa, gracias a los esfuerzos que hace para presentarla a los demás.[10]

Even within the *Sentimiento trágico* itself, however, although language, as shown in the quotation above, can be deemed to represent truth and clarity, it has also very negative aspects. The intellect, though necessary to man's life, is linked for Unamuno to all that is death-bringing, in an existential sense. Language, as the product of the intellect, is consequently also associated with the deathly sides of our activities.[11]

In addition to this type of precise statement that Unamuno makes about the role of language in our lives, we are also given ample evidence of some level of faith in it as a tool for discussion by the frequency with which he resorts to etymological analysis. This natural tendency in one who was Professor of Greek at Salamanca is not motivated simply by a desire for academic exactitude. Derivations interest Unamuno, but in his etymological explorations and discussions he displays a desire not only to formulate a concept of what a word means with greater accuracy, but what matters more to him, a desire to reveal that word's inner vitality. He is equally given to sheer etymological play, rather than etymological exploration. Within this play he conducts his examination of certain words on the basis of preconceived notions about the value of struggle and paradox in our experience, which includes the experience we have of language. The result is that we are given reason to doubt that etymology may be a route to 'truth' in any conventional sense. The conclusions he reaches by his etymological methods are provoking, but ultimately suspect.[12]

A rather different sign that Unamuno has some trust in language as a medium is the degree to which he is prepared to let his characters speak for themselves. In some of his novels there is a noticeably high proportion of monologue and dialogue, at times outweighing the more familiar third-person narrative. This balance within the text seems to suggest that he believes the utterances of his characters to be self-sufficient and self-explanatory, although it does not of course argue for coherence and rationality within the utterances. On the contrary, we find that he displays in both dialogue and monologue an aptitude for coming to terms with man's inability to cope linguistically with his existence. The proportion of the text that is monologue or dialogue varies with the works, with peaks at the *Tres novelas ejemplares*[13] and the plays, in which action and background are reduced to nothing, leaving only the character's words. Even in the dialogue itself there is a frequent lack of communication between the participants, so that language is often a means of apparent rather than real contact, Unamuno's characters having a tendency to remain enclosed in individual anguish. The result is a disconcerting dual text.[14] As we shall see, one of Augusto Pérez's main problems is his desire to break out of this isolation, and to use language as the means of penetrating the world of others.

The insufficiency of language as a tool for describing the most vital processes of life is but one sign of what for Unamuno is the essential duality of man's existence. The very medium of communication that sets man above the animals hinders him from enjoying life with all its natural anima vigour. *Del sentimiento trágico* is the work in which Unamuno gives the first lengthy and direct consideration to the conflict provoked in man by the duality of his existence, but this central issue had already been treated, with humour, parody and exaggeration, in *Amor y pedagogía* of 1902. Despite its schematic nature, its all too obvious trick-playing, and its characters who have no more human reality than the paper figures described in the concluding 'Apuntes para un tratado de cocotología',[15] this novel contains the seeds of all the preoccupations of the later novels.

Avito Carrascal, a man infatuated with dreams of an ideal rational form of humanity, decides to create the perfect human being. The method he proposes is to choose the perfect mate, have a child by her, and then educate the child in a manner wholly and exclusively scientific. Human frailty wins from the beginning. Avito, addressing himself to a suitably robust and wide-hipped girl, 'falls' (the term is one that he himself repeatedly uses) for her friend, the suggestively named Marina.[16] The unfortunate offspring, Apolodoro, is then exposed to the organising and controlling manias of the father[17] and to the dumb yet powerful need of the mother to give and receive emotional nourishment. Unable to form himself into a personality that can survive, he commits suicide, after a last bid for life in leaving Petra (yet another significantly-named character) pregnant with his child. Tragedy, if it can be thought possible within this lunatic travesty of human life, is borne equally by the damaged Apolodoro, by his father, who continues in his blindness and emotional death-state (until he reappears in *Niebla*), and by his mother, whose passive and flexible nature is both her salvation and her undoing, and cannot compensate for the bereavement represented by either the death of her children or her husband's rational lunacy and human abdication.

Although *Amor y pedagogía* is ostensibly about life, since the main character desires above all to control and shape life, the book is inevitably much more concerned with death. Even the vision of a perfect world, governed by logic and language, as outlined by Avito's mentor, don Fulgencio Entrambosmares, is one which has a death-chill of clarity:

Cuando se hayan reducido por completo las cosas a ideas desaparecerán las cosas quedando las ideas tan sólo, y reducidas estas últimas a nombres quedarán sólo los nombres y el eterno e infinito silencio pronunciándolos en la infinidad y por toda una eternidad.   (*A y P*, p.361)

This is the abstract sketching out of what don Fulgencio later elaborates as the death-process which we inflict on our happiness in a contemporary reworking of 'erostratismo'. Erostratus had burnt the temple at Ephesus to save his name from perishing, and as don Fulgencio adds: 'así quemamos nuestra dicha para legar nuestro nombre, un vano sonido, a la posteridad' (*A y P*, p.383). This sacrifice, to our 'name', the piece of language we take to represent ourselves, is a hollow one, and is as absurd as is the notion of regarding as a man someone like Avito who shows himself not only unwilling but also unable to absorb the experience of his daughter's death (*A y P*, pp.391-2).[18]

Language, in *Amor y pedagogía*, is the province of Avito. There is no doubt that it is both masculine and mistaken. If Marina ever uses language it is because she is obliged to do so by society, but the emphasis given to her utterances is on their dream-quality: she lives in a land of moans and mutters, of unexpressed and insatiable need, a need that is as much a need of recognition and response as it is a need for satisfaction. When she does use language, she has to endow it with her own perceptions: hence her insistence on calling her son not Apolodoro (the name chosen by Avito) but Luis (his name received at baptism, an act naturally disapproved of by Avito) (*A y P*, p.343).

For Avito, language is a tool he uses, something that he considers to be the proof that all can be subjected to the order he wishes to impose. We might think that this view is shared by Unamuno, given that the latter argued for a close relationship between language, thought and society.[19] But Unamuno is rarely found to have a single or consistent view on any subject, with the possible exception of his belief in the value of inconsistency. He realises therefore that language may be a necessary tool for our relationship with society, but that it is not a sufficient instrument for the full experiencing of life, just as thought, which is the root of language, is also insufficient for that task. This is a point appreciated by Unamuno,[20] but not by his character Avito, and much of *Amor y pedagogía* is designed to demonstrate both the necessity and the insufficiency of language for the attainment of a full experience of life.

Unamuno suggests the limitations of language by exaggerating Avito's blind belief in it. Thus we have Avito's agonising over the choice of a name for his son, since he desires a name that will be symbolic and suggestive, but which will not be limiting by its associations. He then favours, for economy, a name that will give the child the same initials as himself, so that the family trunk and cutlery will not have to be re-lettered (*A y P*, p.331). We have his reverence for Apolodoro's first babyish mutterings, and his delight at don Fulgencio's discovery that 'gogo' in Basque means 'deseo, ganas, humor, ánimo', so that it may be inferred that Apolodoro, in his infant burbling, is stating a desire, at least in Basque (*A y P*, p.343). We have his reverence for the Latin names of the animals exhibited in the Natural History Museum (for him, the Latin gives an impression of exactitude, and therefore of certainty), contrasted with the real curiosity of his small son about what the animals were like when alive (*A y P*, p.352).

Although Unamuno in the 'Apuntes para un tratado de cocotología' which come at the end of *Amor y pedagogía* appears to follow in his protagonist's faith in language, in that in the *tratado* he equates knowing with naming,[21] there is in the course of the novel itself implied reservation about the adequacy of language as a tool for life. The reservation is expressed in the multiple tragic outcome of the novel, and is outlined by the man who is Avito's mentor, but who shows more essential wisdom within his human frailty, and because of his human frailty, than does his pupil. When Apolodoro's novelette, inspired by a combination of Clarita, his beloved, and Menaguti, a poet and alternative mentor, has just met with a cool critical reception, don Fulgencio, with a cavalier disregard for the niceties of art, advises him not to concern himself with beautiful expression, since feelings and thoughts 'pierden su elevacíon y su hondura por estar bien dichos, eso que llamamos bien dichos' (*A y P*, p.379). This advice shows a frame of mind similar to that shown by Unamuno in his general rejection of musicality and linguistic embellishment[22] in favour of getting to an inner core of feeling and gut-reaction. In this novel, even when Unamuno is using language to describe thought (for which one might suppose it to be adequate and fitting) he uses it in a deprecating manner and, since the word 'idea' pertains to Avito, he distorts and degrades that word, referring to 'ese enjambre de ideas, ideotas, ideítas, idezuelas, seudo-ideas e ideoides' (*A y P*, p.363). In addition, and on a larger scale, there is ample evidence of the rejection of finality of statement as valuable which is conveyed by the structure itself of many of Unamuno's fictional works, in which he aims at non-definition, non-certainty, with multiple and contradictory prologues and epilogues included in an attempt to avoid a single interpretation. Thus, for example, he considers having two endings for *Amor y pedagogía* (*A y P*, pp.399-400), and effectively achieves a double ending to *Niebla* since the question of whether Augusto Pérez committed suicide or not is resolutely left in doubt.

Although language and logic receive a bad press in *Amor y pedagogía*, it would be mistaken to infer that their opposites are shown to be of clear worth. Marina is loving and emotional, but she is also portrayed as bovine and stupid. This impression is softened, but not cancelled out by the fact that this is, in general, how Avito sees her, and the fact that his guilt at having 'fallen' for her may lead him to exaggerate her stupidity so that the stupidity he displayed in marrying her should seem the less. Avito has a similarly low opinion of his daughter, considering her to be of less importance than his son. Only her physical well-being needs to be assured so that she, like her mother, may be the physical vessel for a race of children educated according to rational principles. She is therefore left to the sole care of her mother, and we the readers note that she learns to walk and talk earlier than did her brother. While this might seem to be an argument for the power of Marina's methods and approach, it is common for girls to develop earlier than boys in these respects, and the value of this apparently successful early growth is counterbalanced in the novel by the fact that the daughter dies before reaching full maturity (*A y P*, ch.XV). This is a proof to Avito that death is more powerful than science, and conceivably is also an indication to the reader that she, like Apolodoro, needed the nurturing of both parents in order to survive.

If there is a mid-way of potential common sense, it is in the figure of don Fulgencio, despite the fact that in many respects he is as much a caricature as are the other characters. It is however important that it is as a philosopher that he is parodied, with his *Ars magna combinatoria* which produces philosophical aphorisms by mechanical variations on possible co-ordinations. Despite this caricature, don Fulgencio is the person who is able to be flexible and understanding in his advice to Apolodoro. He is also aware of the tremendous danger to the personality that would result from being able to be classified: 'Que no te clasifiquen; haz como el zorro que con el jopo borra sus huellas; despístales. Sé ilógico a sus ojos hasta que renunciando a clasificarte se digan: es él, Apolodoro Carrascal, especie única. Sé tú mismo, único e insustituible' (*A y P*, p.361). The contrary and perfect state that is at war with individuality is outlined, as I have mentioned above, in the 'Apuntes para un tratado de cocotología', but here receives a much more positive and human treatment. This, however, is no more than one would expect from a man who, while he exchanges trite and condescending banalities with Avito about the general inferiority of woman, who is classified by them as 'un hombre abortado ... el anti-sobre-hombre' (*A y P*, pp.356-7), is nonetheless under the thumb of his wife, Edelmira, and very pleased to be there. Their relationship is one of inter-dependence, humour and mutual recognition of shortcomings, whether his faulty memory (*A y P*, p.356) or her false hair (*A y P*, p.363). It is a relationship in which she protects him, with her reassurance of 'No, hombre, no, nadie lo sabrá, no tengas cuidado' (*A y P*, p.358), and in which he allows himself to be protected, or even occasionally exposed, as when Apolodoro, who has come to receive words of wisdom from his master, sees him engaged in a purely affectionate and predominantly physical exchange with his wife, a woman now no longer obviously young or beautiful enough to incite his desire (*A y P*, p.363).

As Professor Ribbans has already outlined, there are strong thematic and structural relations between *Amor y pedagogía* and *Niebla*. The latter gives nuance and mature questioning to the bald paradoxes of the former, in allowing far more uncertainty to dominate character, plot and attitude of author. The very act of writing *Niebla* is related to what Unamuno had classified as a heroic act in 'Y va de cuento', a short story in the collection *El espejo de la muerte* (1913):

Esto de ponerse a escribir, no precisamente porque se haya encontrado asunto, sino para encontrarlo, es una de las necesidades más terribles a que se ven expuestos los escritores fabricantes de héroes, y héroes, por tanto, ellos mismos.[23]

Niebla itself, as a *nivola*, is the attempt to write within the novel form without being bound by pre-conceived ideas about what constitutes that novel form. As Victor Goti defines it, it is the least containing form possible: 'en esta novela pienso meter todo lo que se me ocurra, sea como fuere' with the protection that it will not even be possible to identify it or classify it as the traditional novel form: 'mi novela no va a ser novela, sino ..., ¿cómo dije?, *navilo* ..., no, no, *nivola*, eso, *¡nivola!* Así nadie tendrá derecho a decir que deroga las leyes de su género ... Invento el género, e inventar un género no es más que darle un nombre nuevo, y le doy las leyes que me place. ¡Y mucho diálogo!'

Niebla is about the attempt of Augusto Pérez to be a person, or a character, and a man. Although many critics have emphasised the generalised nature of Augusto's search, it is Professor Parker who, in remarking on how the central theme of the novel is 'the sadness of the human condition which makes the brotherhood of men impossible on earth, since truth and innocence cannot co-exist in love with sexual passion',[24] has pointed the way to what is the most crucial problem for Augusto himself: to be a man, who can interact as a man with others, that is, a man who is going to have to interact with women, differentiate himself from them and be productive with them in emotional and material or physical terms. One of the things that we need to consider, therefore, is how the already complex core of male-female relationships is made more complex by Augusto's expectations of the male-female roles, and by the fact that language, which is the tool he wants to use to carry out his explorations, while appearing to epitomise rationality (and therefore, wrongly thinks Augusto, truth) in fact impedes him at every turn.

From the beginning, Augusto is aware of his formlessness, his lack of direction, his lack of existential *proyecto*. There seems little doubt that his question in the opening pages, as he stands at the door of his house, 'Y ahora, ¿hacia dónde voy? ¿tiro a la derecha, o a la izquierda?' (*Niebla*, *O.C.*, vol. II, p.557) is meant to express desire for an orientation that is more than geographical. His question also, in the context of the whole of the novel with its intensity of questions and questioning, is more than just the musing of a parodied *fin-de-siècle* young man. It is that as well, and Augusto's incapacities could indeed be defined as those pertaining to the sickly product of a sickly era. But the fact that his questions continue to intrigue and disturb modern readers shows how far Augusto Pérez represents much more than his outward circumstances and confining social status might suggest. His fear that he may be a 'vago' (a suggestion that he immediately squashes (*N*, p.558)), can therefore either be seen as the trivial worry of a silly young man, or, if taken in the general context of his questioning as an existential fear, can be seen as an urgent threat to his sense of himself. His initial confused monologue, therefore, while it introduces him to us as the insignificant character he is in the social setting of the novel, also tells us a great deal about him as an example of confused mankind. His questions, touching continually on apparently chance observation of people he sees in the street, have a single source of coherence and unity: his desire to be what he patently is not, as evidenced by his dizzy and tail-chasing pattern of thought.

Augusto has been left alone in life. Since the death of his mother two years earlier, he has been cared for by a married couple, his servants Domingo and Liduvina. His friends, notably Víctor Goti, are people he sees outside the home, and therefore only in situations which are likely to make him feel exposed and vulnerable, and so more anxious to protect himself. Augusto gives the impression of spending much of his time at home, in a search for security, with occasional risky sorties into the outside world. In general, much of Augusto's experience can be treated in terms of excursion and retreat, with the first one as the most important. The excursion we see him undertake at the beginning of *Niebla* is not just into the street, but into life itself, and it involves for the first time a woman other than his mother.[25]

The *nivola* begins then, not only with Augusto at a point where his character and personality are going to be formed, but where he is both aware of this and about to do something about it. The proposed action is involvement with a woman, with all the problems and implications that Professor Parker has pointed out.[26] One of the most unfortunate consequences that follows on Augusto's proposed simple involvement with a woman, however, is that he is immediately involved in a social act, with its complicated limitations, expectations and requirements.

It could be argued that any relationship between two people is a social act, and indeed it even occurs to Augusto, when in the throes of both love and jealousy, that society and language between them are responsible for love.[27] Moreover, in the context of the particular bourgeois milieu where the action of *Niebla* takes place, the courtship and betrothal of two people could not be other. That there is only one word, 'novio' in Spanish for 'boyfriend', 'fiancé' and 'bridegroom' points to the conclusive implications of making the first approach in a courtship. Thus, as soon as Augusto asks the 'portera' for Eugenia's name, and her social circumstances (*N*, p.558), he is publicly involved in a relationship, from which, if only for the sake of appearances, he cannot draw back: 'Pues señor — iba diciéndose Augusto al separarse de la portera — ve aquí cómo he quedado comprometido con esta buena mujer. Porque ahora no puedo dignamente dejarlo así' (*N*, p.559).

The social commitment is established then by a question. Language, that tool for social interaction as outlined in the *Sentimiento trágico*,[28] is a necessary part of the complexities of society, since it allows us to make statements about what is, or is not. But at the same time, because it possesses qualities of, and apparent adequacy for, definition, it is unable on its own to convey and create all the nuances of a full relationship. One can regard *Niebla* as providing a spectrum of language. At one extremity there is the cut-and-dried categorising type of language that is used inexpertly by Augusto in his relationship with Eugenia, and which leads to an agonising equation of language, as 'la palabra', with honour. At the other extremity there is the wordless but deeply felt relationship between Augusto and his dog Orfeo.

To achieve some sympathetic understanding of why Augusto should see language as some sort of magic key to life, we should perhaps initially focus on the sort of evidence we have in the *nivola* of the functional importance of language. Other critics, for example, have commented on the importance of conversation in *Niebla*. Gullón comments on how the trivialities of conversation instruct the readers about the characters, at the same time as these trivialities instruct the characters about the society within which they live and function, and about what they have in common. This instructive character of conversation and gossip is one which obtains within life as well as within the *nivola*.[29] The concept of conversation as a diversion and time-filler has a similar status, but with added intensity derived from the level of pain from which Unamuno and his characters desire to distract themselves. Thus Goti, the novelist within *Niebla* who is suddenly pushed into the pain of existence by the unexpected pregnancy of his wife, and the resultant awareness of the approach of death with which his child's life endows him,[30] comes to look at conversation as a relief in life, since it is a distraction and may give us the illusion of a comfortable passivity: 'Es el encanto de la conversacíon, de hablar por hablar, de hablar roto e interrumpido ... sí, es la complacencia del hombre en el habla, y en el habla viva' (*N*, p.616). But Goti's view, that a flippant use of language, 'charlar, sutilizar, jugar con las palabras y los vocablos', is what one needs to make the pain of life bearable, or to 'pasar el rato' (*N*, p.663), is one which is reached after painful experience. At the time when he discusses it with Augusto it is a concept of language still unacceptable to the latter who has come by this stage to invest such a weath of existential meaning in language. In the light of this invested meaning, Goti's attitude is a threat and debasement.

Like Avito, Augusto is a man of extremes. While lacking the former's rigidity and obsessiveness, he is nonetheless concerned with absolutes, and this is because of his desire to obtain form, and his belief that it is necessary to use firm and unchanging components in order to create that form. Like many of Unamuno's characters who make unsatisfactory relationships (the vast majority), Augusto thinks to establish one with Eugenia by letter, once the initial contact with the 'portera' has been made. This was also the approach Avito intended to use with Leoncia in *Amor y pedagogía*: his elaborately worded and worked-over letter was, in the event, sent to Marina (*A y P*, p.323), but this does not diminish his rather intellectual, non-spontaneous intentionality in the matter. Augusto's letter is at least unconventional, romantic and lyrical, eccentric enough not to be a string of clichés. The formally begun relationship is then dominated by external preoccupations. The discussions of Augusto and Eugenia are dominated by the question of her mortgage, and negotiation in a manner that smacks of the financial settlements that accompany arranged marriages (*N*, pp.575-6), a gesture that offends the independent Eugenia (*N*, p.581), despite Augusto's assertions that he wished to give her freedom (*N*, pp.597-8). It continues to offend her (*N*, p.605), despite his further retraction and declaration that he will be 'padrino' at her wedding with Mauricio (*N*, p.608). The 'gift' is finally accepted, without commitment, by Eugenia (*N*, p.621), but with Augusto now warning that he is not a piano to be played on by her (*N*, p.622). She in turn refers yet again to his purchase of her mortgage as something that will deter other suitors (*N*, p.625). In Chapter XXVI when she finally agrees to marry him, she immediately insists on formality: Augusto must be more restrained as a 'novio' than as a friend; her uncle must be told immediately (*N*, p.651), and the wedding, she insists, must be a fine one (*N*, p.657).

All of the above emphasises the fierce independence of Eugenia, with her desire for financial autonomy which is the visible manifestation of her desire for personal autonomy. At the same time we have in Augusto a strange mixture of irresponsibility and commitment, which means that he frequently reacts without too much premeditation, and then regards his actions as binding. Thus he 'falls' for Eugenia, binds himself to her, and refuses to release himself from this in the belief that the commitment thus undone will prove his weakness rather than his strength (and, since it will suggest that there may be doubts about the 'love' that inspired the original commitment, will undermine his concept of his personal integrity). The mixture of freedom and commitment which he finds necessary is bound together in the game of chess, a pastime in which many of Unamuno's characters participate with symbolic implications. In playing chess, Augusto adheres to the rules of the game, 'pieza tocada, pieza jugada' (*N*, p.564), while maintaining his right to play in an incompetent and distracted manner: '¿Y por qué no ha de distraerse uno en el juego?' (*N*, p.564). Here there is the double meaning of distraction as non-attention and as amusement or diversion, both contained within 'distraerse'. Similarly, Augusto's attitude to the journey he has said he will undertake to recover from Eugenia's rejection of him (*N*, p.622) is that, having announced it, he cannot go back on his word:

Emprendería el viaje, ¿sí o no? Ya lo había anunciado, primero a Rosarito, sin saber bien lo que se decía, por decir algo, o más bien como un pretexto para preguntarle si le acompañaría en él, y luego a doña Ermelinda, para probarle... ¿qué?, ¿qué es lo que pretendió probarle con aquello de que iba a emprender un viaje? ¡Lo que fuese! Mas era el caso que había dicho que iba a emprender un viaje largo y lejano, y él era hombre de carácter, él era él; ¿tenía que ser hombre de palabra? (*N*, p.625)

The reason why it is so crucial to him to undertake the journey is that he feels bound by his word. The 'palabra' is a sign that he is real, an 'hombre de carácter'. Being a man, for Augusto, is the consequence of accepting commitment, however stupidly or carelessly it is entered into. The language which consolidates and announces intention is therefore central to him in proving to himself, and he hopes, to others, that he is a man. The conversion of language into a proof of honour and integrity takes us back rapidly into the social setting, and perhaps particularly so into the Spanish one. What

Augusto is doing with language here then is using it in an absolute and definite quantity in the attempt to prove something absolute and definite about himself: that he exists. It is also perhaps because he seeks things which are definite and absolute that he is attracted to Eugenia, who is self-defining, tight in her drawing of boundaries and distinctions, a woman who, in Augusto's terms, speaks to his imagination and his head, while Rosario, the laundress, speaks to his heart, and Liduvina, the house-keeper, speaks to his stomach (*N*, p.643). It is because he associates 'la palabra' with honour, reality, affirmation of his existence, that he wants to think of Eugenia as a 'mujer de palabra' (*N*, p.644). Unfortunately he wants her to accept him as a suitor (*N*, p.643), but at the same time, once she has refused him, he wants her to continue to refuse, because she is a 'mujer de palabra'. If she can be this, it will give him some guarantee of her integrity (on an existential rather than on a moral plane). But not only is her refusal something that he does not in fact want, at least on any level other than the theoretical or intellectual, it is, in constituting her being true to her word, something which he suspects may be incompatible with being a woman:

> Tiene que rechazarme. Después de lo pasado, después de lo que en nuestra última entrevista me dijo, no es posible ya que me admita. Es una mujer de palabra, creo. Mas... ¿es que las mujeres tienen palabra? ¿Es que la mujer, la Mujer, así, con letra mayúscula, la única, la que se reparte entre millones de cuerpos femeninos y más o menos hermosos — más bien más que menos —; es que la Mujer está obligada a guardar su palabra? Eso de guardar su palabra, ¿no es acaso masculino? (*N*, pp.643-4)

Without realising it, Augusto has put his finger on the problem. He has been equating reality with masculinity, envisaging as the only worthwhile reality one that is composed of definition, certainty, circumscribed by complete and unrejected actions and commitment to actions, a reality in which language is a counter to be used in precise exchanges. In all of this he follows the erroneous ways of Avito Carrascal. At the same time, however, by suddenly querying whether women can in fact be creatures who keep their word, Augusto has come close to his real dilemma. He has dimly perceived that the key to his reality lies in establishing or re-establishing his relationship with a woman. What he has not perceived is that the relationship has to be with a woman as an individual, not as generalised Woman. What he has to come to terms with is not an objective reality, that can be described or entered into with a language that is precise and mono-valent, but a subjective reality that can be experienced only by giving full attention and response to the complex particularities of each moment. This is a point Unamuno emphasises for us in the enquiries Augusto makes of Liduvina and Rosario about whether women should be expected to keep their word. Liduvina will not accept 'la palabra' as an absolute term: it depends on circumstances, and on one's *sensing* of the situation (something Augusto is not able to or does not trust himself to do): 'Unas palabras se dan para guardarlas y otras para no guardarlas. Y a nadie se engaña, porque es valor entendido' (*N*, p.644). Rosario is even more direct. First of all she refers his question back to himself, and in response to his generalised 'Di, Rosario, ¿qué crees tú, que una mujer debe guardar la palabra que dio o que no debe guardarla?', she particularises in order to reply 'No recuerdo haberle dado a usted palabra alguna' (*N*, p.644). Then when Augusto tries to take the question away from reference to herself ('No se trata de eso, sino de si debe o no una mujer guardar la palabra que dio') she rightly construes that in fact he is *not* making a general enquiry, which might refer to herself, but is concerned with Eugenia: 'lo dice usted por la otra ..., por esa mujer' (*N*, p.645). Since he insists, she says, she will reply that if a word has been given then that was a matter for regret:

— Bueno, ya que usted se empeña, le diré que lo mejor es

no dar palabra alguna.
— ¿Y si se ha dado?
— No haberla dado.   (*N*, p.645)

She will not let him off the hook where he has placed himself. When he tries to test her out, and see if she will make love to him, knowing that he loves another woman, then stops and asks her 'Pero ¿no sabes que quiero a otra mujer?' (thus stating his theoretical and general position), she refers him back to the evidence of reality as she at that moment perceives it, and claims that evidence is sufficient to allow her not to worry about what is *meant* to be his attitude:

— ¿Y a mí qué me importa eso ahora?
— ¿Cómo que no te importa?
— ¡Ahora, no! Ahora me quiere usted a mí, me parece.
                                                             (*N*, p.645)

This is a point which Augusto can accept only grudgingly ('A mí también me parece, pero...') and despite his response to her caresses fails to give in to making love to her, since what he concentrates on is a detached route to self-knowledge, trying to see himself reflected in her eyes rather than on a direct route to self-knowledge through shared experience.[31] As soon as he obtains this view of himself, he loses impetus, and announces that he gives up the love-making, insisting that giving up constitutes a defence of himself and not a rejection of her (*N*, p.646).[32]

The ultimate irony is that Augusto, instead of deriving certainty and reassurance from 'la palabra' is undone by it. When he goes to see Eugenia, to try the 'última experiencia psicológica' which is to see whether she will just allow him to break off their agreement to be friends, and instead marry him, she taunts him. In making the suggestion, he is breaking the masculine attitude of constancy and decision, but she says that this frees her to break her own rigidity, also pointing out that he has paradoxically proved his manhood by the unmanly (or ungentlemanly?) action of breaking his word, since for her all men are 'brutos' and 'groseros' (*N*, p.606): 'Pues bien, Augusto, ya que tú, que eres al fin y al cabo un hombre, no te crees obligado a guardar la palabra, yo, que no soy nada más que una mujer, tampoco debo guardarla' (*N*, p.651). The real consequences of word-breaking come later when Eugenia backs out of the engagement and elopes with Mauricio, ensuring that not only does Augusto suffer the private pain of rejection, but also that he has to suffer the indignity of mockery done to his public person. Since Augusto has staked everything on what was essentially a public, social act, the social ridicule is arguably the pain he feels most bitterly:

— Es que no me duele en el amor; ¡es la burla, la burla, la burla! Se han burlado de mí, me han escarnecido, me han puesto en ridículo, han querido demostrarme... ¿qué sé yo? ..., que no existo. (*N*, p.661)

One could, of course, reason that his awareness of public pain is a last-ditch diversion from his private pain, but we should give due weight to the explicit form he gives to his anguish.

Somewhere in all of this, however, there is Augusto's search for and discovery of his true self, and the discovery of the side of him that recognises that precision and finality are not necessarily to be equated with truth. A flash of this is shown in Chapter XXVIII where he sees Mauricio, who gives yet another threat to his existence in his taunt 'Mírese usted, ahora, don Augusto, en mis pupilas y verá qué chiquito se ve' (*N*, p.656), after which point Augusto trusts none of his senses, and even has to have reassurance from Liduvina that Mauricio's visit has actually taken place. That Liduvina operates on a plane of knowledge that is not the conventional one, or at least not that of men, is commented on by Augusto:

— ¡Cómo las mujeres sabéis tantas cosas que no os enseñan... !

— Sí, y en cambio no logramos aprender las que quieren
enseñarnos. (*N*, p.656)

But this discovery, that there may be a plane of knowledge
and communication other than the clear, rational 'masculine'
one, is not a new postulate within the novel. From very early
on we the readers, and Augusto, are introduced to definition
as destructive. When Augusto is presented with Víctor Goti's
proposition that he, Augusto, has passed from an abstract
notion of or desire for love, to a concrete object of that love (*N*,
p.565), most of the proposition being couched by Goti in
diminutives, Augusto turns to contemplate the nature of love,
and finds that it not only defies definition, but will be
destroyed by it. Following on the principle enunciated in the
Sentimiento trágico[33] that life cannot be analysed, Augusto
rejects by implication Goti's systematising of what is
happening to him, with a statement of his own queries and
ponderings, in which, as is typical of Unamuno, the only
ultimate certainty is doubt: '¿Y qué es amor? ¿Quién definió el
amor? Amor definido deja de serlo' (*N*, p.566). In the course of
this monologue, on the whole incoherent, Augusto touches on a
lot of points vital to him: his defence of *his* love (it is real, not
an abstraction he has just made concrete), his defence of his
distracted manner of chess-playing (he admits careless play,
but accepts the consequences), and the valuation of intuitive
perception and 'niebla' which precede knowledge.

What he does not reach is the next stage of knowledge, that
is, the 'real', carnal knowledge referred to by Eugenia's uncle,
and which relies entirely on spontaneous and non-intellectual
reaction. Eugenia's uncle, don Fermín, mystic and anarchist,
vegetarian, esperanto-speaker and free-thinker (and thus a
parodied figure who cannot fully be trusted) is the character
who most explicitly outlines a scheme for entry into real
existence through physical experience. The social niceties
surrounding a relationship have no significance for him,
compared with the real investigation and knowledge acquired
through experience that follow on the formal commitment: 'El

único conocimiento eficaz es el conocimiento *post nuptias*. Ya
me has oído, esposa mía, lo que en lenguaje bíblico significa
conocer. Y, créemelo, no hay más conocimiento sustancial y
esencial que ése, el conocimiento penetrante' (*N*, p.579).
Augusto, of course, never gets to this Biblical knowledge with
entirety, but there is a pattern of imagery that links his
experience of his mother with part of his experience of
Eugenia, and which is suggestively based on moistness and
fluidity, in contrast with the cut-and-dried unequivocal
associations of a world that is masculine, cerebral and
definitive. This pattern of imagery shows his closest
approximation to experience not processed by language, and
emphasises his need to be received back into an environment
that had originally provided physical — and by extension,
existential nourishment.

There is little mention of Augusto's father, who exists as a
shadow in his memory. He is associated with blood — in
reality, and historically, the blood of death, — but also blood
that symbolises the child's fear: 'De su padre apenas se
acordaba; era una sombra mítica que se le perdía en lo más
lejano; era une nube sangrienta de ocaso. Sangrienta, porque
siendo aún pequeñito lo vio bañado en sangre, de un vómito, y
cadavérico' (*N*, p.571). Of his mother he remembers most
clearly the atmosphere that surrounds her. As a child, he
hides in her, afraid to take his face away from 'la dulce
oscuridad de aquel regazo palpitante' lest he should see the
'ojos devoradores del Coco' — conceivably, one might surmise,
the ghost of his father (*N*, p.571). The house is a refuge, a
welcoming, comforting place: 'Era una casa dulce y tibia. La luz
entraba por entre las blancas flores bordadas de los visillos.
Las butacas abrían, con intimidad de abuelos hechos niños por
los años, sus brazos.' His mother is associated with depths of
quiet, warmth, moistness, and with gentle movement:

Su madre iba y venía sin hacer ruido, como un pajarillo,
siempre de negro, con una sonrisa, que era el poso de las
lágrimas de los primeros días de viudez, siempre en la boca

y en torno de los ojos escudriñadores. 'Tengo que vivir para
ti, para ti, para ti solo — le decía por las noches, antes de
acostarse — , Augusto.' Y éste llevaba a sus sueños
nocturnos un beso húmedo aún en lágrimas.   (*N*, p.571)

There is a re-awakening of this moist atmosphere, with the
addition of flow and energy, after Augusto has seen Eugenia
for the first time in her house, and has had the first contact
with her scorn, independence and lack of interest in him as a
suitor (Chapter VIII). This interview does not have the effect
of depressing him. He neglects the implications of what has
passed between them verbally and simply lets himself expand
into feeling:

El mundo le parecía más grande, el aire más puro y más
azul el cielo. Era como si respirase por vez primera ...
Diríase que para él empezaba a estar el mundo iluminado
por una nueva luz misteriosa desde dos grandes estrellas
invisibles que refulgían más allá del cielo, detrás de su
aparente bóveda. Empezaba a conocer el mundo. Y sin
saber cómo, se puso a pensar en la profunda fuente de la
confusión vulgar entre el pecado de la carne y la caída de
nuestros primeros padres por haber probado del fruto del
árbol de la cíencia del bien y del mal.

Y meditó en la doctrina de don Fermín sobre el origen del
conocimiento.   (*N*, p.583)

Later, in Chapter X, the terms used become more organic,
less ethereal, moving closer to the register of the 'poso' — the
sediment — that had been associated with his mother:
'Sentíase otro Augusto y como si aquella visita y la revelación
en ella de la mujer fuerte — fluía de sus ojos fortaleza — le
hubiera arado las entrañas del alma, alumbrando en ellas un
manantial hasta entonces oculto' (*N*, p.586). It is significant
that it is this vision of Eugenia's strength that brings him the
stronger reminder of his mother — an indication that a more

fundamental quality of his mother than her apparent fragility was some real source of strength.

This type of direct and fluid reaction of Augusto to his experience, which also forms part of his experience, is partly a reiteration of the type of organic, vegetable imagery used by Unamuno to evoke Marina in *Amor y pedagogía*.[34] At the same time we should recognise that while some of this imagery evokes Augusto's potential for life and response, it also underscores his essential passivity, or submissiveness. This is in part a simple desire to remain a child, or become one again, and return to the nurturing of a woman. It is also the result of believing women to be associated with life in a way that men are not. Thus he effectively wants to submit to Eugenia, as a source of power, so that he can acquire a natural power, and be the sort of natural being that Marina was. It is as though he needs to be a woman in order to be a person. This is his instinctive reaction to his undefined existential situation, and seems to rule out the possibility of being a man, which he had also thought of as being co-terminous with being a person, having thought of existence as something which might be achieved by definition, and having associated man with definition. This developmental cul-de-sac that he gets himself into does not, however, diminish the pleasure that he feels in the passivity of submission:

Oyóse un ligero rumor, como de paloma que arranca en vuelo, un ¡ah! breve y seco, y los ojos de Eugenia, en un rostro todo frescor de vida y sobre un cuerpo que no parecía pesar sobre el suelo, dieron como una nueva y misteriosa luz espiritual a la escena. Y Augusto se sintió tranquilo, enormemente tranquilo, clavado a su asiento y como si fuese una planta nacida en él, como algo vegetal, olvidado de sí, absorto en la misteriosa luz espiritual que de aquellos ojos irradiaba. (*N*, p.580)

Passivity is not always desired by Augusto, however. His view of himself, and what he wants to happen to him, undergoes a change which is highlighted in the passage which follows the visit he receives from Eugenia's aunt. During the visit it has become obvious to him that Eugenia intends to use him, to play with him. He goes out to a small park where he looks at the trees. Like him, they have been organised to the satisfaction of others:

Aquellos árboles domésticos, urbanos, en correcta formación, que recibían riego a horas fijas, cuando no llovía, por una reguera y que extendían sus raíces bajo el enlosado de la plaza; aquellos árboles presos que esperaban enjaulados, que tal vez añoraban la remota selva, atraíanle con un misterioso tiro.   (*N*, p.624)

Since the trees have been subjected to man's will, they are no longer themselves. As Augusto says of them:

¡Pobres árboles que no pueden gozar de una de esas negras noches sin luna, con su manto de estrellas palpitantes! Parece que al plantar a cada uno de estos árboles en este sitio les ha dicho el hombre: '¡Tú no eres tú!', y para que no lo olviden le han dado esa iluminación nocturna por luz eléctrica ..., para que no se duerman... '¡Pobres árboles trasnochadores! ¡No, no, conmigo no se juega como con vosotros!'   (*N*, p.624)

The relationship with Eugenia, as we have seen, is complicated because of the social conventions it involves and uses. These are the patterns Augusto feels able to use, and yet is most threatened by, because of his fear of social ridicule. The relationship is also complicated by Eugenia's refusal or inability to be for Augusto the sort of woman he would like her to be. There is, of course, no good reason why she should respond to his advances, or meet his needs. There is no direct response in her except one of fighting him off unlike Rosario who trembled like a leaf when he looked at her (*N*, p.617). Augusto would like Eugenia to provide what his mother did.

He would like her to be a contact for him with the
non-masculine world.

He sees one indication that she may be able to do this in
her profession of teaching the piano. He approves of it, since
he regards music as useless, or at least as not necessary in the
world: 'Pues ahí estriba su mayor encanto, en que no sirve
para maldita de Dios la cosa, lo que se llama servir' (*N*, p.567).
A number of factors come into play here. Although Eugenia's
association with music might seem to indicate that she, like his
mother, has access to the non-rational, non-intellectual world,
her music is in fact part of the artificial decorative trimmings
of society (just as Augusto's poem to her, while it is full of the
misty and liquid imagery that we associate with his inner life,
is nonetheless stilted and conventional). It is the link of music
with the irrational world that disturbs Eugenia. In one rare
moment we are given insight into her as a person and see that
she, like Augusto, may have her existential problems too:
'Sentía la pobre, sin darse de ello clara cuenta, que la música
es preparación eterna, preparación a un advenimiento que
nunca llega, eterna iniciación que no acaba nunca. Estaba harta
de música' (*N*, p.585). A few pages earlier, when Augusto is
confronted by Eugenia's denial that she takes any pleasure in
music, he is reminded that Liduvina had already seen this and
commented that 'ésta, después que se case y si el marido la
puede mantener, no vuelve a teclear un piano' (*N*, p.581). This
aspect of Eugenia which may have rebuffed us as readers to
the same degree as it was intended to rebuff the sentimental
advances of Augusto is one which now acquires a new
dimension. In retrospect we are enabled to see her rejection of
music as an anguished rejection by her of an element in life
that is unbearable because of its apparent potential scope for
personal enrichment. The interplay between this passage and
the earlier one makes it more likely that we can empathise
with her as she hears in the street a parody of music produced
by a barrel-organ: 'Y salió Eugenia con la cabeza alta a la calle,
donde en aquel momento un organillo de manubrio encentaba
una rabiosa polca. "¡Horror!, ¡horror!, ¡horror!", se dijo la

muchacha, y más que se fue, huyó calle abajo' (*N*, p.586).
Although the implications of the music are not spelled out for
us, the possibilities that the music signifies a parody of
herself, or indeed, that she may be a parody of Woman, are
both there. These repercussions between different sections of
the text that deal with music do not end here, for the
barrel-organ, with its sharp and distressing effect upon
Eugenia now sends us back to a still earlier passage where
Augusto is thinking of her, and hears a barrel-organ playing a
polka in the street. He does not hear it for what it is
(mechanical, soulless music) but for what he wants it to be. In
this way the whole basis and scale of his misunderstanding of
Eugenia is exposed:

...un piano de manubrio se había parado al pie de la
ventana de su cuarto y estaba sonando. Y el alma de
Augusto repercutía notas, no pensaba.

' La esencia del mundo es musical — se dijo Augusto cuando
murió la última nota del organillo — . Y mi Eugenia, ¿no es
musical también? Toda ley es una ley de ritmo, y el ritmo
es el amor.' (*N*, p.569)

At times it seems that Augusto has the right idea, unlike
Avito or Apolodoro, his predecessors. He knows that if he is to
define himself as a person, it will have to be in a context
where he relates to other people. He seems to know that it will
be necessary to do this with a woman, he suspects that it may
have something to do with falling in love, he is unwilling to
admit that it may have something to do with sex. The way to
find out about most or all of these things is marriage (the only
route a conventional bourgeois and well brought-up young
man in his situation would contemplate, although Rosario does
not appear to require any promise of matrimony in exchange
for a real level of knowledge of which don Fermín would
approve). He finds the experience of falling in love, or that of
simply becoming aware of women as attractive, to be a

fear-inspiring cataclysm, and does not seem to be able to distinguish between the two states: 'El pobre Augusto estaba consternado. No era sólo que se encontrase, como el asno de Buridán, entre Eugenia y Rosario; era que aquello de enamorarse de casi todas las que veía, en vez de amenguársele, íbale en medro' (*N*, p.636). Marriage, for him, does not seem to be a place where the experience of falling in love might be developed, or even a place of further discovery, but instead a place of retreat: '¿Cómo voy a defenderme de esto hasta que al fin me decida y me case?' (*N*, p.636).

As a temporary measure, he decides to intellectualise his whole approach to women, by making them an object of study. This is an attempt to get away from the disruptive quality of his natural responses, as outlined, for example, in Chapter XI, where he was physically incapacitated by Eugenia's approach: 'De pronto, al oír unos pasos menudos, sintío un puñal atraversarle el pecho y como una bruma invadirle la cabeza' (*N*, p.590). He does not reject this discomfort and its source, but is exalted by it in the flux of the moment: 'Pero es, Eugenia, que yo no pretendo nada, que no busco nada, que nada pido; es, Eugenia, que yo me contento con que me deje venir de cuando en cuando a bañar mi espíritu en la mirada de esos ojos, a embriagarme en el vaho de su respiracíon' (*N*, p.591). Somehow he does not equate marriage with the turbulence he has felt. Marriage, connected with the maternal symbol of the house, will be safe, a haven, to which, in desperation, he decides to return.

So great is this desperation that he is even prepared to give up Orfeo since Eugenia wishes it. The dog represents within the novel the highest potential level of empathy with a human being, but Augusto, while taking comfort in the relationship with the dog, nonetheless fails to see it as a key to his salvation and self-definition: 'Acaso un perro sorprende los más secretos pensamientos de las personas con quienes vive, y aunque se calle ... ¡Y tengo que casarme, no tengo más remedio que casarme ..., si no, jamás voy a salir del ensueño! Tengo que despertar' (*N*, p.657). This is what he thinks directly after the encounter in Chapter XXII with Víctor Goti whose marriage was suddenly brought to life by the birth of a child. Goti's marriage has clarified his existence for him, but only by an event which was not willed. That marriage may represent a possible route to existential salvation not because it is a retreat but because it subjects us to chance in our relation to others is an aspect of it that appears to elude Augusto. No discussion of where Augusto goes wrong in his verbal and non-verbal search for himself would be complete without a consideration of the mute witness of his anguish, the dog Orfeo. Professor Parker has explored a great deal of the necessary ground, but there are some further features of Orfeo's significance which are particularly pertinent here. It could be claimed for Orfeo that he is the character in *Niebla* with whom Augusto has the closest relationship. Recipient of the most agonised monologues, he cannot respond verbally, and thus cannot by example or participation encourage Augusto in his misguided attempts to explore the world via language. As usual, Augusto misunderstands even this: he sees wordlessness as a state to be pitied, not one to be envied, forgetting that his happiest childhood memories are essentially silent and dreamy: 'Pero, ¿por qué me miras así, Orfeo? ¡Si parece que lloras sin lágrimas ...! ¿Es que me quieres decir algo? Te veo sufrir por no tenir palabra' (*N*, p.657).

The way in which Orfeo enters Augusto's life is significant. He is found abandoned, a puppy left to die, looking for his mother's milk. This is at least how he seems to Augusto who has just been remembering his mother's death (*N*, p.572) which has left him as helpless as the puppy. Augusto, by taking Orfeo in, as a response to his feelings of pity for the animal, is not acting within a social norm (it is more unusual in Spain than in England to adopt a stray animal). He is, significantly, acting in a spontaneous and instinctive manner.[35] The naming of the dog also has special significance, despite Unamuno's assertion that the name was given 'no se sabe ni sabía él tampoco por qué' (*N*, p.573). Since the dog is Augusto's *alter ego*, as shown by Professor Parker, the name is of ill portent in two respects. Firstly, that just as Orpheus lost Eurydice by turning to look at her, so Augusto will lose Eugenia, or any woman, by his attempts to make safe the relationship by 'looking' at her in a detached and analytical way. Secondly, after Orpheus lost Eurydice, he refused to have anything to do with women. Later, the Thracian women, during a Dionysian orgy, set upon him and tore him to pieces. We can either see the analogy here as being that Augusto, having lost his mother, is devoured by his need for women, and is destroyed by it, or that Augusto, in being misguided in his attempts to relate to women, is destroyed by their reactions to him.

Orfeo is invested with additional significance by being linked with the concept of the house, and the inner life. When we find that Eugenia cannot tolerate the dog in the house we are given a clear sign that she cannot or will not be what Augusto wants her to be after they are married. Orfeo, this 'símbolo de la fidelidad', as his master calls him, is closely associated with all the feelings of warmth and security that a house ('casa') has, and that a marriage ('casamiento') ought to have. But Augusto, after all his unproductive grapplings with language as a possible entry into life, is finally faced with the prospect that experience, as in marriage, is maybe not a simple alternative to his present fumblings. He realises unconsciously perhaps that his marriage will not be a step back into the comfort of the home, but will be a step out into the painful experience of life. The house both is and is not life. It is the dream, the 'sueño' in which Marina of *Amor y pedagogía* lived, and thus something from which Augusto feels he must escape if he is to reach 'realidad'. Hence, as we have already seen, his insistence on participating in a 'real' act: '¡Y tengo que casarme, no tengo más remedio que casarme ..., Si no, jamás voy a salir del ensueño! Tengo que despertar' (*N*, p.657). At least here Augusto has reached a more mature view of what his contact with life is likely to mean: a simple return to maternal comforting is not possible.

Orfeo, the dumb animal, is given his due importance by

having the last word. In this way Unamuno closes the circle or paradox that language represents for him. We are forced by our nature as articulate beings to approach or explain those areas of life where language is bound to be inadequate. Without words we could not begin to question why it is that life will not fit into tidy systems, and yet at the point where life ceases to fit such systems our methods of describing it break down. Augusto pities Orfeo for his lack of speech: Orfeo pities man for his inability to express what really matters: 'Y luego habla, o ladra, de un modo complicado. Nosotros aullábamos y por imitarle aprendimos a ladrar, y ni aun así nos entendemos con él. Sólo le entendemos de veras cuando él aúlla. Cuando el hombre aúlla o grita o amenaza le entendemos muy bien los demás animales' (*N*, p.680). Augusto was blind in his belief in words, and never learnt to emancipate himself from them.

To many readers, Unamuno may seem to have suffered the same fate as his most famous character. So many words, contradictory, warring, playful, attempting to define, being used to construct systems that they can then be used to take apart: this seems to be the essence of Unamuno, and source of frustration to his readers. The solution is not retreat. Augusto Pérez, whether or not he committed suicide (which to him and his creator, but perhaps not to all readers, seems to be the crucial detail on which the reality of his existence hinges) does have an existence that is far more real than that of any other character created by Unamuno, precisely because of the painful nature of his struggle to be. Within this, language is a seemingly conclusive factor in the question of whether he will win the struggle or not. His success lies in his distress and his realisation of man's limitations, and in the conclusion that his example suggests to us that life, experience and language are only valid insofar as they are experienced by individuals as individuals. As general propositions they are sterile.

When Unamuno was invited to a dinner in Christ's College, Cambridge, as a guest of the late Professor J.B. Trend, he found that his command of English was insufficient to allow him to join in the conversation at High Table. For once language eluded him, rather than his characters. His solution was neither anger nor passivity, but a creative search for the limited perfection open to him in that situation. He made a number of paper birds. The 'Apuntes para un tratado de cocotología' tell us little about communication, but a lot about perfection as something which is at odds with individuality. On the surface, the practice of origami at Christ's high table looks like a retreat. Carried out by a man who knows that the struggle for perfection in origami is doomed to failure, because of the imperfections in the raw material, just as the struggle for communication in human speech is doomed to failure because of the imperfections and inadequacies of words, the creation of paper birds was Unamuno's elegant proof of his individuality, and an assertion that struggle is worthwhile, even if failure is ultimately inevitable. Both Unamuno and Augusto Pérez might have described it as a question of dignity.

NOTES

1. E.g. R.E. Batchelor, *Unamuno Novelist*, (Oxford, 1972), p.250.

2. For an examination of how this formlessness is only apparent, see Geoffrey Ribbans, 'The structure of Unamuno's *Niebla*', *Spanish Thought and Letters in the Twentieth Century*, edited by Germán Bleiberg and E. Inman Fox, (Tennessee, 1968), pp.395-405.

3. See Ribbans, 'La evolución de la novelística unamuniana: *Amor y pedagogía* y *Niebla*', *Niebla y Soledad: Aspectos de Unamuno y Machado*, (Madrid, 1971), pp.83-107.

4. 'Es que la fantasía y la tragicomedia de mi *Niebla* ha de ser lo que más habla y diga al hombre individual que es el universal, al hombre por encima, y por debajo a la vez, de clases, de castas, de posiciones sociales, pobre o rico, plebeyo o noble, proletario o burgués', Unamuno, 'Prólogo a la tercera edición, o sea, historia de *Niebla*', *Obras completas*, edited by Manuel García Blanco, (Madrid, 1966-71), 9 vols., vol. II, p.553. All other references to Unamuno's work will be from this edition of the *Obras completas*. References to *Niebla* and *Amor y pedagogía* will be given in the text. They refer to vol. II of the *O. C.* and will be preceded by the abbreviations *N*

and *A y P* respectively.

5. There seems to be an intended echo of the expression 'es un Pérez', i.e. 'He's just an ordinary bloke' here.

6. Ribbans, *Niebla y Soledad*, p.93.

7. Ribbans, *Niebla y Soledad*, p.105.

8. See R.E. Batchelor, *Unamuno Novelist*, p.130: 'Being a protracted monologue, *Niebla* involves the reader in a series of unanswered and unanswerable questions that Augusto asks himself'.

9. Unamuno, *Poesías, O. C.*, vol. IV, p.362. The poem is dated Salamanca, 28 September, 1910.

10. *Del sentimiento trágico de la vida, O. C.*, vol. VII, p.124.

11. See, for example, in the *Sentimiento trágico*: 'Es una cosa terrible la inteligencia. Tiende a la muerte como a la estabilidad la memoria. Lo vivo, lo que es absolutamente inestable, lo absolutamente individual, es, en rigor, ininteligible. La lógica tira a reducirlo todo a identidades y a géneros, a que no tenga cada representacíon más que uno solo y mismo contenido en cualquier lugar, tiempo o relacíon en que se nos ocurra ... La identidad que es la muerte, es la aspiración del intelecto. La mente busca lo muerto, pues lo vivo se le escape.' *O. C.*, vol. VII, p.162.

12. Some nice examples are collected by Adolfo Jiménez Hernández in *Unamuno y la filosofía del lenguaje*, (Puerto Rico, 1973), pp.183-5, arguing links betwen 'nombrar' and 'conocer', 'fe' and 'confianza', 'conseguir' and 'consecuencia', 'habla' and 'fábula', 'palabra' and 'parábola', 'museo' and 'musa'.

13. See Turner, *Unamuno's Webs of Fatality*, (London, Támesis, 1974), p.78: 'In the *Tres novelas ejemplares* ... nothing is learnt of Raquel, Carolina or Alejandro, except what is revealed in their words, actions and gestures, or occasionally from assumptions made by other characters'.

14. This is elaborated by Batchelor, op. cit., p.132: 'The characteristic and exceptional feature of the dialogues in the *nivola* arises from the disregard that each character manifests towards the interlocutor. In other words, we witness two opposed yet parallel monologues and not, in fact, a dialogue of question and answer, incrimination and repartee ... The protagonist never exhibits any emotional appreciation of other people's problems, the solipsist question involving exclusively experiences and impressions recorded by the protagonist alone'.

15. This closing section, a twenty-page article on the art of origami, is at once Unamuno's way of cocking a snook at the whole process of writing novels, and giving them artistic form, and also an underlining of the potential frailty and inadequacy of human life. There are constraints in origami, since the imperfections of the paper mean that the ideal form can never be achieved (*O. C.*, vol. II, *A y P*, p.418), just as the imperfections of the human condition prevent Avito Carrascal from forming his perfect and rational progeny. It is in the 'Apuntes' that Unamuno queries most insistently and seriously Avito's desire to create perfection, since perfection is the antithesis of individuality: 'La perfección se adquiere a costa de personalidad, y ... cuanto más perfecto o arquetípico es un ser, tanto menos personal es, y veamos por aquí, mirándonos en las pajaritas como en espejo, si nos conviene aspirar al sobrehombre, al hombre inscribible en óvulo perfecto, y si para lograr semejante perfección hemos de renunciar a nuestra personalidad cada uno.' (*O. C.*, vol. II, pp.418-9).

16. In addition to the traditional connotations of sexuality and the unconscious that are carried by the watery echoes of Marina's name, there are all the sea-associations of the changeless and ever-changing which are so powerfully evoked in Unamuno, 'La tradición eterna', *En torno al casticismo*, *O. C.*, vol. I, pp.783-98, and, in Spanish, the possible dual sexual nature of the sea. As 'el mar' or 'la mar' it can be all things to all people, a duality of reference exploited with delicacy in the poetry of Juan Ramón Jiménez and Rafael Alberti.

17. Avito Carrascal displays most of the characteristics of the Freudian anal character, as does Emeterio Alonso of 'Un pobre hombre rico', *San Manuel bueno, mártir y tres historias más*. Avito's passion for order, system and hygiene (see *A y P*, p.326) are not merely those of the modern scientific and rational man he would like to think himself to be, but are on the level of the obsessive. Compare with Freud's essay 'Charakter und analerotik' of 1908: 'The people I am about to describe are noteworthy for a regular combination of the three following characteristics. They are especially *orderly*, *parsimonious* and *obstinate* ... "orderly" covers the notion of bodily cleanliness, as well as of conscientiousness in carrying out small duties and trustworthiness.' Sigmund Freud, 'Character and anal eroticism', the Pelican Freud Library, 16 vols., general editor Angela Richards, vol. VII, *On Sexuality: Three essays on the Theory of Sexuality and other works*, translated by James Strachey, (London, 1977), p.209.

18. See also Gregory Ulmer, *The Legend of Herostratus: existential envy in Rousseau and Unamuno*, (University of Florida Monographs, Humanities, no.45, 1977).

19. See above, pp.190-91.

20. 'el *ego* implícito en ... *ego cogito, ergo ego sum*, es un *ego*, un yo irreal o sea ideal, y su *sum*, su existencia, algo irreal también. 'Pienso, luego soy', no puede querer decir sino 'pienso, luego soy pensante'; ese ser del soy, que se deriva de pienso, no es más que un conocer; ese ser es conocimiento, mas no vida. Y lo primitivo no es que pienso, sino que vivo, porque también viven los que no piensan. Aunque ese vivir no sea un vivir verdadero.' *Del sentimiento trágico, O. C.*, vol. VII, p.130.

21. '¿Qué es, en efecto, conocer una cosa sino nombrarla? Conocer una cosa es clasificarla, nos dicen los filósofos, es distinguirla de las demás, y cuanto mejor la distingues es que la conoces mejor.' (*A y P*, p.414)

22. See, in this connexion, S. Serrano Poncela, *El pensamiento de Unamuno*, (Mexico, 1953), pp.226-7, on Unamuno's dislike of 'la lengua literaria' for being 'muerta' and 'petrificada', in contrast with 'la lengua popular, anónima, coloquial, ... lengua viva, siempre, en el tiempo.' The comparison is much the same as the distinction made by Bécquer in the prologue to A. Ferrán, *La Soledad*, in G.A. Bécquer, *Obras completas*, edited by J. García Pérez, (Barcelona, 1956), pp.539-40.

23. 'Y va de cuento', *El espejo de la muerte, O. C.*, vol. II, p.539.

24. A.A. Parker, 'On the interpetation of *Niebla*', *Unamuno creator and creation*, edited by José Rubia Barcia and M.A. Zeitlin, (University of California Press, 1967), p.130.

25. The house representing Augusto's mother, and the notion of retreat, or isolation from the world for the sake of safety, is common as a motif in Unamuno's work. See for example 'Don Sandalio, el jugador de ajedrez' of the *San Manuel* collection, where the narrator retreats successively to the isolation of the country, to an oak tree and to a ruined house, *La tía Tula*, where Tula concludes that she is strongest in her own house, and 'Nada menos que todo un hombre' of the *Tres novelas ejemplares* where Alejandro isolates both himself and his wife in the house. Above all, when Unamuno's characters wish to control and (possibly) nurture others, they isolate them: hence Augusto's education at home by his mother, Apolodoro's education principally conducted at home by his father, and Joaquín of *Abel Sánchez* who takes care to keep his daughter away from the world. It is significant in this context that Augusto finds the dog Orfeo in the street, and needing nourishment (*N*, p.573), a need which Augusto meets with a feeding bottle, wanting to provide the nourishment of a mother for him.

26. See above, note 24.

27. 'Probablemente no nace el amor sino al nacer los celos; son los celos los que nos revelan el amor. Por muy enamorada que esté una mujer de un hombre o un hombre de una mujer, no se dan cuenta de que lo están, no se dicen a sí mismos que lo están, es decir, no se enamoran de veras sino cuando él ve que ella mira a otro hombre o ella le ve a él mirar a otra mujer. Si no hubiese más que un solo hombre y una sola mujer en el mundo, sin más sociedad, sería imposible que se enamorasen uno de otro.' (*N*, p.620)

28. See above, note 10.

29. R. Gullón, *Autobiografías de Unamuno*, (Madrid, 1964), pp.108-9.

30. As Goti remarks, 'Ver crecer al hijo es lo más dulce y lo más terrible, creo. No te cases, pues, Augusto, no te cases si quieres gozar de la ilusión de una juventud eterna' (*N*, p.636).

31. Augusto is particularly reliant on the sense of sight, and thus especially vulnerable to all that he sees. It is Eugenia's eyes which attract him. It is of some interest in this context that, according to a concordance of Quevedo's *Poesía amorosa* prepared by P.J. Smith with the assistance of the Literary and Linguistic Computing Centre, Cambridge, the most frequently occurring noun after 'amor' (the most common noun) is 'ojos'. This is not the order that necessarily obtains in other writers. In Lorca's poetry, for example, the order of noun frequency runs 'luna', 'agua', 'corazón', 'amor', 'noche', 'cielo', 'ojos' (*A Concordance to the Plays and Poems of Federico García Lorca*, edited by Alice M. Pollin, (Cornell University Press, 1975).

32. Cf. the failure of Augusto's other attempt to define himself in Chapter XIX. Having rejected passivity ('que yo no soy un piano en que se puede tocar a todo antojo, que no soy un hombre de hoy te dejo y luego te tomo, que no soy sustituto ni vicenovio, que no soy plato de segunda mesa' (*N*, p.622)), he affirms his independence: 'Lo que sobran son mujeres ... No, no, conmigo no juega nadie, y menos una mujer. ¡Yo soy yo! ¡Mi alma será pequeña, pero es mía!' (*N*, p.623). He makes this affirmation only to find that when he goes into the street, he does not appear to exist for others, since they do not notice him. He consequently does not have an existence that feels real to him. Whereas he suspects that being recognised by society at large will prove his reality, he is forced to conclude that in fact only his subjective, individual perception will do this: 'Sólo a solas se sentía él; sólo a solas podía decirse a sí mismo, tal vez para convencerse: '¡Yo soy yo!', ante los demás, mejido en la muchedumbre atareada o distraída, no se sentía a sí mismo' (*N*, p.623).

33. See above, note 11.

34. E.g. 'de otra parte Marina, la inductiva por misteriosa ley de contraste branqui-morena, sueño hecho carne, con algo de viviente arbusto en su encarnadura y de arbusto revestido de fragrantes flores, surgiendo esplendorosa de entre los fuegos del instinto, cual retama en un volcán' (*A y P*, p.322).

35. For similar reasons, Jacinta's reaction to the drowning kittens in Galdós's *Fortunata y Jacinta* is striking if less interesting. See Benito Pérez Galdós, *Obras completas*, edited by F.C. Sainz de Robles, 6 vols., (Madrid, 1967), vol. V, pp.70-71.

Towards a Poetry of Silence: Stéphane Mallarmé and Juan Ramón Jiménez

Mervyn Coke-Enguídanos

Si fuese el fablar
de plata figurado,
debe ser el callar
de oro afinado.

Sem Tob

Stéphane Mallarmé was already thirty-five years old when Juan Ramón Jiménez was born, and his death occurred sixty years before that of the Spanish poet. Yet despite this difference in age, both poets shared in a particular epoch: one which marked and shaped the aesthetic ideal of each in a singularly like manner. I refer to that era of 'fin de siècle' Europe — or 'fin du globe', as Oscar Wilde caused Dorian Gray dismally to observe — in which prevailed a profoundly disturbing sense of the destructiveness of Time. That metaphysical Angst is borne out in Mallarmé's own poetic expression of it in his summary phrase: 'un tremblement du voile du Temple trouble mon époque'. Using the same metaphor he again declares: 'on assiste, comme finale d'un siècle, pas ainsi que ce fut dans le dernier, à des bouleversements: mais, hors de la place publique, à une inquiétude du voile dans le temple avec des plis significatifs et un peu sa déchirure.'[1] The ubiquity of this feeling is confirmed when we remember that these very words were taken up by the Anglo-Irish poet, W.B. Yeats, to form the title of his book *The Trembling of the Veil*, the Preface to which, written in 1922, bears witness to the continuing prevalence of this special brand of anguish. There can be little doubt that Mallarmé felt himself to be living in a terminal phase of civilisation; felt therefore, too, that it was his responsibility as poet and thinker to transcend the ravages of Time and create the Work — that saving crucible of all experience. 'L'Œuvre' of Mallarmé, like 'la Obra' of Juan Ramón, has for its goal the attainment of timelessness. The transcendence of Time is an aesthetic ideal which bears radically upon the nature of the Work. It is necessary here to confine myself to the study of a single aspect arising from that goal, and that is the treatment in Juan Ramón's 'Obra' and in Stéphane Mallarmé's 'Œuvre' of silence.

In a very beautiful metaphor, in his 'Estética y ética estética', Juan Ramón envisages his completed work as a 'Casa de tiempo y de silencio',[2] yoking together the concept of absolute Time, the timelessness of eternal Time, with the ideal of silence. But what does he mean by silence? Is it that silence which is the only recourse left in the face of the sheer inadequacy of language? The kind of silence to which Wittgenstein referred when he declared in his *Tractatus Logico-Philosophicus*: 'What we cannot speak about we must pass over in silence' ('Wovon man nicht reden kann, darüber muß man schweigen')?[3] In his *Diario poético*, Juan Ramón wrote the following: 'Si yo hubiero podido desenvolver, conservar, imprimir mi obra poética, en la forma, en una de las formas soñadas y pensadas, durante tantos años, por mi fe y mi duda, hubiese regalado, a lo último, un libro en blanco, con el título *Poesía No Escrita.*[14]

What emerges from this is the fact that Juan Ramón conceives silence — the unwritten page or book — as a *goal*, as the desirable and proper culmination of the poetic process. Here, there is no question of that negative defeat suggested by Wittgenstein. For the silence to which Juan Ramón refers is the silence of Perfection; a silence which does not occur *before* any attempt at expression, but which is attained as a result of and conclusion to a whole commitment to expression. His particular brand of silence will be that of the unending soundless reverberation and resonance of 'la vibrante palabra muda, / la inmanente'.[5] It is the kind of silence which Mallarmé likewise apprehended and which he came as close to evoking as possible, within the poetic frame. Through a technique of abolition and of negation, silence alone remains in his sonnet 'Une dentelle s'abolit'. But it is a miraculous silence for, out of the vacant and dormant 'mandore' issues a music whose very fabric is that same silence. Again, it is this strange silence, precious and perfect, which pervades the poem 'Sainte' and from which the image of the saint, that enigmatic 'musicienne du silence', draws her unheard melodies. In 'La musique et les lettres', Mallarmé expresses his own aspiration to silence: 'Je réclame la restitution, au silence impartial, pour que l'esprit essaie à se rapatrier, de tout — chocs, glissements, les trajectoires illimitées et sûres, tel état opulent aussitôt évasif, une inaptitude délicieuse à finir, ce raccourci, ce trait — l'appareil; moins le tumulte des sonorités, transfusibles, encore, en du songe' (*OC*, p.649). This music, bereft of sound and rendered into silence, is none other than poetry itself, the 'musicienne du silence' of 'Sainte'. That this silence is indeed transcendental, released from contingency and unfettered from the accidents of Time, is indicated by Mallarmé's frequent use of epithets such as 'impartial', 'juste' and 'égal'. Thus, for example, in 'Variations sur un sujet', he says: 'Evoquer, dans une ombre exprès, l'objet tu, par des mots allusifs, jamais directs, se réduisant à du silence égal, comporte tentative proche de créer' (*OC*, p.400).

The silence to which both Juan Ramón and Mallarmé aspire is attainable only through and beyond expression, for it is situated, as it were, on the farther side of language. It is a Utopian silence. If this is not borne carefully in mind, Juan Ramón's statement that his ultimate wish was to render a blank book with the title *Unwritten Poetry*, made without either humorous or ironic intent, would border perilously on the grotesque — perhaps even on 'lo esperpéntico'. (Comparable, in the medium of visual art, might be the humorous invention of the avant-garde painting entitled 'Charcoal in a black tunnel'.) It is imperative therefore to remember that the blank book, the perfected silence, is a dream. A direction. Similarly, if the extradordinary paradox of Mallarmé is that he spent years in the mental conception of an inexistent Book of the Universe at the expense of actual poetic achievement, it is precisely because it was this *direction* which for him most mattered. A path that led above and beyond expression to the silence of pure thought — that 'cime menaçante d'absolu, devinée dans le départ des nuées là-haut, fulgurante, nue, seule: au delà et que personne ne semble devoir atteindre' (*OC*, p.546). The hesitation and immobility which Mallarmé suffered in the face of his own expression of the ineffable is the penalty of the gulf interposed by reality: the reality of those 'chocs' and 'glissements' mentioned earlier, which he sought to efface. The Utopian silence, that 'trop lucide hantise', is recognised equally by Juan Ramón and by Mallarmé for what it is: an *orientation* towards the Ideal. In their single-minded pursuit of that sublime course, Stéphane Mallarmé and Juan Ramón Jiménez are outstanding among poets.

In her book *The Aesthetics of Stéphane Mallarmé in Relation to His Public*, Paula Gilbert Lewis has pointed out that Mallarmé's desire was for a 'pure, silent, and immediate communication among men where true thoughts would be neither misrepresented nor obscured by the imperfections of people and language'.[6] In 'Crise de vers', Mallarmé observes: 'Les langues imparfaites en cela que plusieurs, manque la suprême: penser étant écrire sans accessoires, ni chuchotement mais tacite encore l'immortelle parole, la diversité, sur terre, des idiomes empêche personne de proférer les mots qui, sinon se trouveraient, par une frappe unique, elle-même matériellement la vérité' (*OC*, pp.363-4). Bearing this in mind, let us turn to a poem by Juan Ramón Jiménez. 'Eloquence of silence' might indeed be an adequate title for the following untitled poem from *Eternidades*:

> Me respondió en lo que no dijo,
> a lo que, sin decirlo, dije,
> afirmando en un no lo no pedido
> por mi pregunta falsa.

> ¡Sentí que lo más puro
> se me cuajaba en su alegría,
> cual si esa rosa que el rócio yerto
> hace en la rosa suave,
> la suplantara para siempre!

(LP, p.660)

The first stanza is precisely concerned with the speech of silence, which is perfect communication far transcending ordinary language. How, we may ask, has Juan Ramón been able to convey such a silence when words alone, indicative of sound and utterance, are at his disposal for the task? He has achieved it by that same process of abolition through negation which I have already alluded to in Mallarmé. The not-ness of the reply ('me respondió en lo que *no* dijo'); the not-ness of the ensuing affirmative ('afirmando en un *no*') to the not-ness of the request ('lo *no* pedido'): all these are positive communicating strands interwoven and comprehended by the two interlocutors, and they are authentic. In fact they are more perfectly so than their vocal utterance could ever be. The full realisation of this truth is brought out only at the very end of the stanza, with the brilliant introduction and positioning of the adjective 'falsa'. The significance of this word is that it throws into relief the fact that throughout the entire non-conversation, the sole pronouncement lacking in authenticity is the one which has actually been given utterance: the verbally articulated 'pregunta' which evidently initiated this silent intercourse. Thus the falsity of language as communication is denounced, by contrast with the absolute integrity and truth of the speech of silence. The perfect eloquence of the unsaid is then, in the second stanza, translated on to the plane of pure aesthetics and sensorial Beauty, incarnate in the symbol of the rose.

Mallarmé recognises a dual condition in the word, 'brut ou immédiat ici, là essentiel' (*OC*, p.368). The raw word 'a trait à la réalité des choses', and narration and description present things before us; whereas the essential word, which is pure suggestivity, causes them to retreat, to disappear. The apprehension of things in and through their absence is the privilege of thought, and so for Mallarmé the pure word is thought. In his poem 'Nada', Juan Ramón declares: 'A tu abandono opongo la elevada / torre de mi divino pensamiento;' and closes with the line: '...¡y soy yo sólo el pensamiento mío!' (*LP*, p.19). For Juan Ramón, thought seeks the purity of flame, and in *Belleza* he refers to his Work, the creative Thought *par excellence*, in these terms:

¡Qué puro el fuego cuando se ejercita
— ¡corazón, hierro , Obra! —
¡Cómo salen de claras
sus llamas, del trabajo rojo y negro!
¡Con qué alegre belleza se relame
con sus lenguas de espíritu,
en el aire por él trasparentado
— ¡corazón, Obra, hierro! — ,
después de la pelea y la victoria!

(*LP*, p.1011)

The poetic language is the silent language of thought; and the idea, the Mallarméan 'notion pure', becomes the poet's sole concern, since it is that which liberates things from their material contingency. Poetry, 'proche l'idée', inclines to silence. 'Parler', for Mallarmé, 'n'a trait à la réalité des choses que commercialement' (*OC*, p.366), and it is his lifelong endeavour to find himself 'face à face avec l'Indicible ou le Pur, la poésie sans les mots' *OC*, p.389). It is this realm of the ineffable which is sought by Juan Ramón Jiménez too, a realm in which the voice of man is at its most naked, freed from practical — and partial — meaning. For Juan Ramón, the poetic concept of 'depuración' offers a means to that ultimate goal. The expression of the ineffable requires a perfect transparency, a luminous clarity, in the word; and this can be achieved only by the strict eradication of all that is superfluous. 'Cultivemos, ante todo, la voluntad de rechazar', he declares in his 'Estética y ética estética'. The same necessity to whittle away and purge is experienced by Mallarmé in the attempt to render the silence of the ineffable: words must be 'comme disséqués, réduits à leurs os et à leurs tendons, soustraits à leur vie ordinaire'. He too writes by expunging, and his statement 'Je n'ai créé mon oeuvre que par élimination' might no less have been pronounced by Juan Ramón.

It could be argued that Juan Ramón's desire to attain the silence of a blank book is none other than a recognition of the finite nature of the printed word and the voicing of his fear of the destructive interference of worldly temporality and the dangers of misinterpretation by posterity. Or indeed it may be that he is contemplating the destruction of thought itself, symbolised in the intuition of the possible death of his Work:

> Tú, así labrada con mi vida ardiente
> hecha diamante para ti;
> tú, con tanto soñar perfeccionada,
> como una estrella por los siglos...
> ¡Qué pálido pensar que tú, obra bella,
> te has de morir, lo mismo
> que se muere de siglos una estrella...![7]

Ultimately, however, silence is for Juan Ramón a
transcendence of language, a triumphant state, reached only
after apprenticeship and mastery of the word. It is that
'langue sans paroles' sought by Mallarmé. Not silence itself,
but the articulation of silence in Eternity. The following poem,
the first of the collection called *Belleza,* answers the poet's
own fears of the finite character of the Work and is a
reassuring affirmation that, veritably, the Work will be that
'Casa de tiempo y de silencio' which Juan Ramón desired:

> Sé que mi Obra es lo mismo
> que una pintura en el aire;
> que el vendaval de los tiempos
> la borrará toda, como
> si fuese perfume o música;
> que quedará sólo de ella
> — sí arruinado en nóes —
> al gran silencio solar,
> la ignorancia de la luna.
>
> — No, no; ella, un día, será
> (borrada) existencia inmensa,
> desveladora virtud;
> será, como el antesol,
> imposible norma bella;
> sinfín de angustioso afán,
> mina de escelso secreto... —
> ¡Mortal flor mía inmortal
> reina del aire de hoy!

(LP, p.985)

That 'hoy' is the today of Eternity.

The concept of the relation of space and silence is realised
by Mallarmé in 'Un coup de dés', where the distribution of the
printed text allows the blank paper to intervene in such a way
that phrases fade into its whiteness as sound into silence. This
physical structure, visible to the eye, of a language of silence

spatially oriented, is first and foremost intellectual. For the importance which Mallarmé accords to these 'blancs' or spaces between word-groups is, as he himself puts it, that 'l'armature intellectuelle du poëme se dissimule et tient — a lieu — dans l'espace qui isole les strophes et parmi le blanc du papier: significatif silence qu'il n'est pas moins beau de composer, que les vers' (*OC*, p.872). The measure of the silent text of 'Un coup de dés' is taken by Paul Valéry when he compares it with the 'texte' of 'l'univers silencieux'. And again: 'Il a essayé, pensai-je, d'élever enfin une page à la puissance du ciel étoilé!'[8] There is no question that Juan Ramón, too, fully apprehended both the aspiration behind 'Un coup de dés' and its significance. In the notes for the course on *Modernismo* which he gave in 1953, he refers to the French poet: 'Mallarmé escribió: "una jugada de dados no abolirá jamás el azar". Yendo con Valéry [le decía] "Yo quisiera hacer un libro que fuera como las estrellas en el firmamento". Idea abstracta. Dentro de la cabeza de un poeta puede residir la poesía [sin necesidad de escribirse] como [las estrellas y] constelaciones [en el firmamento]. Idea cósmica.'[9] Or as he expresses it in terms of his own similar experience, in a poem which concludes *Piedra y Cielo*:

¡Quisiera que mi libro
fuese, como es el cielo por la noche,
todo verdad presente, sin historia.

Que, como él, se diera en cada instante,
todo, con todas sus estrellas;...

¡Temblor, relumbre, música
presentes y totales!
¡Temblor, relumbre, música en la frente
— cielo del corazón — del libro puro!

(*LP*, p.828)

It is in his own 'Ciudad del cielo', in a night 'brillante / de

limpieza primera' that Juan Ramón detects the 'total murmullo verdeoscuro, / alrededor de la inmortal ausencia' (*LP*, p.1145). Indeed, for both poets there is an intrinsically spatial quality about the silence of absolute poetry. If Mallarmé speaks of the opulent silence of words, as if to give it geographic location, or coaxes that audible silence out of the terrain of absence, no less does Juan Ramón relate the sounding silence of perfection and of mystery to remote places, stressing absence and distance as its hallmark. The adjective 'lejano' and the adverb 'lejos' recur time and time again; the stars 'allá en el cielo, / conversan lejanamente'[10] and 'Lo que llora... llora más allá, en el mar; / llora más allá, en la aurora'.[11] As the critic Fernand Verhesen has pointed out, it is the interior space of the poetic word which reflects and accords with the dimensions of the cosmos: 'Más que las palabras dichas, las cuales pudieran cerrar sobre ellas mismas el mundo del poeta, importa ese rumor de caravanas que ensancha el espacio en que la palabra no pertenece realmente sino al silencio expresado, al puente sonoro que se tiende entre un alma y otra alma situada en algún sitio del mundo donde nada *que no sea este canje de resonancias interiores puede encontrar sitio*.'[12] The reference here is to a poem from the 1912 collection entitled *Pureza*, the central part of which reads:

> Es cual una inminencia
> de algo infinito y trastornado,
> que, aunque viene muy lejos, ya se siente
> llorar, reír — nacer —, a nuestro lado...
> Pensativa inconciencia
> de un remoto rumor de caravanas,
> que sobre tierra oyera amedrentado
> centinela... Palabras ya cercanas,
> ya lejanas,[13]

It is out of the absence of things that Mallarmé evokes their essential definition: 'Je dis: une fleur! et hors de l'oubli où ma voix relègue aucun contour, en tant que quelque chose

d'autre que les calices sus, musicalement se lève, l'idée même et suave, l'absente de tous bouquets' (*OC*, p.368). And it is out of the silence and the void that he conjures the sound of the poetic word. The sonnet 'Ses purs ongles' is a fine illustration:

Ses purs ongles très haut dédiant leur onyx,
L'Angoisse, ce minuit, soutient, Pampadophore,
Maint rêve vespéral brûlé par le Phénix
Que ne recueille pas de cinéraire amphore

Sur les crédences, au salon vide: nul ptyx,
Aboli bibelot d'inanité sonore,
(Car le Maître est allé puiser des pleurs au Styx
Avec ce seul objet dont le Néant s'honore).

Mais proche la croisée au nord vacante, un or
Agonise selon peut-être le décor
Des licornes ruant du feu contre une nixe,

Elle, défunte nue en le miroir, encor
Que, dans l'oubli fermé par le cadre, se fixe
De scintillations sitôt le septuor.

(*OC*, pp.68-9)[14]

The absent seashell, doubly non-existent for it is both 'nul' and 'aboli', is a silent void, an 'inanité'. Yet mysteriously it is a sonorous hollow, its resonance parallel to the utterance of the poet whereby the void of the universe is overcome. This sound issuing out of the silent emptiness is evoked by Mallarmé through the internal interplay of words: a technique to which he alludes in 'Variations sur un sujet': 'L'oeuvre pure implique la disparition élocutoire du poëte, qui cède l'initiative aux mots, par le heurt de leur inégalité mobilisés; ils s'allument de reflets réciproques comme une virtuelle traînée de feux sur des pierreries, remplaçant la respiration perceptible en l'ancien souffle lyrique ou la direction personnelle enthousiaste de la phrase' (*OC*, p.366). If we take

the second stanza of the sonnet as an example, this kind of reciprocal echoing can be seen at work between the first and second lines, in which 'aboli' reflects 'nul', 'inanité' reflects 'vide', and 'bibelot' reflects 'ptyx'. Again there is mutual interaction between the fourth and second lines of this same stanza: 'seul objet' echoes 'aboli bibelot', 'Néant' doubles with 'inanité', and 's'honore' reflects 'sonore' through the parallel of shell and poet. The echo both of rhyme and meaning creates this taut network. The rare structural rhyme pattern of the sonnet too, with its interplay of masculine and feminine endings: 'yx — ore', 'or — ixe', evokes a certain audibility amid the silence. It is that 'mirage interne des mots mêmes' of which Mallarmé spoke in his 1868 letter to Henri Cazalis which achieves the effect. Each word reflects and resumes a preceding one while simultaneously heralding a successor; each line mirrors a former line. Thus the sonnet in its entirety is a system of oscillations, now back, now forward. Out of the void of 'une nuit faite d'absence', as Mallarmé himself described this sonnet, emerges the vibrancy of the poetic word.

Returning to Juan Ramón, I think it is important to remember the title which he gave to his 1908 collection of poems, namely *La soledad sonora*. For San Juan de la Cruz, in his *Cántico espiritual*, the immanent music that inhabits silence ('la música callada') and the immanent sound within the heart of solitude ('la soledad sonora') are attributes of the 'Amado', the Godhead. Juan Ramón adopted this expression of the Divine in order to express his own — profane — conception of the silent ineffable. In his dedicatory poem he addresses solitude thus:

> ¡Qué latiera, en un sueño, tu corazón sonoro
> sobre mi corazón sediento de ideales;
> que mi palabra fuesa la palabra de oro
> de tus inagotables y puros manantiales!
>
> (*PLP*, p.903)

The golden word is the ideal word, the word of silence which is perfect expression. And so the exhortation to a wordless purity rings out:

> ¡Canción mía,
> canta, antes de cantar;
> da a quien te mire antes de leerte,
> tu emoción y tu gracia;
> emánate de ti, fresca y fragante!

(LP, p.697)

It is of course an impossibility. In a letter to Luis Cernuda, written from Washington, D.C. in July 1943, Juan Ramón speaks of his ideal — and it is noteworthy that he does so in terms of a cherished dream: 'Creo que en la escritura poética, como en la pintura o la música, el asunto es la retórica, "lo que queda", la poesía. Mi ilusión ha sido siempre ser más cada vez poeta de "lo que queda", hasta llegar un día a no escribir. Escribir no es sino preparación para no escribir, para el estado de gracia poético, intelectual o sensitivo. Ser uno poesía y no poeta'. The nearest approximation to that silence of the ineffable forever remains 'un no sé qué que quedan balbuciendo', the tentativeness of a stammer. But indeed, it is ironically at this very point, when the word becomes impotent to express the poet's feelings, that the poet is actually in possession of something worthy of revelation to other men. With great conviction this has been stated by Ramón del Valle-Inclán: '¡Qué mezquino, qué torpe, qué difícil balbuceo el nuestro', he says, 'para expresar este deleite de lo inefable...! Hay algo que será eternamente hermético e imposible para las palabras.' And yet arrival at this recognition of the failure of words is a vital and requisite stage in the poetic process for, as he continues, 'tal aridez es el comienzo del estado de gracia'.[15] It is another way of expressing what Juan Ramón implies in his enigmatic avowal that writing is but the preparation for the state of poetic grace.

What ultimately bears witness to the success of a poet in

nearing that state is — paradoxically of course — the written evidence. In Mallarmé we have a very small corpus of poetic work compared with the perhaps ironically voluminous output of Juan Ramón. It is the 'suprasiderales únicas melodías' emerging from Mallarmé's 'divino secreto del silencio' that Rubén Darío calls to our attention in his tribute written on the poet's death. And it is significantly with these words that the Nicaraguan closes his homage: 'hé aquí que traza un signo nuevo, sobre el lago en silencio, el Cisne que comprende'.[16] It is doubtful that Juan Ramón underwent direct influence from Mallarmé or from the example of that 'alfabeto enigmático de la poesía pura' which he attributed to him.[17] But that he understood and appreciated the direction of his endeavour is unquestionable. And the written evidence of Juan Ramón's own great 'Obra' confirms his continued advance towards the golden silence.

NOTES

1. Stéphane Mallarmé, 'Variations sur un sujet', *Œuvres complètes*, ed. Henri Mondor and G. Jean-Aubry (Paris, 1945) p.360. Future references to this edition are included in the text in the abbreviated form *OC*.

2. Juan Ramón Jiménez, 'Estética y ética estética', "Ideolojía lírica", *Pájinas escojidas; prosa*, selected by Ricardo Gullón (Madrid, 1970) p.147.

3. Ludwig Wittgenstein, *Tractatus Logico-Philosophicus*, German text with translation by D.F. Pears and B.F. McGuinness; introd. Bertrand Russell (London, 1961) p.151.

4. Juan Ramón Jiménez, *Diario poético*, 1936-37 (fragmentos), *Poética*, I, (number dedicated to Juan Ramón Jiménez), La Plata, 1943.

5. Juan Ramón Jiménez, 'Poeta y palabra', *La estación total, Libros de poesía*, ed. Agustín Caballero (Madrid, 1972) pp.1171-2. Future references to this edition are included in the text in the abbreviated form *LP*.

6. Paula Gilbert Lewis, *The Aesthetics of Stéphane Mallarmé in Relation to His Public* (London, 1976) p.169.

7. Juan Ramón Jiménez, 'De Siglos', *Rueca*, Mexico, V, 1954, p.3.

8. Paul Valéry, 'Le coup de dés', *Variété II* (Paris, 1930) p.181.

9. Juan Ramón Jiménez, *El modernismo, notas de un curso (1953)*, ed. R. Gullón (Madrid-Mexico-Buenos Aires, 1962) p.94.

10. Juan Ramón Jiménez, *Pastorales, Primeros libros de poesía*, ed. Francisco Garfias (Madrid, 1973) pp.549-50.

11. Ibid., pp.543-4. Future reference to this edition is included in the text in the abbreviated form *PLP*.

12. Fernand Verhesen, 'Tiempo y espacio en la obra de Juan Ramón Jiménez', *La Torre*, V, núms. 19-20, julio-diciembre 1957, p.103.

13. Juan Ramón Jiménez, *Tercera antolojía poética*, ed. Eugenio Florit (Madrid, 1970) pp.381-2.

14. My analysis of this sonnet is based on the exegesis by E. Noulet in *Vingt poèmes de Stéphane Mallarmé* (Geneva, 1967) pp.177-92.

15. Ramón del Valle-Inclán, *La lámpara maravillosa, Obras completas* (Madrid, 1944), I, p.780.

16. Rubén Darío, 'Stéphane Mallarmé', *El mercurio de América*, Buenos Aires, Oct. 1898.

17. Juan Ramón Jiménez, letter to Alfonso Reyes written Nov. 11, 1923. In Alfonso Reyes, *Mallarmé entre nosotros* (Mexico, 1955) p.31.

Sticks and Stones: the Weaponry of Words in *Vous les entendez?*[1]

Valerie Minogue

'Sticks and stones may break my bones — But names will never hurt me...' The well-known playground jingle testifies sharply if paradoxically to the very real effectiveness of 'names' as offensive weapons. The atmosphere of Nathalie Sarraute's fictional world is thick with 'naming' aggressions and the defensive manœuvres they produce. In the Sarrautean world 'name', of course, must be taken in a very wide sense, to embrace not only proper and common nouns but even personal pronouns — the use of the collective 'vous' can be neatly damaging![2] All may serve a defining and consequently wounding or caressing purpose.

To look at the function and operation of the 'Sticks and stones' generated by language in the Sarrautean novel is simultaneously to look at the tension between language as an agreed meeting-place and language as a creative effort. On the one hand we have the language of the commonplace — 'la présence de tout le monde en moi' as Sartre remarked in his preface to *Portrait d'un inconnu*[3] — and on the other, the effort to formulate things anew in response to the conviction that, as Proust put it, 'ce qui était clair avant nous n'est pas à nous'.[4] The old 'clarities', indeed, whenever emotions are involved, are usually the product of stereotypes and moral clichés embedded in our language. The merest word is often quite sufficient to set off a whole emotional melodrama. We can, like Gisèle in *Le Planétarium*, responding to her father's description of a celebrated writer as 'une jolie femme', develop the formula.[5] The strength of 'names' lies in such formulae and the patterns of typologies and roles they so conveniently summarise. The effort to reach new perceptions means steering a course through old ones that have not only the might of apparent Truth, but the almost irresistible force of congruence with deep-seated stirrings of feeling.

Vous les entendez? offers a particularly fruitful field for this discussion since all the language of which it is composed may be seen as expressing, with varying degrees of irony and exaggeration, the tenuous movements that occur in a father's heart and mind in response to a specific situation. It is the moment when his aesthetic enjoyment of a small stone figure, which he is admiring in the company of a visiting friend, is disturbed by the sound of his children's laughter. Innocent laughter? — the 'rires cristallins' of children laughing out of sheer exuberance? Or is the laughter a mocking defiance and rejection of the father and his friend, joined in reverence before their little stone idol? Is it indeed a rejection of the father's entire mode of life with its established values, its hierarchies, its secure order? In the reverberations of the laughter, the novel sounds out the father, the children, the relationship between them, and the ambivalent relation between Life (spontaneity and vitality? or anarchy and vulgarity?) and Art (the mature values of civilisation? or the dead hand of conformism?).

For Sarraute, the very language in which inner responses are formulated is suspect, and the novel focuses our attention on the encounter between experience (what Sarraute calls 'le ressenti'[6]) and verbal formulation with all its hidden purposes and perils. We see efforts to use language as a 'clean' and neutral vehicle, but we also see highly-charged language sparking off emotional explosions.

In spoken exchanges, is it the speaker who, with more or less awareness, throws charged material into the discourse? Or is it the hearer who, by his own emotional charge, creates the weaponry of words? Or is it language itself, with its uneasy compromise between public and private, that generates a charge in speaker and listener alike? For Sarraute, it is the exploration of the virtualities of language in its relations with the non-verbal that is of prime interest. She is not concerned with the personal psychology of speaker or 'receiver' but with the inter-personal area — the peripeteia of communication and response, whether verbal or non-verbal, spoken or unspoken. Vague unformulated feelings latch on to available words or phrases that give them weight and form, while a tremor of tone or the merest muscular flicker may be enlarged into a whole scenario. Words exercise a polarising function, offering crude dramatic structures, moral simplifications, granting emotion the momentary relief of appearing in congruent but simplified form. Basic feelings like humiliation, beatitude or righteous indignation surge up with crude clarity, briefly shedding the ambiguity and contradictions that characterise inner experience. A critical self-consciousness, however, soon restores the balance and returns to the turmoil and uncertainty of experience.

Whence comes this polarising force in words? Though there are deeper sources that will concern us later, it largely derives from stereotypes both social and cultural, from proverbs, commonplaces, and other repositories of universal wisdom, whose moral simplicity makes them peculiarly attractive and effective. Sometimes too it may derive from more personal typologies whose force depends on their correspondence with personal fears and sensitivities. The seizing of such images on the wing is usually accompanied by a deep sense of certainty — a certainty based on the recognition of familiar 'names'. Such certainty is an indicator of sensitivity, but no yardstick of accurate perception. What was intended may differ in varying degrees from what is communicated and the variation may derive on the one hand from unconscious impulses betrayed in the tone, gestures or words of the speaker and/or on the other hand, from the grid of fears, hopes and preoccupations through which the receiver receives and interprets.

Neutrality is virtually impossible: amorphous and unformulated feelings quickly take on gross shapes when they wrap themselves around the crude but magnetic structures lurking beneath the apparently bland surfaces of everyday words. No words are safe in this world of quivering sentience: all are capable of becoming 'names' that are at least as effective as sticks and stones. The effort to formulate experience accurately and precisely is a prodigious effort of creation, for individual expression is constantly invaded by the discourse of others. The language of others, the common language, is after all the only language available, and the creative effort involves scrutinising, rejecting, selecting, juxtaposing, and making new constructs out of old building-blocks.[7] And that indeed is the effort represented in the battle with words in the pages of *Vous les entendez?*[8]

Many of the words and phrases that beset the father in *Vous les entendez?* derive from commonplaces and accepted ideas — ideas from all sides. 'Vivre et laisser vivre' from the tolerant; rage at the 'chenapans' and 'dégénérés' of the younger generation from the Old Guard; 'C'est de leur âge' and 'ça leur passera' from the benign; 'Des goûts et des couleurs' ... 'oui, il ne faut pas demander l'impossible, vouloir la lune...' (81) from the peace-makers; the value of 'la curiosité, le besoin de savoir' (53) from the educators, and a vision of school in terms of 'mornes salles vitrées où des médiocres ingurgitent docilement des bouillies insipides' (54) from those who see education as the suppression of spontaneity and free development — and so on. In the midst of such sayings and slogans the father picks a cautious way, not, however, without falling into excesses of self-castigation ('Je sais, je suis impardonnable, je me méprise, je suis un monstre...' (80)) or outraged vengefulness ('Vite. Menottes. Paniers à salade. Passages à tabac. Pas d'autre argument avec eux.' (94)) or gross self-pity ('étalez vos tripes pour qu'ils s'en nourrissent, ils cracheront dessus, ils saliront tout...' (64)).

Clearly language is potentially dangerous: words create prisons of definition and category, words paralyse. Words threaten that which is free and changing: 'C'est grave d'enfermer dans des catégories rigides, d'étiqueter ce qui est encore fluctuant, changeant...' (51). Yet it is paradoxically words that warn us of the paralysing power of words; it is language that reveals the traps and undercover operations of language. The father shows an acute sensitivity to his own use of language as well as to the language of others: 'Il a été maladroit' (42) he acknowledges, reflecting on his use of the simple word 'Regarde' — 'Il ne fallait surtout pas de ce mot, pas de ce verbe à l'impératif' (43). He retrospectively recognises the implicit demand in his 'casual' comment in an art gallery: 'C'est tout de même rudement beau' (45). It required (but did not receive) a minimal acknowledgement — 'une pure formalité, une brève génuflexion' (45). Self-conscious reflection draws attention to the latent but spiky thrusts of demand or provocation in his words. Phrases uttered at various times lurk around menacingly — papering the mental walls, as it were. The phrase 'ces regards enfiévrés d'intelligence', used in conversation by the children, returns to haunt the father's consciousness, making him guiltily sensitive to his own feverishness or posturing. His consequent self-castigation takes the form of a verbal caricature, based on stereotypes of guilt: 'pris la main dans le sac, en flagrant délit, se reboutonnant encore tout échauffé, se redressant, se tournant vers nous, toussotant pour gagner du temps' (137). In the 'reddition complète' that follows this humiliating vision, it is by his vocabulary that the father most clearly indicates submission: 'Et cette balade?' he asks, 'comment ça s'est passé?' (137). The use of 'balade' rather than 'promenade' indicates a 'climbing down' to reach the right idiom.

Within the family code, the direction and purpose of words is instantly subject to examination and some words are instantly recognisable as 'special agents'. They have become, perhaps, attached to recurrent sequences of discourse or entrenched attitudes (the phrase 'Nous connaissons tous la musique' often accompanies such familiar passages). The word 'goût' instantly condemns the user: 'Quel est le mot qui révèle aussitôt chez qui l'emploie que la chose que le mot désigne lui manque?' (169) runs the mocking riddle. 'Facile' is another word to beware: it is one of the older generation's 'mots garde-fous, un de leurs mots chien de berger' (179). With such density of signs and meanings it is not surprising that 'messages' are not always clear, and rarely what they seem to be. Transmission and reception are equally liable to distortion.

The conflicts centring on the word 'collectionneur' well illustrate some of these general points as well as pointing to the way that individual instances of verbal clash become polarised by fundamental oppositions established by the novel. The word is, of course, semantically associated with the question of the relation between life and art, the question focused by the stone animal and the children's laughter. Asked about the provenance of the sculpture which he has been showing to his visitor, the father explains that it belonged to his father before him, adding 'Moi, vous savez, je ne suis pas un collectionneur. Je dirais même qu'au contraire...' (14). Even as he makes the remark, he recognises it as an ignoble (and futile) attempt to abdicate responsibility for his possession. A further effort is outlined in which he now dissociates himself from the visitor and tries to convert his remark into an expression of solidarity with the children: 'Je crois qu'il ne partira jamais... Vous avez vu comme il m'a regardé, quand j'ai dit que je n'avais rien d'un collectionneur?' (18). Emphatic reiterations ('Moi... je dois dire que je n'ai jamais été un collectionneur... Jamais, n'est-ce pas? Au contraire.' (22)) underline his fear of the threatening classification: 'Qu'ils ne le mettent pas là, pas dans le même sac, pas dans la même section' (22). The name 'collectionneur' isolates him from the children, links him indeed with a band of hoarders and aesthetes — 'tous ces vieux enfants aux visages extatiques ... ceux qui cherchent, fouinent, s'emparent'. His rather comic 'au contraire' is in fact a claim to freedom from the cupidity associated with 'collectors': 'de savoir que ça m'appartient, voyez-vous... je dois dire que ça ternit, en quelque sorte, oui, ça rend moins parfait... mon bonheur' (24). The hesitations here betray the self-consciousness, the fear of falling into the grotesque, while the reassuring interpolated 'oui' indicates that this statement, under examination, does seem to tally with experience and lies within the bounds of the decently sayable. He then struggles on, trying to clarify his position — 'ce qu'il préfère' — and here he comes unstuck as his attempt at self-definition meets the mocking batteries of self-criticism. What he really prefers, he now reflects, is only safety and certainty. He is a coward and a parasite, a pretentious 'connaisseur' claiming exquisite sensibility.

The throwing-off of one name leads only to other equally undesirable ones. Anxious self-consciousness reveals posturings latent in his language and seems to justify the children's laughter as a well-deserved punishment. Now all he wants is to be forgiven and accepted. He will utter 'les mots de passe qui lui permettront de passer dans leur camp: Alors, et cette promenade?'; then, as the friend extends his hand towards the stone animal, he extends his hand to the children's dog, the living animal — 'la bonne grosse vie qu'on saisit à pleines mains' (32). In comparison with the dog, the stone figure is only 'une bête grossièrement taillée dans une matière grumuleuse, d'un gris sale: La ligne du dos trop droite: Les pattes disproportionnées... trop courtes?... trop écartées?... Mais toi... toi... mon joli...' (33). These manœuvres, despite instant classification as 'ces jeux suspects', carry him on to the point where he is tempted to dash the stone figure against the wall. His allegiance to the carved figure returns, however, and he recalls his friend's edict that it is 'digne de figurer dans un musée' (40) though he will, of course, swing back to a mode of self-accusation as the emotional tug-of-war continues.

The menace of 'collectionneur' is that it cuts him off from the children and imprisons him in a category that gives art the ascendancy over life. It indicates a mode which prizes a stone animal more than a live dog, a mode that makes the visitor seem 'ce noble ami venu en toute innocence' (45) and the children 'des oreilles ennemies... des yeux ennemis' (45). A shift of allegiance will make the friend the 'étranger', the 'intrus', and the children and the dog will be once more 'la bonne grosse vie'. Whether a man is called 'collector' or not hardly seems much of a subject in itself — this surely is a name that shouldn't hurt him? But that name and the response to it take the reader into a ding-dong tussle of emotions and values, apprehending the tugs of emotional attachment and self-definition in the very act of speech and in the encounter with the language of formulation.

Within the 'collectionneur' framework, the descriptive phrase 'digne de figurer dans un musée' (38) ushers in a further dramatic sequence. It at once polarises the father's sense of the value of the figure and offers the balm of reassurance. But it also hardens his attitudes and provokes a sense of exasperated outrage at any dissent. Those who refuse proper respect must be 'des dégénérés. Des abrutis...' (40): the children, in this light, become 'ces petits privilégiés, boudant les trésors' (41). However, in a surge of warm feeling for the children ('vous intacts, vous purs, innocents... poulains, agneaux, petits chats...' (68)) the friend's remark will seem a pretentious piece of attitudinising that invited and justified deflating laughter:

> Chaque mot est à retenir. Chaque mot — une perle. Comment a-t-il dit ça? 'Ça mériterait' ... la plus haute distinction. Résultat de la plus sûre sélection. 'De figurer'... le mot à lui seul... mais a-t-on besoin entre nous de commenter? ... 'Dans un musée' ... parmi les sarcophages, les momies, les frises du Parthénon, près de la Vénus de Milo ... devant laquelle autrefois les gens entraient en transe, parfois le choc était si fort qu'ils perdaient

connaissance... (69)

The friend's remark has become, to borrow a phrase from Celia Britton, 'less a communication than an object in its own right',[9] an object to be turned over, valued and revalued. If such repetitions and revaluations devalue communication, they do, however, show the freedom of the self to align itself in a number of different ways to any proffered verbal 'object', and thus escape from the prison of automatic responses. But the search for the truth of experience, whether for inward apprehension or for communication, remains a perilous venture, for words constantly threaten to deform feeling. In moments of deeply-felt experience, the father rejects words and their fixing power. In a moment of intense communion with the stone figure, he briefly casts about for words to express what he feels emanating from it: 'Un rayonnement? Un halo? Une aura?' But at once he thrusts aside the words that dress his experience in false costume: 'Les mots hideux touchent cela un instant et sont rejetés aussitôt' (131). The negation of language becomes a mode of positive expression.[10]

Celia Britton sees Sarraute's novels as 'emphasising the point that language is not an integrated element of the self. It comes from society in the first place and remains a tool which we can manipulate for social purposes but never really assume as our own...'.[11] In the Sarrautean world, she argues, in a passage worth quoting at some length,

> ...the position of language as a social institution which has become cut off from the individual subject deprives him not only of a means of authentic communication but also of the possibility of self-definition.[12]

Dr Britton goes on to argue that Sarraute reduces characters to 'a set of empty mechanisms who react to external stimuli in a perfectly predictable manner' and cites, in support of this view, the following passage from *Vous les*

entendez?:

> C'est vraiment étonnant, admirable, comme une fois déclenché cela se déroule inéluctablement avec la précision d'un mécanisme d'horlogerie minutieusement réglé. Il n'y a jamais de ratés. Il suffit d'une première impulsion, si légère soit-elle... mais rien ici ne peut jamais être trop léger... pour que tous les fins rouages exactement imbriqués les uns dans les autres se mettent en branle. (29-30)

This is followed by the comment: 'Such a conception of the self is already implicit in Sarraute's notion of *tropismes*, but it can be seen more specifically as a necessary correlate of the fact that the self has no language'.[13] But the words quoted here from Sarraute's text in no way represent a 'conception of the self'. They are merely a 'metaphorisation' of a brief inner movement, an ironic recognition of helplessness before a trivial but unstoppable action — the picking up by the visitor of the stone animal, which indeed takes place with clockwork precision, If here the action is seen in terms of a perfectly-regulated mechanism, it is expressed a few lines further on in the same paragraph as a supernatural intervention: 'Quel mauvais sort le pousse? Quel démon s'amuse à jouer cette farce?' (30) The mechanistic view has no more authority than the supernatural one, and neither view represents a conception of the self. Both are metaphoric expressions of an instant of distressed helplessness and both, by virtue of being both exaggerated and self-contradictory, are ironic. To ignore the irony is to ignore the possibility of freedom which the distancing of irony provides. Stereotypes and automatic reactions may unfurl within the inner self, and stereotyped reactions may be attributed to others, but all are submitted to an ironic and critical gaze. One might well ask why, if Sarraute's 'characters' are empty and predictable, it is necessary to imagine so many possible reactions in such diverse modes, and why it proves so impossible to find any point of rest or certainty in the manifold possibilities. The self is not 'empty': it is full of thoughts, feelings and emotions, and it treats language with caution, sensing at all points the treacherousness of instantly available language and the extreme difficulty of making language coincide with felt experience. As Dr Britton very perceptively remarks, 'salvation... can come only from the reappropriation of language, by making it true to our individual subjective perception of reality. This transformation of language is the main creative project presented in the novels.'[14]

Vous les entendez? itself enacts the drama of formulation and communication which is the substance of its peripeteia. Each word emerges into an atmosphere vibrant with resistance and the threat of reinterpretation, vibrant too with eager responses that enlarge, emphasise and move far from the initial effort. The whole text develops the unrollings of resistances and alliances that ripple out from each 'mise en mots', and it moves through expansions and rejections to create a fine and almost invisible balance — a sort of balance in filigree — that centres on concern for the truth of experience. This provides the central axis that controls extravagances, rejects distortions, and returns inexorably to the tentative mode.

Sarraute's characters endlessly pursue freedom in the very processes of articulation. This involves an attentive exploration of the 'formulae' latent in instantly available language: such exploration and self-correction ultimately provide a means of escape from the pre-articulated fixed forms in which they are otherwise likely to be trapped. Freedom in the Sarrautean world is battle with words and fixity. Battle for the novelist and battle for all the various selves that merge with one another and speak with each other's voices — as we all do. It is a combat in which irony and humour play an important role. The stereotypes and posturings that burst from the words in the very process of formulation are not allowed to take command. Enlarged and dramatised, they show their colours, and are engaged by opposing forces — the sequences of conflicting attitudes represent effectively the conflicting forces acting upon and within the father's inner self. They show his failures and defeats, his transitory alliances, but above all they show movement, refusal of fixity. Beneath the armour-plated words, trails of dots suggest the quiverings of a feeling self, struggling for its freedom, struggling indeed for self-knowledge. Besieged he may be, but he is neither empty nor mechanistic. He does not find clear solutions nor make profound moral decisions, but maintains precarious equilibrium in the midst of contradictions: he goes on sifting in his shifting world.

There is comedy in the desperateness of some of the responses he projects, but each movement of feeling and each choice of word is charged with significance by its relation to a set of basic polarities: guilt and innocence, Heaven and Hell, love and rage, life and death. The very formulation of the disturbance caused by the children's laughter is therefore necessarily subjected to anxious scrutiny. The adverb 'sournoisement' which slips into his mind in the train of a mindless burst of indignation gives the father just the word he needs to describe the laughter: 'sournois': 'Voilà qui est de taille. Voilà qui peut lutter contre innocents. Contre frais... Rires sournois ... Sournois. Ça tout le monde le comprend. Sournois est admis. Sournois est légal.' (195) The verbs 'se dégageaient', 'coulaient' and 'déferlaient' are all rejected in favour of the cooler 'provenaient': 'D'où provenaient... ça c'est propre, aseptisé, parfaitement salubre... d'où provenaient des rires sournois.' At last he finds an acceptable way of expressing his situation: 'des rires sournois ont provoqué chez lui un sentiment bien naturel de malaise.' (196) All is clear and well-defined: briefly these seem strong safe words, but, just as when, earlier, he came close to referring to his children as 'des natures médiocres', the words explode in his face. The apparently 'antiseptic' formulation turns out venomous. 'Sournois' is more powerful than he had thought and the pain it causes seems an illustration of the proverb that 'people in glass-houses shouldn't throw stones', for this 'name' becomes a stone that threatens to shatter the fragile and vulnerable dwelling-place of his fatherly love.

The effort to find a neutral language, by its very evasions and negations, outlines the distress experienced by a man torn between his children and the values he holds dear, between his wish to educate them and his fear of suffocating them. He is constantly divided between what is vital, graceful and natural in the children and fear of their possible mediocrity and lack of culture: imperfections in the loved ones are intolerable. His worry about the children leads him to diagnose 'des lésions', 'une tare héréditaire' and to wish to cure them, then turns into a guilty sense of the inadequacy and demanding nature of his paternal love — in the eyes of an imaginary social worker he becomes his children's 'tortionnaire' (103). To escape the endless alternations of guilt, reproach, tenderness, fear and fury, he turns to an 'outside', a 'legal' view, but no external testimony can withstand internal erosion. There is no accusation of the children that cannot turn to self-blame, no 'fact' impervious to interpretation. Small wonder that when critics complained of what seemed to them the lack of love in this novel, Nathalie Sarraute replied 'il y a même trop d'amour'.[15] Love for Sarraute, as for Proust, is no single monolithic thing but a series of 'intermittences du coeur', of conflicting and contradictory states. The 'trop d'amour' is indicated in the intensity of the internal conflict, by the strength of the sympathy (and empathy) with the children, and by the passion that informs the father's linguistic sensitivity.

If at one level, then, *Vous les entendez?* may be seen as a sounding-out of 'names' and their repercussions, at another level it reaches into regions of universal feeling that make it not so much a metalinguistic exploration as an Everyman drama. It is more than a battle of words, more than a conflict between life and art, and more than a study of the vicissitudes of a specific relationship. It centres on the relation between parent and child; it explores the language they live in and the language that lives in them; it sounds the affective charges of the discourse between parent and child. The novel is so structured as to link the most diverse and minute verbal vicissitudes with fundamental poles of feeling.

The novel opens with the question: 'Vous les entendez?' and we hear 'des rires clairs, transparents...' (8) in an Eden of chintz, white lace and sweet peas in porcelain vases. In that Eden, father, children, dog and visiting friend are all joined in family-album love and harmony and respect for art and beauty. It is that Eden that the children's laughter puts at risk. The children's spontaneity, courage, freedom, vitality may come to seem anarchy, rebellion and vulgarity, while the respect for the values of Art and Beauty may become gutless conformism, withdrawal from life, authoritarianism. The play of archetypes and stereotypes gives powerful body to phantom feelings all parents (indeed most adults) have met at some point or other. The simple concept of 'the thankless child' provides a focus for confused visceral feelings whose truth is, as it were, self-evident. Parents, after all, die and children take over. Children grow up as their parents grow old. There is a primitive melodrama here — Proust indeed outlined it from the guilty filial point of view in *Sentiments filiaux d'un parricide*: 'Au fond, nous vieillissons, nous tuons tout ce qui nous aime par les soucis que nous lui donnons, par l'inquiète tendresse elle-même que nous inspirons et mettons sans cesse en alarme'.[16] Children, however, are inevitably bullied by adults and parents: most parents are intermittently and painfully aware of this, just as children are intermittently conscious and resentful of their parents' incomprehensions, injustices and disapprovals. Love itself is inevitably fraught with guilt; perfect harmony is unattainable, and imperfections cause pain. It is such basic cruelties of the human condition that give such emotional power to the dramatic structures which briefly embody them. The 'names' which emerge as sticks and stones are the surfacing-points of monsters of the deep. Cloaked in triviality and particularity, they derive poetry and power from universal and visceral experience. It is not surprising if their rising to the surface is often charted first in physical terms ('Tout s'éloigne, vacille, prend un air irréel... comme avant les crises d'épilepsie...' (62)) for they usually proceed from faint stirrings of the gut, then, focusing on a word or phrase ('Ha éduquer, vous en avez de bonnes... ha inculquer... Essayez donc un peu...' (63)) they outline their 'clarities' in familiar shapes that look and feel like self-evident truths.

From the first sounds of the laughter and the question 'vous les entendez?' in the opening paragraph, the father's features are softened by 'un attendrissement mélancolique'. The laughter is 'de leur âge', and the two men recall their own childhood: 'Nous aussi, on avait de ces fous rires...' The face moves into 'un sourire bonhomme' which gives the mouth 'un aspect édenté'.

The remembering of childish gaiety imposes a sense of toothless old age upon the elders. The attempted solidarity of the 'nous aussi' and the irremediable distance between youth and age are thus instantly introduced into the text where they will be two sides of a perpetual see-saw. At the tenderest and sweetest moments, a rumbling unease makes itself felt at the fixed roles that youth and age impose:

> C'est vrai, c'était touchant, il s'est senti ému quand ils se sont penchés vers lui, quand ils lui ont tapoté la joue tendrement, quand ils se sont retirés pour laisser les deux vieux fous, les gentils maniaques discuter sans fin... rires enfantins... voix fraîches... fillettes taquines qui grimpent sur les genoux des barbons, passent leurs doigts sur les mèches blanches dans leur cou, leur font des chatouilles... et ils se laissent faire...' (37)

'Ils se laissent faire'; but there is awareness here of greater complexity than is allowed by these hallowed roles — the language of stereotypes can make sudden incursions, creating inward transformations even in the moment of joy: 'il pousse de petits cris séniles d'excitation, de satisfaction, il ouvre toute grande sa bouche édentée, il rit aux anges...' (86) Acquiescence in the simple formula of 'Vivre et laisser vivre', if it brings peace, also brings a sense of abdication, acquiescence in old age, marked once more by 'un bon sourire édenté' (125). The toothless smile separates the father from the children, and makes them inhabitants of a different world, to be bridged only by tolerance and consideration: 'il faut les laisser s'abandonner à leurs lubies, à leurs manies, il est très bon qu'ils conservent leurs dadas... éviter surtout de les contrecarrer... S'approcher, comme ils le désirent, se pencher, contempler avec respect... et puis se retirer. Chacun à sa place. Chacun chez soi' (127). The dreamed-of fusion with the loved ones becomes, in this light, parental acceptance of an allotted role, and filial consideration from the children — 'nous serons comme eux un jour... il faut faire un effort' (128).

To his friend the father confides his sense of having been overtaken: their values, their ideas, their life, have all become part of 'un monde mort. Nous sommes les habitants de Pompéi ensevelis sous les cendres' (155) — yet he does not want to be identified with his friend — 'ce balourd, à demi sourd' (156). It is with his beloved children that he seeks union — despite age, and despite the inevitability of death. It is to them that he gives the animal figure — the figure to which he attributed the power to 'tenir en respect la mort' (186) and in so doing, seems to make a symbolic acceptance of death. They may as well have the figure, for 'elle sera à vous de toute façon' (208), and they accept it with the 'gravité triste et détachée qui convient aux héritiers en vêtements sombres' (215). Towards the end of the novel, the father's image of himself is more and more as 'le petit vieux' (218, 220) with his 'bon sourire édenté' (218) till he visualises himself as 'Ah ce pauvre papa' existing only in memory (222). The vicissitudes of the parent-child relationship and the conflict about the nature and role of art are all caught up into the larger and deeper dramas of love and mortality.

In this framework, love is apprehended as the longing for a perfect but impossible fusion with the loved object, whether human or inanimate. It is not only age and death that separate

— love has its own inbuilt disturbances. In the context of the father's feelings, the 'public' formula for the children's laughter — 'Des-gosses-qui-s'amusent' — can find no anchorage, buffetted as it is by the contrary winds of fear and hope that form part of his mental climate. All his diverse interpretations and reactions, however much they seize on commonplace and stereotype for their expression, derive from within himself: 'Où a-t-il été chercher tout ça? Mais en lui-même évidemment. Chez qui d'autre? En lui seul. Il est seul. Seul portant cela en lui...' (28) That expression of a fundamental solitude, buzz as it may with public words, the voices of others, and different modes of self-hood, frames and fills the manifold dramas of *Vous les entendez?*

The beloved stone animal at times represents a harbour of peace and harmony that no words can touch, but infiltrated by possible mockery it too becomes a centre of self-doubt. When contemplating the stone animal with a fullness that drowns self-consciousness, the father rejects words as worthless and distorting: 'Aucun mot ne peut fusionner avec cela, conclure avec cela une alliance. Pas de familiarités. C'est là. Seul. Libre. Pur. Aucune exigence... plus de mots mesquins, précis, coquets, beaux, laids, enjôleurs, trompeurs, tyranniques, salissants, réducteurs, amplificateurs, papoteurs, dégradants' (130-1). But after the momentary purity, words return once more, draping the figure in heavy protective folds:

Elle se tient bien sage tandis que sur elle les mots sont épinglés, elle se prête à de longs essayages. Elle se présente aux yeux attentifs de ceux qui l'observent sous toutes ses faces, elle fait valoir ses formes, des mots scintillants la recouvrent. Vêtue et parée comme elle est, c'est à peine s'il peut la reconnaître. Elle se tient un peu raide, comme consciente de son rang. Elle exige, elle obtient le respect.

(132)

Thus classified and presented, the figure becomes almost unrecognisable. Words ('Ces mots dont elle est entourée sont

comme des fils de fer barbelés' (132)) establish and protect the dignity of art, but at the same time desecrate, define and limit. They return the art-object to the world of 'names' and judgments, judgments that jeopardise not only the loved object but the loving self, and set up waves of antagonism between conflicting evaluations. The two men, rapt in contemplation, become two misers with their precious casket (73), or else, 'comme deux tendres parents qui se penchent sur leur enfant, ils se rejoignent, ils se confondent... moments d'entente parfaite...' (75). That perfect understanding, however, cannot last:

> Si fragile, on le sait bien. Qui ne sait que les fusions les plus complètes ne durent que peu d'instants. Il est imprudent d'engager trop souvent, de prolonger trop longtemps l'épreuve, même entre proches, même entre soi... Une autre forme, une autre ligne ramenée d'ailleurs ne suffit-elle pas pour qu'aussitôt se séparent, s'éloignent l'une de l'autre, encerclées de solitude, les deux âmes sœurs? N'est-ce pas là notre lot à tous, notre inévitable sort commun?

The comparison of the art-lover/art-object relation with that of parent and child is no accident. The comparison imposes itself throughout the novel, where similar patterns of communion and detachment, admiration and disappointment make themselves felt in both areas.

The wordless joy of the contact with the stone animal is paralleled in the wordless joy of communion with the children. The brief sense, in the response to the art-object, of stepping out of time and out of words: 'il est cet infini... que cela emplit... non, pas "infini", pas "emplit", pas "cela". Même "cela", il ne faut pas... c'est déjà trop... Rien. Aucun mot' (131) is echoed in the sense of freedom and deliverance from words and judgments which the children seem to offer: 'Il n'y a plus rien à craindre, plus de juges, plus de lois...' (178). The momentary exhilaration of fusion with them is 'metaphorised' in terms of an invitation to join them in a world free of words or imprisoning images, a world where they will all join together in perfect harmony. But in *what*? 'Est-ce une pièce de théâtre? Est-ce un ballet?' (179) His questions and fears are tossed aside — 'Ça n'a pas de nom, comprends-tu... Plus de noms, plus d'étiquettes, de définitions ... lance-toi à corps perdu...' (179). But he may indeed be 'perdu' — 'dans un espace vide, sans pesanteur... il sent comme son gros corps lourd...' (180). Here his fear, his sense of inadequacy and age, focus on the phrase 'gros corps lourd' which already appeared earlier in the text. 'Qui a dit cela?' he asks, 'Qui a dit gros? Qui a dit corps? Qui a dit lourd?' (180) He see the words as a constraining verbal panoply to be thrown off — like the words that seemed to disfigure the stone animal: 'D'où viennent ces mots? Ils sont sur moi. Ils sont plaqués sur moi... les mots me recouvrent... arrachez-les...' Briefly he loses age and fear and self-consciousness: 'Il regarde ces vieux mots qui se sont détachés de lui, il les piétine en riant... Voilà ce qui a collé à moi toute ma vie... gros corps lourd... je n'ai plus peur... regardez ce que j'en fais... mais tandis que le mouvement l'emporte toujours plus fort cela aussi se détache de lui, squames qui tombent de la peau des scarlatineux en voie de guérison... il n'y a plus de "regardez", plus de "je", plus de "fais"... Plus rien que ce qui maintenant en lui, à travers lui, entre eux et lui se propulse, circule, ils ne font qu'un...' (180) Inevitably a sense of excessiveness, of going beyond the limits, closes in, and familiar words surge up to outline a familiar role; the heady joy is relegated to a zone of abnormality: 'Vous voyez ce que vous me faites faire... Vous me faites faire des folies...' (181)

It is clear that in the most intense moments, the self loses itself, loses the need for definition, and fuses with the object of its love. But outside these moments of fusion, the self returns to the world of words and definition, where it must pick a careful way through the postures and attitudes latent in the very words in which thought or feeling is formulated. This is not a merely linguistic endeavour, for it involves the consciousness of fear and death, shame at the imperfections of the self, the inadequacies and disappointments of love, the unquenchable longing for the infinite, for innocence and perfect love — for Paradise, in short — and it is that deeper layer of awareness that gives the apparently trivial dramas of *Vous les entendez?* their power.

The idyllic image created by the décor in which the novel unfolds, becomes a structural device, underpinning the alternations of guilt and innocence, serenity and despair: 'Amples housses de chintz aux teintes passées. Pois de senteur dans les vieux vases. Des charbons rougeoient, des bûches flambent dans les cheminées...' (8)[17] The children become perfect emblems of the impeccable family-album: 'Fossettes, roseurs, blondeurs, rondeurs, longues robes de tulle, de dentelle blanche, de broderie anglaise, ceintures de moire, fleurs piquées dans les cheveux, dans les corsages...' (8). The protective power of this serene and ordered world is expanded in a further passage (13) and various elements of this Edenic décor recur strategically throughout the novel. Facing the accusation of ill-treating his children, from the 'protectrice de l'enfance malheureuse', the father appeals to the décor to testify for him: 'Mais madame, vous vous êtes trompée de porte, de quartier. Regardez donc autour de vous. Voyez cette pièce paisible, ce vieil ami assis en face de moi, ces rideaux de percale, ces pois de senteur...' (108). That ordered décor seems to provide a haven of peace where the father and his friend can indulge their appreciation of art, but it may after all be a suspect haven, a well-constructed defence against the disorder of the real world:

voyez-vous ça, lui aussi, tout comme l'autre, en sécurité parmi les percales glacées, les pois de senteur, les prairies, les poneys... si loin tous deux de là où nous sommes, des arrière-cours humides et sales...   (139)

When the stone animal is suffering from one of its recurrent devaluations, and is no more than 'cette statuette en pierre rugueuse, d'un gris sale' (152), the former icon clashes with the idyllic décor (153) but the room itself, a construction of well-chosen language, is not impregnable. It too can be devalued and seem no more than a careful display of elegance and good taste: 'tout lisse et rond, satiné, parfumé, pois de senteur, vieux vases et percales glacées, sculpture précolombienne aux lignes si pures, délicieusement naïves et savantes?... Les gens bien nés savent du premier coup d'oeil où ils se trouvent...' (169) The harmony and order of that perfect setting for perfect family life may after all be an obstacle to the very reality it seeks to represent, for when the father enjoys his moment of fusion with the children — 'ils ne font qu'un' — the union seems to be accomplished at the expense of the harmonious setting: 'l'eau coule des vases renversés... une fleur toute droite se balance comme un cierge dans sa main' (181). The heedless joy that disrupts the shrine is all too quickly quenched and classified as folly: 'Vous me faites faire des folies'. The décor also turns into a weapon against the father when he is seen to be disgracing its perfections by his capacity for manufacturing 'des gaz asphyxiants' (194) out of innocent childish laughter — he who grew up 'parmi les percales glacées et les pois de senteur'! The external Eden cannot preserve the paradise of the heart.

Nothing is proof against the power of names: they drop like stones, deep into the pool of thought and feeling where the inner being, in contact with words, meets other beings and other versions of the self. Agitated eddies appear on the surface, but it is the novelist's art to make audible, through the intricate patterns of language itself, the sonic boom of language in its encounters with the profound and universal disturbances of human life.

NOTES

1. Nathalie Sarraute, *Vous les entendez?* (Paris, 1972). Page references, given in brackets in the text, are to this edition.

2. The uncle's 'vous' in *Martereau* (Paris, 1953), for instance, transforms his hearers into 'petits moineaux alignés sur un fil,

grappe tremblante de singes souffreteux...' (p.35).

3. N. Sarraute, *Portrait d'un inconnu* (Paris, 1956) p.9.

4. M. Proust, *A la recherche du temps perdu* (Pléiade edition) III, p.880.

5. N. Sarraute, *Le Planétarium* (Paris, 1959) p.109.

6. Cf '...ce que j'appelle l'innommé. C'est une impression, c'est du "ressenti" d'une manière extrêmement globale et confuse et dont l'attrait principal c'est précisément qu'il ne se laisse prendre dans aucun mot.' (N. Sarraute, in *Nouveau roman: hier, aujourd'hui*, vol. 2, *Pratiques* (Paris, 1972) pp.44-5).

7. Cf 'Entre ce non-nommé et le langage qui n'est qu'un système de conventions, extrêmement simplifié, un code grossièrement établi pour la commodité de la communication, il faudra qu'une fusion se fasse pour que, patinant l'un contre l'autre, se confondant et s'étreignant dans une union toujours menacée, ils produisent un texte.' (N. Sarraute, 'Ce que je cherche à faire', in *Nouveau roman: hier, aujourd'hui*, pp.32-3).

8. Celia Britton discusses the metalinguistic element in Sarraute's novels in 'The Self and Language in the novels of Nathalie Sarraute', *Modern Language Review*, Vol. 73, no.3 (July, 1982), pp.577-84.

9. Strictly speaking, Dr Britton uses these words to refer to the use of the commonplace. In 'The Function of the Commonplace in the novels of Nathalie Sarraute', *Language and Style* XII, 1979, pp.79-80 (p.85).

10. Ann Jefferson discusses the way in which Sarraute's prose indicates 'the inadequacy of the linguistic order when it comes to matching the order of reality. This disparity becomes a sign of authenticity...' In 'Imagery versus description: the problematics of representation in the novels of Nathalie Sarraute', *Modern Language Review*, vol. 73, no.3 (1978), pp.513-24.

11. Celia Britton, 'The Self and Language in the novels of Nathalie Sarraute', cited above, p.577.

12. ibid., p.578.

13. ibid., p.579.

14. ibid., p.580.

15. N. Sarraute, in an interview with Guy Le Clec'h, 'Drames

microscopiques', *Les Nouvelles Littéraires*, 28 Feb - 5 March, 1972.

16. M. Proust, *Pastiches et Mélanges* (Paris, 1919) p.223.

17. Nathalie Sarraute has often used images of England to express the idyllic, no doubt partly because of very happy youthful memories (see for instance *Tropisme* XVIII, where, indeed, we already meet the 'rideaux de percale'). It is interesting to observe how 'English' this drawing-room seems! The father and his friend also become anglicised as 'Les gentlemen' (p.8), and later in the novel, a brief reference to the 'fresh and innocent' children who 'dilatent leurs narines emplies de l'odeur juteuse des prairies, des pelouses, ils ouvrent leurs lèvres encore humides de thé, de porridge laiteux...' also has a distinctly English flavour!

AUSTERITY

Those plain flowers whose strict stems aim
accurately at the jug that is no vase
and claim quite nothing, white strait nothing,
regarding any loveliness, cause tears.

Their shadows on the wall fall clinical,
dependent on their source:
so small a comment on the world makes each
petal and stalk that a fleet thought
dwells more.

Those chins propped on a long green bone
turn stern and moral from the laughing room:
precisely this austerity it is which
twists in me tight sticks,
recalls.

Mervyn Coke-Enguídanos